# The Visual Language of Comics

# ADVANCES IN SEMIOTICS

Semiotics has complemented linguistics by expanding its scope beyond the phoneme and the sentence to include texts and discourse, and their rhetorical, performative, and ideological functions. It has brought into focus the multimodality of human communication. *Advances in Semiotics* publishes original works in the field demonstrating robust scholarship, intellectual creativity, and clarity of exposition. These works apply semiotic approaches to linguistics and non-verbal productions, social institutions and discourses, embodied cognition and communication, and the new virtual realities that have been ushered in by the Internet. It also is inclusive of publications in relevant domains such as socio-semiotics, evolutionary semiotics, game theory, cultural and literary studies, human-computer interactions, and the challenging new dimensions of human networking afforded by social websites.

**Series Editor**: Paul Bouissac is Professor Emeritus at the University of Toronto (Victoria College), Canada. He is a world-renowned figure in semiotics and a pioneer of circus studies. He runs the SemiotiX Bulletin [www.semioticon.com/semiotix] which has a global readership.

### Titles in the Series:

Buddhist Theory of Semiotics *Fabio Rambelli*
Introduction to Peircean Visual Semiotics *Tony Jappy*
Semiotics of Drink and Drinking *Paul Manning*
Semiotics of Religion *Robert Yelle*
The Language of War Monuments *David Machin and Gill Abousnnouga*

**BLOOMSBURY ADVANCES IN SEMIOTICS**

# The Visual Language of Comics

## Introduction to the Structure and Cognition of Sequential Images

### NEIL COHN

B L O O M S B U R Y

LONDON • NEW DELHI • NEW YORK • SYDNEY

**Bloomsbury Academic**

An imprint of Bloomsbury Publishing Plc

| | |
|---|---|
| 50 Bedford Square | 1385 Broadway |
| London | New York |
| WC1B 3DP | NY 10018 |
| UK | USA |

www.bloomsbury.com

**Bloomsbury is a registered trademark of Bloomsbury Publishing Plc**

First published 2013

**British Library Cataloguing-in-Publication Data**
A catalogue record for this book is available from the British Library.

ISBN: HB: 978-1-4411-7054-5
PB: 978-1-4411-8145-9
ePub: 978-1-4411-8324-8
PDF: 978-1-4411-7451-2

**Library of Congress Cataloging-in-Publication Data**
Cohn, Neil.
The visual language of comics : introduction to the structure and cognition of sequential images / Neil Cohn.
pages cm.
Includes bibliographical references and index.
ISBN 978-1-4411-7054-5 (hardcover : alk. paper)– ISBN 978-1-4411-8145-9 (pbk. : alk. paper)– ISBN 978-1-4411-7451-2 (ebook (pdf) : alk. paper) – ISBN 978-1-4411-8324-8 (ebook (epub) : alk. paper) 1. Semiotics–Psychological aspects. 2. Visual literacy. 3. Comic books, strips, etc.–Psychological aspects. 4. Sequence (Linguistics) 5. Cognition. 6. Psycholinguistics. I. Title.
P99.4.P78C64 2013
302.2'019–dc23
2013018690

Typeset by Fakenham Prepress Solutions, Fakenham, Norfolk NR21 8NN
Printed and bound in India

*This book is dedicated to my best friend, John Pacheco*

# CONTENTS

# LIST OF FIGURES

# INTRODUCTION

While growing up, reading and drawing comics were a particularly enveloping set of obsessions, and I had every intention of becoming a professional comic artist. As I grew into my teens in the mid-1990s, I began to consider the theory behind how the medium worked. I religiously studied books and magazine columns about storytelling techniques and pored over Scott McCloud's groundbreaking book *Understanding Comics*. This focus was mostly directed into my creative endeavors, as I played with these theories in experimental ways in the thousands of comic pages I wrote and drew as a teenager.

It was not until I stumbled upon linguistics and cognitive science as an undergraduate at the University of California, Berkeley that I began to notice the similarities between language and my understanding of comics. I then realized that my meditations on my art form could extend beyond creating comics, and that what really intrigued me was how our minds are able to make sense of sequential images. As often happens with research, the more I learned about language and the brain, the more my conception of the medium changed, and each discovery yielded dozens of new questions. Before too long, it felt like I had begun to see all drawing and sequential images in a novel way.

This book summarizes some—but not all—of the research I have undertaken since that time. My hope is that it can provide an *introduction* to "visual language theory"—the broad architecture of my thinking about the visual language of comics, drawing, and graphic communication. As will quickly become apparent, despite its title, this book is less about comics, and more about language and the mind. While I have written it as a scholarly treatise, I tried to make this book understandable for anyone with an interest. Hopefully I have hit my mark in this balancing act and it does not just sound like a lot of academic-y gobbledygook.

In many ways, this introduction also serves as an invitation. While I am ever appreciative of the growing community who recognize my work, few have actually begun research in this paradigm. I therefore hope that those who find this perspective intriguing, interesting, and/or objectionable will enter the fray and pursue the questions I've posed throughout (you'll likely find me a willing collaborator). If anything, this book is meant as a starting point.

Mostly though, I aim to give the reader a taste of what it's like to see drawing and sequential images through my eyes. Hopefully you'll like the view.

*** *

A note on terminology: In this book, I argue that the study of the structure and comprehension of graphic images—particularly sequential images—should parallel the study of verbal and signed languages. Building this research over the past decade has required me to formulate a lot of new terminology. Many of the terms have been reworked several times, and have been "tested" with scholars and fans of comics, linguists, psychologists, and lay-people. In most cases, I have opted to borrow terms from linguistics (in line with the practice from sign language research), or to create new terms to be explicit about my intents. I have found this to be preferable to pursuing niche terms from research on comics or film that may carry additional connotations or stereotypes. This is done deliberately, to further highlight the parallels of the graphic domain with other linguistic domains.

Adopting linguistic vocabulary is consistent with the spirit of the overall endeavor of this book. Using a different type of terminology would only serve as a subtle separation between the natures of the verbal and visual expressive modalities, which would run counter to the argument pursued throughout. To the extent you might agree with these intents, I encourage you to do the same.

*** *

I have chosen the images in this book quite explicitly to highlight authors whose work I enjoy and also want to promote. Please check out their works if you haven't already. I drew all the images you see that don't have attribution.

*** *

Since I first had the idea of a "visual language" as an undergraduate in 1999, I have benefited from the insights of many people. Scott McCloud's work was a profound early influence, and he has thankfully always encouraged my pursuits, even when they started to drift from his original thinking. I am very grateful for the support of Dan Slobin, to whom I am indebted, along with David Wilkins, for introducing me to Australian sand narratives. This research proved pivotal in forming my conceptions of visual language, which I hope is successfully conveyed by Chapter 9. Along those lines, Jenny Green's willingness to share the newest research on these systems and to offer feedback on my work has been invaluable.

Christopher Johnson and Jason Merchant provided good guidance in my year at the University of Chicago. I thank my friends Ian Christian Blanche, Kevin Cannon, Alexander Danner, and Tim Godek for allowing me to bounce ideas off theoretically minded comic/film creators, along with my editor, Kelly J. Cooper. Comic scholar Kent Worcester offered helpful feedback on previous drafts. Paul Bouissac is thanked for presenting me with the opportunity to write this book.

Even more, I am eternally grateful for the continued advice, guidance, and insights from my mentor, Ray Jackendoff, who saw how a research project slightly outside the norm could connect with a broader understanding of language and the mind. His fingerprints and influence permeate this whole endeavor. My other mentors from my years at Tufts University, Gina Kuperberg and Phil Holcomb, taught me how to think beyond the theoretical domain and how to test these ideas experimentally. Their influence is especially noticeable in Chapter 6.

Several other people from Tufts University deserve mention for their continual insight, advice, and feedback on the development of these theories over many years: Laura Babbitt, Patrick Bender, Naomi Berlove, Ariel Goldberg, Stephanie Gottwald, Suzi Grossman, Steve Maher, Martin Paczynski, Anita Peti-Stantic, Chelsey Ott, Eva Wittenberg, and the students of my 2009 "Visual Linguistics of Comics" class. My time as a graduate student in the Tufts Psychology Department was funded by the Tufts Center for Cognitive Studies, and my postdoctoral fellowship at UC San Diego was hosted by the Center for Research in Language.

Finally, I am always grateful for the many family and friends who have supported me as I have pursued this research, especially my parents, Leigh and Lindsey Cohn, and my brother Charlie. Thanks.

Neil Cohn
La Jolla, CA
March 2013

# CHAPTER ONE

# Introducing Visual Language[1]

Several authors of comics have compared their writing process to that of language. Jack "King" Kirby, celebrated as one of the most influential artists of mainstream American comics, once commented: "I've been writing all along and I've been doing it in pictures" (Kirby, 1999). Similarly, Japan's "God of Comics" Osamu Tezuka stated: "I don't consider them pictures ... In reality I'm not drawing. I'm writing a story with a unique type of symbol" (Schodt, 1983). In his introduction to *McSweeny's (Issue 13)*, comic artist Chris Ware stated that "Comics are not a genre, but a developing language."

Other comic authors have described the properties of comics like a language. Will Eisner (1985) compared gestures and graphic symbols to a visual vocabulary, a sentiment echoed by Scott McCloud (1993), who also described the properties governing the sequence of panels as its "grammar." Meanwhile Mort Walker (1980), the artist of *Beetle Bailey*, has catalogued the graphic signs and symbols used in comics in his facetious dictionary, *The Lexicon of Comicana*.

This intuitive link between comics and language in the minds of their creators is a belief shared by a number of researchers of language who, with growing frequency, are discussing properties of comics in a linguistic light (for review, see Cohn, 2012a). Despite this, the comparison of comics to language has remained controversial (Duncan and Smith, 2009; Hick, 2012), possibly due to a misunderstanding of what exactly is being compared. What place do comics have in the study of language and the mind, and what exactly is being (or should be) analyzed?

Comics do not fall within the normal scope of inquiry for contemporary linguistics and psychology—not because they are an inappropriate topic, but because *language* is a human behavior while *comics* are not. Comics are social objects created by incorporating the results of two human behaviors: writing and drawing. Believing "comics" are an object of inquiry would be akin to linguists focusing on "novels" as opposed to studying English, the language that novels are written in. Analogously, the sequential images used in comics constitute their own "*visual language.*" Thus, the behavioral domains of *writing* (written/verbal language) and *drawing* (visual language) should be the object of cognitive inquiry, stripping away the social categories like "comics," "graphic novels," "bande dessinée," "manga," etc.

Comics then become the predominant place in culture where this visual language is used, often paired along with writing (a learned *importation* of the verbal modality into the visual-graphic). That is, contrary to the metaphor used by their authors: **Comics are not a language**. I emphasize this greatly, because the title of this book might lead some to believe that "The Visual Language *of* Comics" means "comics are a visual language" and that this is the ultimate message of the book. That is *not* the case. Rather, comics *are written in* visual languages in the same way that novels or magazines *are written in* English.[2]

Potentially, comics can be written in both a visual language (of images) and a written language (of text). This combination reflects the capacity for humans to express concepts through multiple modalities, such as in co-speech gestures (e.g. Clark, 1996; McNeill, 1992). While "visual language" is the biological and cognitive capacity that humans have for conveying concepts in the visual-graphic modality, "comics" are a socio-cultural context in which this visual language appears (often with writing). Just to emphasize this again: *Comics are **not** a language*, but they are written in a visual language of sequential images.

By separating the "system of communication" (visual language) from its sociocultural context (comics), we can allow comics to not be defined by their structural properties. This directly contrasts with the work of those who define "comics" by the contributions of images and/or text, such as the requirement of sequential images (McCloud, 1993), the dominance of images (Groensteen, 2007), or the need for multimodal text-image interactions (Harvey, 1994). By recognizing "visual language" as a system divorced from its predominant sociocultural context, a "comic" can use any combination of writing and images: single images, sequential images, some writing, no writing, dominated by writing, etc. In fact, all permutations of these combinations appear in objects we call "comics."

Ultimately, the definition of comics includes a network of ideas composed of their subject matter, format, readership, history, industry, the specific visual languages they use, and other cultural characteristics. Visual languages also appear outside the cultural institution of comics as well, such as when sequential images appear in instruction manuals, illustrated books, and various other contexts that are *not* labeled as "comics." Indeed, illustrated books and comics both use sequential images and/or writing (most often) to tell stories, but they play different roles in culture and carry different stereotypes. Both may use visual languages, but both are not called "comics" because they belong to different cultural contexts. Similarly, historical instances of sequential images like cave paintings, medieval carvings, or tapestries (Kunzle, 1973; McCloud, 1993) should not necessarily be called "comics" (or "protocomics"), but rather can be viewed simply as visual language usage, tied to unique and specific cultural and historical contexts (Horrocks, 2001).

This split between the sociocultural context ("comics") and the structural/cognitive system ("visual language") is essential for how each part is studied. While "comics" can be studied in a primarily sociocultural light (literary studies, political science, economics, history, etc.), visual language should be studied in the linguistic and cognitive sciences. For this latter field of study, the focus is not on "comics," but on the visual language they are written in, how the mind works to create meaning through various modalities, and how graphic expression relates to other systems of the mind.

Truly, the ultimate object of inquiry in linguistics and the cognitive sciences is not a physical or social phenomenon "out in the world" at all. Rather, the units of investigation are the representations and principles in the human mind that motivate comprehension, from understanding form and meaning to usage in social settings. These principles are not tied to any sociocultural context (like comics or novels). Thus, while glossed over as the study of "comics," really the cognitive study of this visual language aims to illuminate the links between domains that can paint a broader picture of the nature of human expression.

## What is "visual language"?

"Visual language" here has been framed by its relationship to comics, but this notion ultimately extends beyond these contexts. Rather, the idea of a visual language contributes toward filling a gap in the cultural category regarding the channel of graphic expression. While we readily acknowledge that verbal communication uses a *system* of expression, graphic communication has no equivalent system recognized (i.e. I speak in the verbal *language* of English, but I draw in _____?). While language is viewed as a rule-governed system acquired through a developmental period, drawing is looked at as a "skill," conditioned only by the expressive aims of the artist and their abilities, which are assumed to develop through explicit instruction or innate talent. While sentences can be grammatical or ungrammatical, the predominant intuition is that there is no unacceptable way to structure images.

Humans use only three modalities to express concepts: creating sounds, moving bodies, and creating graphic representations.[3] I propose further that when any of these modalities takes on a structured sequence governed by rules that constrain the output—i.e. a grammar—it yields a type of language. Thus, structured sequential sounds become spoken languages of the world, structured sequential body motions become sign languages, and structured sequential images literally become *visual languages*.

This notion of a "visual language" fills the gap for categorizing the cognitive system at work in graphic expression. When individuals acquire or develop the ability to systematically draw, along with the structures necessary to string them into sequences, they are effectively using a visual language. Just as spoken language does not have a universal manifestation, visual language varies by culture. We would expect diverse cultural manifestations of visual languages throughout the world, perhaps even not resembling comics at all (such as the sand narratives used by Aboriginal communities in Central Australia, discussed in Chapter 9). This theory provides a context to explain why, for example, Japanese and American comics vary in graphic styles and narrative patterns: they are written in different visual languages, used by different populations. However, while "Japanese Visual Language" and "American Visual Language" feature unique patterns for their "speakers," overall this use of sequential images for expressing concepts belongs to a broader system of "visual language" in the same way that English and Japanese are both types of "verbal language."

It is important to stress that this notion of "language" is *not* merely a metaphor or analogy. The notion of a "visual language" is here meant to be on par with verbal and signed languages as a primary human ability for the expression of concepts using a grammatical system. Three primary components underlie the structure (and definition) of languages, motivated by their underlying cognitive architecture:

1 *Modality*—Languages are produced in a *modality*, be it creating sounds from the mouth (verbal), moving the body (manual/bodily), or making marks on a surface (visual-graphic). These expressions are in turn decoded by a sense organ (eyes, ears). While features of language may be (to some degree) transferable to other modalities (as in Braille or writing), natural languages have a predisposition for the modality they use.

2 *Meaning*—Languages use modalities to express *meanings*. These meanings may be abstract or concrete, and may use different manners of reference (discussed in the next chapter).

3 *Grammar*—Languages use a system of rules and constraints for sequential expressions of meaning. If sequences obey these principles, we consider them to be comprehended acceptably (i.e. grammatically), while those that violate these principles read unacceptably (i.e. ungrammatically).

In addition to these three primary components, language also has two important traits—it is both **systematic** and **combinatorial**. First, all of these components combine to create systematic units of expression. A "lexicon" or "vocabulary" of a language is built of systematic pieces of a modality (like sounds) that have a meaning (as in words) and can be placed in rule-bound sequences (grammar). The most recognizable piece of a lexicon is a word, which is a systematic pattern stored in people's heads. To the degree that these systematic pieces are shared between the minds of individuals, we say that they speak a common "language" in the world. Language is also a combinatorial system, allowing for these finite pieces to combine in infinite ways. For example, small units of the modality (sound) can be combined to create innumerable words, while units of the grammar (words) can be combined to create innumerable sentences. This combinatorial nature applies to *all three* of the traits of language: modality, meaning, and grammar (Jackendoff, 2002).

Individually, none of these components are special to language and all represent facets of cognition that are present in other domains (Jackendoff, 2011). Nevertheless, only language engages all three of these components. For comparison, research on music has emphasized that it too uses a hierarchic, combinatorial grammar (Lerdahl and Jackendoff, 1982), but music does not express conceptual meaning in the same way that language does. It certainly evokes *emotions*, but does not match specific sensorial forms to explicit meanings.

Dancing—as in ballet, salsa, and waltz—likely uses many of the same grammatical properties as music, only expressed through the bodily modality.[4] These bodily actions may also use their own grammar: certain movements can combine with others to create "grammatical" sequences, although some combinations of movements do not fit together in comprehensible ways (i.e. "ungrammatical"). However, unless the dancing starts bordering on pantomime, it too does not express explicit meanings.[5]

Other actions might be similar, especially those learned in athletics. Martial arts training teaches people movements in the bodily modality (punching, kicking, blocking, grabbing) and also has a system of combining these actions in intuitive ways (a grammar) that makes some orderings less intuitive. Yet, these actions only have their intrinsic meanings: a punch is just a punch (versus a punch being a representation for some other meaning). All of these forms involve "grammars" of combinatorial rules and constraints that are tailored to each domain—it is just that they are not built of nouns and verbs like the grammar of sentences (i.e. syntactic structure).

Conversely, some behaviors are meaningful but lack a grammar. For example, we gesture alongside speech to add meaning to our expressions, and these gestures often feature very systematic signs. Gesture alone does not use a grammar to create full sequences though—they usually only arise about once per spoken clause, and coincide with the grammar of speech (McNeill, 1992). This limitation applies both to novel gesticulations (like widening your hands to convey "large") and to systematic gestural emblems (like "thumbs up" or "OK"). When the manual/bodily modality does use a full grammar, it becomes a sign language, with far more systematic representations and rules. It is important to note that sign language grammar is not merely pantomime and is not a conversion of verbal speech into the manual form. Rather, sign language grammars use properties similar to verbal syntax (like nouns and verbs), with all the potential complexity of a verbal language, albeit tailored to the unique characteristics of the manual modality (Liddell, 2003).

Similarly, individual drawings, paintings, diagrams, charts, etc. also do not use a sequence governed by a grammar. They are still meaningful expressions in the visual-graphic modality, but they lack the grammar of a sequence. Here's an analogy: individual manual expressions (which have no grammar) are to sign languages (that use a grammar) what individual drawn images (no grammar) are to visual languages (grammar). One step further removed would be abstract art: these images play with the modality alone, and have neither grammar nor meaning. Individual images—meaningful or not—may have combinatorial properties within the *visual features* alone (the modality), just as the sound component of language (phonology) also uses combinatorial rules to create units, but lacks a larger grammatical system to string these units together.

I should also mention how written language factors into all of this. By my definition, one might think that writing—which uses visual-graphic signs in a sequence—is also a visual language. However, writing is based on the correspondence that graphic signs have with sound, and is essentially a type of learned *synesthesia*—a crossing of wires in the brain that achieves an "unnatural" mix of senses (like the ability to smell colors or taste sounds). Writing is the importation of the natural verbal language into the natural visual-graphic domain to make an unnatural (albeit very useful!) connection. This is why writing is so hard to learn and must be acquired through instruction. Even highly pictorial writing systems like Egyptian hieroglyphics still have a mapping of sound to meanings (unlike the fully pictorial Egyptian wall carvings). Thus, the grammar of writing is always tied to the grammar of the verbal language.

What does this comparison tell us? As represented by Table 1.1, various human behaviors use the same underlying principles as language, but they may lack certain parts. Some behaviors may not express meaning but still use a grammar (music, dance), while some might lack a grammar but still express meaning (gesture, single images). Only language uses all three of these components. Thus, while language shares its cognitive architecture with other domains, it is still "special" as it is the confluence of all three components at once. Furthermore, these behaviors often join each other in expression: we gesture when we speak, writing can join visual languages, music and dance can accompanying singing, dancing could accompany drawing, etc. Ultimately, we can conceive of these expressive capacities as interweaving parts of the broader whole of human expression and meaning-making.

**TABLE 1.1** Varying human behaviors involving similar underlying cognitive capacities.

| | Modality | Meaning | Grammar |
|---|---|---|---|
| *Verbal/Written Language* | X | X | X |
| *Sign Language* | X | X | X |
| *Visual Language* | X | X | X |
| Music | X | | X |
| Dance | X | | X |
| Athletic skills | X | | X |
| Gestures | X | X | |
| Meaningful images/paintings/diagrams/etc. | X | X | |
| Abstract art | X | | |

Through this book, I will describe how visual language shares the same key traits (modality, meaning, and grammar) as verbal and signed languages, with particular emphasis on the systematic and combinatorial features of these components. Broadly, like other modalities of language, this system uses the confluence of a Modality, Meaning, and a Grammar. However, the nature of those components manifest in particular ways suited to the visual-graphic domain.

# The structure of visual language

So, what are the structures underlying this visual language? What mental representations does a reader construct in the course of understanding sequential images, and on the basis of what principles? The guiding questions of linguistics can be applied to the study of this visual language:

1   How is the *form* (i.e. graphics or sound) of the expressive system organized?
2   How is *meaning* conveyed by a form?
3   How do perceivers encode both *form* and *meaning*?
4   How do perceivers draw connections between and encode *sequential units*?

   **5**   How do perceivers *learn* all this given *cultural variability* across systems?

These are the fundamental motivating questions of various subfields of linguistics and all apply to the study of the expressive system used in comics (i.e. phonology, morphology, semantics, grammar, acquisition). While these questions have specific ways in which they are answered in linguistics proper, direct analogies between the verbal and graphic modalities (i.e. like "words = panels") are less important than the fact that the same questions are being addressed in both the verbal and graphic forms. Also, it is significant that these questions are situated as an examination of cognition. The approach outlined here seeks to understand how people comprehend and produce the structures of this visual language, and how those structures manifest in different cultures of the world, by using the methodologies that researchers use to look at language. These notions can better be understood with an example.

On the surface, images in sequence appear simple to understand: images generally look like objects in the world, and actions in the world are understood perceptually; thus, the argument would go, understanding sequential images should be just like seeing events. Although such an explanation appears intuitive, it ignores a great deal of potential complexity. Consider Figure 1.1, which is excerpted from *Copper* by Kazu Kibuishi.

We can interpret this sequence as depicting Fred, the dog, running to catch a frisbee. He runs and sees another dog (his nemesis), who in prior panels performed a magnificent frisbee stunt resulting in the adoration of the other dogs. Fred then attempts a fantastic stunt to catch the frisbee,

**FIGURE 1.1** *Visual narrative. Copper © 2003 Kazu Kibuishi.*

only to face embarrassment in front of the other dogs, and slinks away with his owner. Let's examine all the different structures that factor into understanding this sequence.

First, a reader must be able to comprehend that these drawings mean something. How do we know that the lines and shapes depicted in panels create objects that have meaning? Physical light waves hit our retinas, and our brains decode them as meaningful, not just nonsense lines, curves,

a. Graphic schema of Fred the dog

b. Surface navigational structure

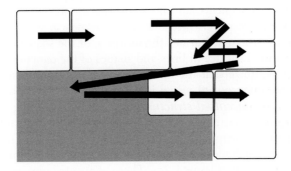

c. Some conceptual, morphological, and event structure

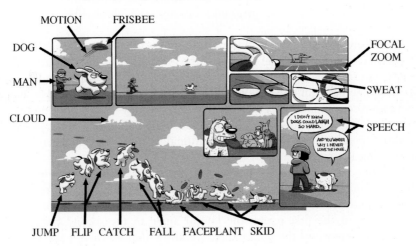

**FIGURE 1.2** *Component parts of Figure 1.1 with regard to meaning and graphics.*

and shapes. Here, we decode a *graphic structure* of lines and shapes that underlies our recognition of drawn objects in perceptually salient ways. Some of these lines and shapes may form as patterns in our head as well. Notice, each time Fred (or his owner) is drawn in Figure 1.2a, Kibuishi uses the same patterns of lines, sometimes with slight alterations, but the same basic lines and arrangements persist. This consistency is evidence of a *schema*—a cognitively stored pattern—in the mind of the author, used to draw each character.

On a larger level, we also must recognize visually that this is not just one image, but a *sequence* of images, facilitated by the shapes of the panel borders. This already creates a problem: how do we know which direction the sequence progresses? Left-to-right and down? Right-to-left and down? Zigzagging up and down? Center outwards? This sequence even contains *rows inside of a row* (panels 2, 3, and 4), creating more complexity (Figure 1.2b). This moves beyond the meaningful aspects of the images to encompass a *navigational structure*, an aspect of graphic structure that tells us where to start a sequence and how to progress through it. Indeed, we could rearrange these panels into one linear sequence, which would alter the navigational structure, but not the meaning of the sequence.

Beyond the visual surface of lines and shapes of the panels and sequence, we must also recognize that the individual images mean something. How do we create meaning out of visual images? This must involve connecting graphic marks to *conceptual structures* that encode meaning in (working and long-term) memory (e.g. Jackendoff, 1983, 1990). For example, nearly all the panels in this strip show a dog (indeed, the *same* dog) with a man in panels 2, 3, and 4 (indeed, the *same* man). Other panels show clouds, a frisbee, and other dogs (Figure 1.2c). These elements compose the objects and places involved in the sequence's meaning. We understand that these representations have these meanings because they look like what they represent.

This sequence has some additional meanings, however, such as the lines that trail the frisbee in panel 1 to show the motion of the disc (Figure 1.2c). These motion lines are different in meaning from the lines surrounding the inside of the panel in panel 3, which convey a "zooming" effect. These are more conventionalized aspects of visual *morphology*—the stored pieces of meaning of a language—which also includes the balloons in the last panel to show speech. These signs are conventional, with little or no resemblance to their meaning.

Additionally, how do we know that these images are not simply flat drawings on a page? We know that these 2D representations reference 3D objects, and thereby can vary in perspective, such as between the depth perspective in the first panel, the lateral angle in the second panel, and the rear viewpoint of the final panel. We know that all these panels depict the same dog and man, despite being from different viewpoints. These are all manipulations of a *spatial structure*, which combines geometric

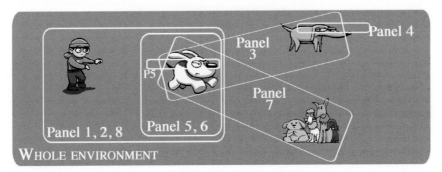

**FIGURE 1.3** *Spatial structure of the whole environment from Figure 1.1 and the portions highlighted by each panel.*

information with our abstract knowledge of concepts. We know that the first panels depict a dog and a man because we know what men and dogs look like, and we retain what *this* man and *this* dog look like as we read. In fact, although the same characters appear in different states of a continuous progression across panels (and within panels), we know that each image does not depict wholly new people in new scenes.

Consider also panels 4 and 5. Although they only show individual characters (Fred, nemesis), we recognize that they belong to a common environment. Figure 1.3 shows the overall environment of this scene—which we never see as a whole—as well as the portions each panel highlights. In this sequence, the whole environment is provided prior to these panels, yet we retain these spatial relationships in our minds through a higher level of spatial structure. This is the unseen spatial environment that we create mentally. Panels can thus be thought of as "attention units" that graphically provide a "window" on parts of a mental environment (Cohn, 2007). Within a frame, attention can be guided to the different parts of a depicted graphic space: the whole scene (Fred, owner and nemesis), just individual characters (Fred or nemesis), or close-up representations of parts of an environment or an individual (Fred's eyes).

Beyond just objects, how do we understand that these images also show these objects engaged in *events* and *states*? For example, the first panel does not just depict a man and dog—it depicts the man *throwing a frisbee* and the dog *chasing after it*. Panel 6 shows Fred *jumping, flipping, catching the frisbee, face-planting into the ground, and skidding to a stop*. Panel 7 depicts Fred *holding the frisbee and looking at other dogs*. These concepts relate to the **event structure** for each panel that is depicted by each panel's **morphology**. An event might extend across several panels (as in the frisbee in flight) or constrained into a single panel (as in Fred's stunt in panel 6). Events may also not be depicted, such as the spectator dogs laughing in the final panel, which is not seen—only mentioned in the text. By the end of the sequence, we understand that all of these things have taken place in relation to each other, and they are not just isolated glimpses of unconnected events.

Finally, how do we understand the pacing and presentation of events? Why does the sequence start with an event and end with a state? Couldn't it start with a passive state? Why bother showing the second panel of the frisbee just hanging in air (omitted in Figure 1.4a)? Why depict Fred's whole stunt in a single panel instead of letting each figure have an individual panel or simply highlighting certain portions of that trajectory (like panels only for jump, grab, and face-plant, as in Figure 1.4c)? These questions relate to the sequence's ***narrative structure***—the grammar of sequential images— which guides the presentation of events.

Consider also, what roles do the fourth and fifth panels play here in the overall meaning of the sequence? Semantically, they show the eyes of Fred and his nemesis (omitted in Figure 1.4b). This relationship is also provided by panel 3—why bother to zoom in on their eyes? Narratively, these panels also provide extra units of pacing that prolong Fred's interaction with the frisbee, and further accentuate the tension with his nemesis. These panels do not necessarily prolong "time" within the event structure of the characters' actions or the situation. Since they zoom into information provided in panel 3, it is ambiguous whether time progresses or it just shows a shift in space to focus on more detail. The prolongation in the *narrative* pacing provided by these panels builds the tension leading to the event in the sixth panel— the climax of the sequence where Fred does his stunt.

a. Figure 1 with no panel 2

b. Figure 1 with no zooming panels

c. Figure 1 with segmented events

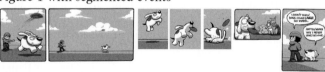

**FIGURE 1.4** *Different possible manipulations of the narrative structure of Figure 1.1.*

So what overall issues are involved with understanding visual narratives? A graphic structure provides information about lines and shapes that are linked to morphological meanings about objects and events at the level of the individual panel. The graphic structure also connects to a spatial structure that encodes the spatial components of these meanings, from which the reader constructs an environment in which they are situated. The narrative structure orders this information into a particular pacing, from which a reader can extract a sequence's meaning—both the objects that appear across panels and the events they engage in. It is significant to note that these structures are separate: while event structure is the knowledge of meaning, narrative structure organizes this meaning into expressible form. Altogether, these different components mutually interact with each other in the process of comprehending a sequence of images.

Clearly, one additional element has not been discussed much so far: the expression of the verbal language in writing. Comics are essentially written in two languages: the visual and written/verbal. Throughout this book, we will be focusing predominantly on the structures of visual language alone, without connection to written language. Just as people gesture while they talk, in actual usage, visual language most often occurs in conjunction with written language in the creation of meaning. Ultimately, human expression in the visual-graphic domain must include this complex multimodal inter-action. However, if we are to fully understand this union, it makes sense to first establish a basis for the understanding of each modality alone. This is especially true when, as of now, the linguistic status of only one of those modalities is fully recognized (and it is not the visuals). Thus, while the structure of verbal language in writing can be found throughout research in linguistics, this volume begins to address the structure of the visual language.

# Outline of the book

Through this book, we will explore most of these structures in more depth. In the first major section, we will discuss the structure of visual language: its lexicon and grammar. Here we explore what systematic parts of visual languages are stored in people's minds. In Chapter 2, we explore visual morphology: how individual images are constructed and how systematic signs like motion lines or zoom lines use structures similar to those in verbal and signed languages. Then, in Chapter 3 we look at patterns at the panel level and in full sequences of images. We then address the question of "what representations do people use to make sense out of a sequence of images?" In Chapter 4, I outline the visual language grammar, its narrative structure. In Chapter 5, we then depart from discussing the lexicon and grammar to address the strategies that people use in making their way through the panels of page layouts—the navigational structure.

Having established this systematic structure, we then turn away from the domain of theory to focus on how sequences of images are actually comprehended. In Chapter 6, I review what we know so far about the processing of sequential images by the mind/brain. Insofar as a theory of language—no matter the modality—is psychologically valid, it must be supported by evidence about how people actually process that structure. Therefore, this chapter draws from the existent evidence provided by psychological experiments looking at participants' behaviors and brains while they interact with sequential images.

The next section of the book brings us beyond structure in an abstract sense to the sociocultural realm. Like language in the verbal and signed modalities, there is not just one visual language in the world. The second section addresses cultural diversity by describing the structure of three different visual languages. In Chapter 7, we discuss American Visual Language, and whether the diversity found in American styles warrants being described as a whole cohesive system. We then turn in Chapter 8 to Japanese Visual Language, found in manga from Japan. Here, we address a system far more systematic than is found in America, and ponder the ramifications of such conventionality. In Chapter 9 we then consider a visual language found in the sand drawings of Aboriginal communities from Central Australia. This system is very different from the visual languages found in comics, yet still adheres to the principles and definition of a visual language framed at the outset. By describing the properties and usage of this system, we can get a better understanding of the overall idea of visual language as a cognitive system not bound to cultural contexts like comics.

Finally, Chapter 10 reflects on the implications of this theory on language and cognition. I propose a broad principle for the cognitive connections between different expressive domains, and frame other ventures for visual language research.

# Notes

1  Parts of this chapter appeared previously in Cohn (2012a).

2  Here's a useful check for distinguishing these notions: when you talk about them, substitute "English" for "visual language" and "novels" for "comics."

3  Although we only use three modalities to communicatively *produce* concepts, we use more than three to understand them! For example, smells can inform us that someone is cooking in another room, but we cannot willfully emit specific smells from our bodies to communicate. It's also within the realm of biological possibility that we could secrete chemically sensitive mucus from our skin and lick each other to communicate, but we don't do it (for better or worse…).

4  Of course, *playing* music also can involve the bodily modality as well when instruments are involved. Here again the bodily motions use a system that is likely tied to the grammar of music.

5  This may differ on context. For example, some forms of Indian dancing use
   particular movements to express particular meanings. We may think of these
   meanings as the integration of a system of sign language/gestural emblems with
   dancing.

# Structure of visual language

Despite the intuitions by comic authors that sequential images constitute a language, several scholars have raised objections to the notion of a visual language (e.g. Duncan and Smith, 2009; Hick, 2012). Before detailing the structure of visual language, we must first directly address two primary criticisms that have motivated the skepticism of a visual language. First, critics note that the panels that make up a sequence of images are not drawn from a set of arbitrary signs, in contrast with the arbitrary words that make up sentences. Second, critics contend that, since most panels vary greatly between each other, no identifiable "lexicon" or "vocabulary" is easily recognized (i.e. there is not a "visual language dictionary" of panels). Because of these features, they claim that sequential images cannot be considered language-like. Let's address each of these concerns.

## Concern #1: Panels are not arbitrary signs

The idea that language is made up of arbitrary signs has been emphasized since the early part of the twentieth century. The Swiss linguist Ferdinand de Saussure (1857–1913) was the first to prominently emphasize that the sound patterns of words had no motivated relationship with their meaning (de Saussure, 1972).[1] For example, nothing about the sound string "d-o-g" inherently connects to four-legged canines who happen to be man's best friend. Rather, an arbitrary relationship connects the sounds "dog" to the meaning "DOG," which is why different sounds can mean the same thing in different languages. This idea that language was arbitrary was revolutionary when it was introduced in the mid-1900s, and linguists quickly championed it as a defining feature of language, especially in contrast with other systems of human communication (like drawings) and systems of animal communication (Bloomfield, 1933; Hockett, 1977).

Despite the growth in the study of language facilitated by the focus on arbitrariness, earlier linguists lacked several of the insights that we now have about language. First, these theories predated the recognition of a modality of language *outside* verbal speech (and its conversion to the visual domain in writing). Most prominently, sign language was not yet recognized *as a language* in the visual-manual modality until the second half of the twentieth century. Sign language is not entirely arbitrary, and many of its signs and even grammatical functions look like what they represent. However, because of the emphasis on arbitrariness as a "defining feature" of language, early researchers arguing for sign language's rightful linguistic status focused solely on the arbitrary features, while often denying any non-arbitrary features. Contemporary views of sign language are more accepting that sign language uses *both* arbitrary and non-arbitrary features (e.g. Liddell, 2003).

Another major insight lacked by early researchers of language was the "semiotic" theories of the American philosopher Charles Sanders Peirce (1839–1914). Although he was a contemporary of Saussure's, Peirce's ideas were not recognized widely until the middle of the 1900s, long after his death, and were not adopted into the mainstream study of language until almost the end of the century. Peirce described the relationship between an external stimulus (like sound or graphics) and its meaning in much more detail than Saussure's focus on arbitrariness, as in Figure 2.0a (Peirce, 1931).

First, Peirce noticed that some "signs" derived their meaning by *resembling* what they meant, an **iconic** form of reference. For example, a picture of a dog resembles a real dog. Similarly, a person saying "Luke, I am your father" is *iconic* of Darth Vader, but *only* if it is said in a deep, breathy voice. The iconicity disappears if it is spoken in, for example, a Texan accent.

Second, some signs derive their meaning by *causing* or *indicating* meaning in something else, an **indexical** form of reference. An *index* finger or an arrow pointing towards a dog do not in and of themselves mean "dog," but point towards that other meaning. Similarly, in verbal language, pronouns like "this, that, he, she" etc. do not directly refer to any sort of meaningful thing, but indicate that meaning should be culled from other parts of a scene or discourse.

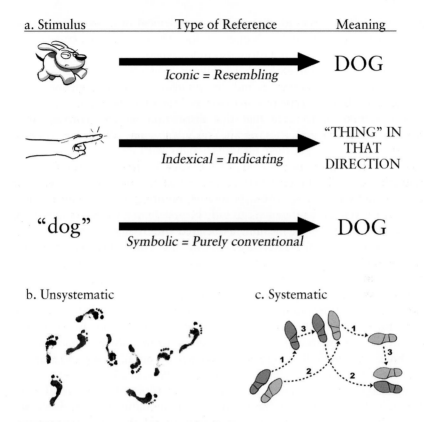

**FIGURE 2.0** *Peirce's three forms of reference.*

Finally, some signs cannot have their meaning derived from resemblance or indication, and only can be recognized as meaningful through a conventional relationship between a stimulus and its meaning, a ***symbolic*** form of reference. This is Saussure's arbitrariness. Again, the word "dog" neither resembles nor indicates an actual dog, and in the visual form, a heart-shape does not actually look like the concept of "love" (or a human heart).[2] Of crucial importance is to recognize that these relationships describe how a form connects to its meaning, *not* the actual nature of the form itself (i.e. technically there are no "symbols," just "symbolic" signs).

These three forms of reference are the most well-known of Peirce's contributions, but they only constitute one part of his broader system for understanding meaning. While his classification system has hundreds of distinctions, we will focus here on two essential points that are often overlooked. Not only did Peirce describe the types of *reference* between a stimulus and its meaning, but he also directly described traits of the stimulus itself. Some stimuli are wholly unsystematic and novel each time they appear, while others are systematic and conventionalized. For example, footprints left in the sand on a beach are indexical of a person's step, but they are unsystematic and each one is unique (Figure 2.0b). In contrast, the footprints used in dance notation also index where feet should go, but they are systematic and conventionalized (Figure 2.0c).[3] Both of these are iconic (*resembling* feet), function as indexes (*indicating* where someone did or should step), but one type is systematic and the other is not.

It is significant to note that this distinction of unsystematic versus systematic signs (properties of the stimulus) cuts across the types of reference (how they get their meaning). Signs with iconic reference can be both unsystematic (photographs, direct quotes) or systematic (smiley faces, onomatopoeia), and indexical reference can also be unsystematic (footprints in sand) or systematic (arrows, pronouns, pointing with an index finger). However, a symbolic reference can *only* be systematic, because it derives its reference solely from the meaning associated with that conventionalization. In this way, symbolic references wholly use conventionality to derive meaning, but conventionality exists outside of symbolic reference.[4]

This insight offered by Peirce's semiotic theories is important for the conception of a language built only of images as well as for the conception of language's features more generally. All forms of language (verbal, signed, and visual) use all three forms of reference described by Peirce (iconic, indexical, and symbolic). While the verbal form may be dominated by symbolic reference (allowing Saussure to pick up on it), iconic and indexical references are also prevalent (Clark, 1996; Silverstein, 1976).

Sign language also uses a mix of all three types of reference (Liddell, 2003). Similarly, although the visual-graphic modality may be dominated by iconic reference, it too uses indexical and symbolic signs. Furthermore, as will be emphasized in the following chapters, many aspects of iconic reference used in drawings are systematic and conventionalized. Thus, each type of language uses all three forms of reference—they just do so in ways that are tailored to the modality.

Given this expanded view of meaning offered by Peirce's conception of signs—beyond the limitations of Saussure's arbitrariness—we can reframe what is important in questioning the existence of a visual language. The issue is *not* "languages are arbitrary and thus is this type of expression arbitrary or not?". All languages use all three forms of reference, and the visual-graphic modality is no different. What is important then is identifying what features might be *systematic* in the sign systems used by people to draw, no matter how those marks connect to their meaning. To be more specific, what aspects of the visual-graphic modality do people store in their long-term memory that enables them to generate an infinite array of unsystematic expressions? What is the "lexicon" of this visual language?

# Concern #2:
# There is no systematic lexicon of panels

This concern has also generated concern by critics, who question the degree to which a lexicon exists or could exist in a visual language of sequential images. They argue that panels, which make up the primary units of this language's sequence, are far too unsystematic to constitute a lexicon of graphic signs. This is very different from words, which are each conventionalized units of meaning that can be combined to form sentences. How can this be a language if every unit is different?

One answer to this question lies in looking beyond languages structured like English. Many languages do indeed use conventionalized units of "words" that become ordered in novel ways by a grammar. These *analytic* languages, like English or Japanese, use consistent word forms at the grammatical level that often place a smaller role on the internal structure of those units. In contrast, *synthetic* languages like Turkish and West Greenlandic use a different strategy. The systematic pieces in these languages are smaller than whole words, and these meaningful pieces combine productively in *novel* ways to create grammatical units. The smaller pieces alone cannot operate as grammatical units—they *must* combine.

Panels in visual language might be thought of similarly to grammatical units in synthetic languages. They are novel units built of smaller systematic parts. This is not to say that visual languages using panels are *equivalent* to Turkish or West Greenlandic. Rather, we can say that they exhibit a similar method of organizing information into workable units (synthetic) rather than letting meaningful information stand alone as units unto themselves (analytic).

Another answer to doubts about the existence of a visual language lexicon lies in what is contained in a "lexicon" in the first place. Critics have emphasized that there is no specific lexicon of *images* the same way that there is a lexicon of *words* in speech. However, contemporary conceptions of language have stressed that the lexicon extends beyond storing whole "grammatical units" like words (or here, panels), but rather consists of *systematic units or combinations of units that create form-meaning pairings* of various sizes across numerous levels of linguistic structure (Goldberg, 1995; Jackendoff, 2002). For example, some signs might be smaller than words, such as affixes like *pre-*, *de-*, *-ness*, and *-ize*. Because these forms are stored in memory as units, not only can they be understood in conventionalized combinations (like "*dee*mpha*size*"), but they can also be used to create novel words (like "manga*ness*"—which could mean "the property of being like a Japanese comic").

Language also encodes patterns that are larger than words. Idioms like *kick the bucket* use multiple words to convey a meaning that goes beyond the composition of their parts (as an idiom, *kick the bucket* means "die" rather than "strike a pail"). More abstract patterns also go beyond the word level. For example, the pattern *VERB-ing the TIME away* refers to spending a time period doing something, as in *twistin' the night away* or *lounging the day away* (Jackendoff, 2010). Even though it is not a word, or even a specific combination of words, we store this pattern in our lexicon (long-term memory) and use it to create novel expressions.

Like verbal language, visual languages also use systematic signs stored at various levels of structure. It is true that panels are *most often* not systematic. Some conventionalized panels do exist, but we find even more systematic patterns in the components that make up panels and the broader sequences in which they are placed. On the whole, visual-graphic expression uses far more systematic patterns than might be recognized. In the next chapters, we turn to exploring this lexicon of visual language.

# Notes

1  Technically, Saussure's ideas were understood from the writings compiled by his students after his untimely death as a young man. Recent discovery of his actual writings in the 1990s have revealed some differences with the accounts handed down; however I will here refer to "Saussure" in the sense of the original posthumous interpretations of his ideas.

2  While the heart-shape does not currently have any relationship to its meaning, it apparently originates in being iconic to the silphium seed of Africa, which was used as an ancient aphrodisiac (Favorito and Baty, 1995), hence the association with love. Besides being a fun fact, this also serves as a disclaimer: most often, the origin of a sign's meaning has little bearing on its active meaning in the mind of a person!

3  For completeness, Peirce called unsystematic stimuli "sinsigns" and systematic stimuli "legisigns." Peirce also recognized the difference between types and tokens in this distinction. "Legisigns" are the base conception of a systematic sign (a type), but a "replica" refers to the unique "token" that occurs each time the "type" of a legisign is expressed. I'll generally avoid these more opaque instances of Peirce's jargon.

4  This point of Peirce's often goes unnoticed by theorists who claim that systematic iconicity somehow warrants iconic signs to also have "symbolic" traits. Peirce did conceive of mixed signs, but blurring iconic/symbolic types of reference is unnecessary if all—or even *some* other parts—of Peirce's system is recognized.

# CHAPTER TWO

# The Visual Lexicon, Part 1: Visual Morphology

In general, people think of drawings as being very diverse and unsystematic, which leads to a persistent belief that whole panels in sequential images cannot belong to a larger vocabulary. Yet drawings are a lot more systematic than people might believe, especially in the context of the visual language used in comics. One reason for this belief might be the dominant iconicity of the visual-graphic modality. By and large, people can understand iconic drawings no matter what country the sign originated in, because they look like what they represent. But, despite the universality of *comprehension*, regularity may be present in the minds of drawers in *production*. After all, drawings must still come from a human mind, which stores its building blocks as schematic patterns. In this chapter, we examine some of the components of drawings that are stored in the lexicon of visual language.

## A visual lexicon

In language, *morphology* is the study of units of meaning manifested in a modality. *Morphemes* are the smallest units of meaning in a language. Words might be morphemes, like *dog*, *afraid*, and *happy*, which can all stand alone. Other morphemes like the affixes *–s*, *un–*, and *–ness*, cannot stand alone and must attach with other morphemes to express their meanings, as in the multi-morphemic words *dogs*, *unafraid*, and *happiness*.

In a similar manner, visual languages use morphemes to express meaning as well, although it is often harder to identify the *smallest* elements of meaning in drawings. In a picture of a face, is the face the smallest morpheme? The eye? The pupil of the eye? The ambiguities of decomposing images into their smallest parts have historically fueled doubts about an analogy between language and drawings. I do not aim here to merely categorize or subdivide meaningful elements, nor do I pursue a "structuralist" theory that seeks to reduce the structure of visual language to smaller and smaller parts (e.g. Gubern, 1972; Hünig, 1974; Koch, 1971; Nöth, 1990). The distinction of what is or is not a "visual morpheme" at an irreducible level is irrelevant. Rather, I am more concerned with what parts of visual morphology are stored in people's memory as part of a broader lexicon—no matter their size—and how they combine with other signs to create additional meaning.

Linguists have identified that the lexicon of languages consists of two broad classes: *open-class* items and *closed-class* items. An open class of items can be added to easily and these signs can often be manipulated. Nouns and verbs contain open-class lexical items, evident since we frequently add new words to the lexicon. The verb *to email* or the noun *blog* did not exist as words until recently, yet we had no problem accepting them as new forms into our vocabularies. Further, we have no problem manipulating these words, as you can probably understand what "re-email" might mean. In contrast, closed-class lexical items include things like articles (*the, a*) or prepositions (*under, in*). Rarely do new words become added to these grammatical categories.

Similarly, visual languages also have open- and closed-class lexical items. Most iconic drawings are open-class items. It is easy to invent new ways to draw actual (or imaginary) things in the world, like people, lamps, or aliens. The visual lexicon also includes signs like thought bubbles, motion lines, or stars above people's heads to show pain. These types of signs are often more symbolic, and belong to a relatively closed class of visual lexical items. New signs of this type are much harder to invent. In the rest of this chapter, we will explore the properties of open- and closed-class lexical items in visual language.

## Open-class lexical items

Most people do not recognize that iconic drawings use patterned parts. The stereotypical belief is that drawings reflect (or "should" reflect) the way that we see the world. The story goes that each person views the world differently, and drawing reflects each individual's unique viewpoint (e.g. Wolk, 2007). When drawing something in front of us, we articulate that perception through our drawings ("life drawing"). If we cannot see something in front of us, we simply imagine it in our minds—using our visual memory of objects—and draw from that ("drawing from memory"). These views echo the conscious experience people have of drawing.

I will argue that both of these conceptions of drawing are short-sighted. Rather, all drawing—from vision or from memory—uses patterned schematic information stored in our long-term memory. These schemas belong to an open class of visual lexical items and often combine with each other in ways that can yield highly variable novel representations (for further detail, see Cohn, 2012b).

The idea that drawing is simply a reflection of perception (either by the eye or the mind) cannot account for conventionalized patterns that permeate the drawings of both individuals and groups. For example, people can readily identify the geographic and temporal origins of drawing "styles." While people may not have pinpoint accuracy, it should be easy to recognize at a glance whether a drawing comes from the ancient Mayans, Greeks, or Chinese, or modern Japanese versus American comics. The very notion that there are cultural drawing styles confounds a purely perception-based notion of drawing, because "styles" are built from conventional patterns shared by people of a culture.

There are many examples of specific graphic schemas. My childhood drawing teacher, "Commander" Mark Kistler (1988) described an activity that highlights people's conventional schematic knowledge for drawing. When he asks adults to very quickly draw a house, an airplane, and a person, they consistently draw the same conventionalized representations (as in Figure 2.1).

While these figures are iconic images of houses, airplanes, and people, they reflect conventionalized *schemas* of drawing (do you know anyone whose house actually looks like that?). The "stick figure" is also a conventionalized representation of a person. Not all cultures use the stick figure, but they do have diverse yet systematic ways of drawing people (Cox, 1998; Cox, Koyasu, Hiranuma, and Perara, 2001; Paget, 1932; Wilson,

**FIGURE 2.1** *Conventional drawings of basic objects.*

1988), and some even have difficulty discerning what the American-style stick figure represents (Wilkins, 1997). Even people who do not consider themselves proficient at drawing likely use the same visual vocabulary of simple graphic schemas for houses, airplanes, people, mountains, the sun, flowers, and many other objects.

Schematic representations are particularly apparent in drawings by authors of comics. These patterns combine to make larger novel forms, thus masking their systematic nature. Consider the representations of hands in Figure 2.2 by three comic artists. The first row (2.2a) depicts consistent patterns used for drawing open hands and fists by Jack Kirby (1917–94), an early and highly influential comics artist, along with drawings of hands by two other popular contemporary artists, Jim Lee (2.2b) and Erik Larsen (2.2c). All three artists remain internally consistent with their own patterns for the whole hand as well as the fingers, knuckles, fingertips, palms, etc. that comprise them. Lee and Larsen clearly use the same schematic representations as Kirby, in a sense validating his influence (at least in the small scale).

Similar schematic patterns can be found in drawings by most comic authors, especially in the small details. Most artists draw noses, jawlines, ears, lips, and other small details in systematic ways. Sometimes the schemas are much larger, like the shapes of heads, bodies, or other ways of drawing. These types of patterns within and between drawers are particularly evident in America between artists who belong(ed) to the same studio. For example, in the 1990s, the most popular artists from Image Comics all had their own studios: Wildstorm (Jim Lee), Extreme (Rob Liefeld), and Top Cow (Marc Silvestri). Books from these studios show a pervasive influence of the founding artist's style—other artists in that studio had recognizable similarities in the patterned way that they drew.

a. Jack Kirby

b. Jim Lee

c. Erik Larsen

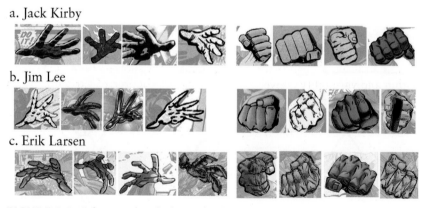

**FIGURE 2.2** *Schematic hands drawn by three comic authors. All artwork © their respective owners.*

The disparaging viewpoint of this similarity would claim that the other artists were simply "knock-offs" or "clones" of the original. From a linguistic perspective, let's consider a different viewpoint: these drawers all use similar cognitive patterns in the way that they draw, and those similarities constitute a shared visual vocabulary that reflects and reinforces an identity of belonging to a particular group of people (i.e. their studio and their subculture). Though the styles of individual artists within the aforementioned studios each had idiosyncratic traits, stylistic similarities also appeared between studios, reflecting another level up in the "visual language community" of those artists. While less direct in their influence, these popular artists also inspired comic authors throughout America (and these popular artists often shared common influences to begin with), contributing to a more general visual vocabulary of American Visual Language used in superhero comics (as we will discuss further in Chapter 7).

The graphic structure of Japanese manga features well-recognized schematic patterns, such as the stereotypical style of drawing people with large eyes, pointy chins, and big hair (Cohn, 2010; Gravett, 2004; Schodt, 1983). This "style" is not constrained to manga, and recurs ubiquitously in cartoons, advertisements, and visual culture. Truly, in Japan, one is pressed to find graphic representations that do *not* demonstrate this style. This style originated with the Japanese "God of Comics" Osamu Tezuka, who was influenced by Walt Disney and Western cartoonists (Gravett, 2004). Due to his unprecedented popularity at the birth of the contemporary Japanese comic industry, many other comic authors imitated his style. As the industry grew and developed, the style moved away from association with any individual author and became characteristic of Japanese Visual Language tied to the whole nation (as we will discuss further in Chapter 8).

Further evidence for schematic graphic representations comes from studies by Brent Wilson and colleagues of how children draw. In a seminal study, Wilson and Wilson (1977) examined the drawings of American high school students and found that virtually all of them were in some way imitative of other drawings, particularly comics and cartoons. Further examination of drawings throughout the world showed both consistency within and variability between the drawings by children of various cultures. For example, rectangular bodies were drawn by children in Islamic countries (Wilson, 1988; Wilson and Wilson, 1984) while bottle-shaped bodies were drawn by English children in the late 1800s (Sully, 1896). One corpus of drawings by Mexican children in California from the 1920s used a method of drawing legs with crossing lines that attached to the torso in a systematic pattern (Wilson, 1988). In this corpus, 100 percent of the drawings used this pattern, and one example showed an initial attempt to draw legs another way, only to be erased and completed in this "correct" conventional method.

These findings led Wilson and colleagues to conclude that drawing involves the transmission of culture-specific schemas, not drawing from perception (Wilson, 1988). They argued that people store hundreds to thousands of these mental models in their long-term memory and then combine these parts to create what on the whole appears to be a novel representation (Wilson and Wilson, 1977). Drawing then becomes similar to language: it uses a lexicon of schemas stored in memory that combine in innumerable novel ways. These schemas can range in size from the small-scale (fingers and hands) to the large-scale (whole bodies and whole images), and these components end up creating a person's drawing "style."

This view goes against the perceptual viewpoint of drawing, since schematic information often has nothing to do with the way things actually look in perception or in visual memory. Rather, these schematic representations—on their own or in novel combinations—map with an iconic form of reference to meanings in the mind.

Given this view of drawing as using a visual vocabulary, it is worth asking to what degree do drawers create their own unique systems of drawing—their own idiolects—and to what degree do they participate in the patterns reflecting a larger visual language of their culture? This question touches directly on aspects of cultural diversity, and will be explored in the second section of this book.

## *Combining schemas*

If "fluent" drawers do indeed store thousands of graphic schemas in their minds, what sort of system governs how these pieces combine? Drawers use rules of combination to construct the meaningful aspects of drawings, similar to the way that various morphemes combine to create different words. For instance, in English, the word *recital* is different from *recitation* because the last morpheme creates a different meaning of the whole word. However, we know that *recitize* is not an actual word, despite also adding a morpheme to the end of the root *recite*. Similarly, the combination of meaningful parts of images contributes to changes in meaning of the whole image.

Artists have long recognized that parts of images can be altered to create subtle changes in meaning, especially related to the face. In the mid-1800s, Swiss educator and "cartoonist" Rodolphe Töpffer (1799–1846) analyzed the regularities of his own drawings (Töpffer, [1845] 1965). He believed that by slightly changing facial features, such as using a shorter versus longer nose or large versus small eyebrows, he could influence stereotypical interpretations of those characters' personalities. Researchers in semiotics have continued this tradition, albeit with more complexity, looking especially at how *graphemes*—basic graphical shapes like lines, dots, and shapes—combine to influence meaning in the drawings from

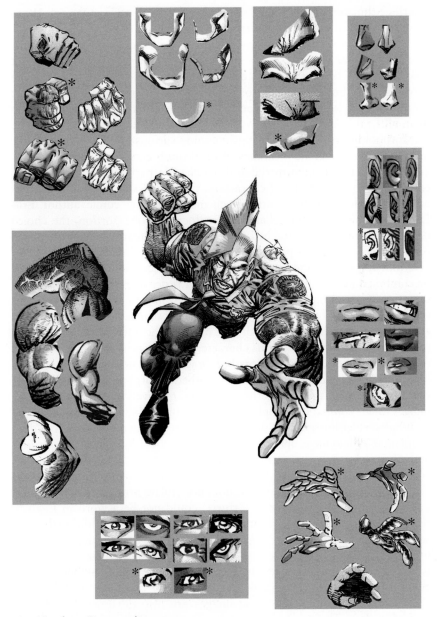

\* = Not from Dragon character

**FIGURE 2.3**  *Combination of numerous schemas using the visual vocabulary of the comic author Erik Larsen. The Savage Dragon and all related artwork © Erik Larsen.*

Charles Schulz's *Peanuts* (Gauthier, 1976; Kloepfer, 1977; Oomen, 1975; Sonesson, 2005). For example, the same physical lines may play different roles depending on their contexts. The same curved semicircle can both be Charlie Brown's nose or his ear (or that of other characters). Other schemas might be particular to different characters, such as how Charlie Brown's head (both from the front and side) is different from Linus's, but Linus's head is similar to Schroeder's, despite different hair schemas for them all.

Morphologically then, drawings combine various graphic schemas that ultimately map to iconic meanings. With *Peanuts* characters, head schemas and hair schemas can be mixed and matched in particular ways to derive consistent representations of characters. Figure 2.3 shows a more complicated example, depicting various schemas from the comic author Erik Larsen and his "Dragon" character. To focus on one portion, the choice of hand schema (to be attached at the end of a forearm schema) depends on what type of hand position is desired: open, closed, or some other position? If a novel hand position is called for, pieces of other schemas may be combined and/or "averaged together" in order to get the desired representation (for example, two fingers open, two fingers closed). However, it would be unusual if a "foot schema" or a "head schema" was placed on the end of a forearm (at least normally). It may also be unusual to use schemas that are not appropriate for this character, such as using a rounded jawline typical of another character instead of Dragon's square jaw, or using fuller lips. This is how novel images with "synthetic morphology" may be built out of systematic parts, whether they are relatively simple "cartoony" images (like *Peanuts*) or complex "realistic" ones (like Larsen's).[1]

What sort of fine-grained properties might also factor into the building of images? In language, speech-sounds are governed by rules of **phonemics** and **phonology** that ensure that speakers do not produce "illegal" sound combinations. For example, English speakers can recognize that "flurp" is not a word, but it *could* be, since it does not violate properties of the sound patterns in English. In contrast, "tfurp" could not be a word in English, since the sound string "tf" cannot legally start a word. Additionally, the sounds within a word may change based on its environment. The "c" in *elastic* changes from a "k" sound to an "s" sound when a morpheme is added to become *elasticity*. In this way, the sounds in a language are governed by rules of combination.

Similar to phonology, graphic images are also governed by *"photological"* rules.[2] The psychologist and artist John Willats (1997) carefully detailed rules of combination between lines that are analogous to those found in phonology. For example, conjoined lines in T-junctions often depict occlusion, Y-junctions show corners, and L-junctions show edges (see Figure 2.4a). Just as starting a word with an illegal string of sounds leads to violation of phonetic rules, "illegal" images result from using contextually inappropriate line junctions. For example, in Figure 2.4b, instead of using a T-junction of intersecting lines, Y-junctions or +-junctions make occlusion impossible or simply look "wrong" (Huffman, 1971; Willats, 1997).

Similar problems occur when lines "run into" others to look like a single continuous line, instead of better contrasting occluded shapes with T-junctions. These line junctions are purely graphic aspects of under-standing drawings—they do not intrinsically rely on any aspects of meaning (re: morphology).

It is also important to remember that, while *completed* drawings end up—and are comprehended—as static, unchanging spatial representations,

a. Different types of line junctions.

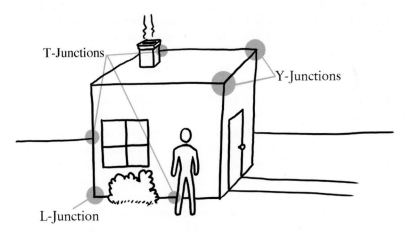

b. Alteration of line junctions to become illegal.

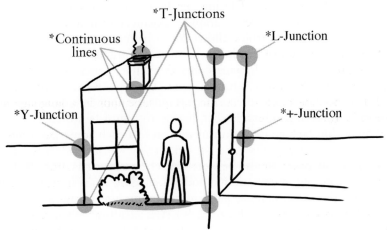

**FIGURE 2.4** *Legal and illegal line junctions.*

they are produced across a span of time. ***Production scripts*** specify the order that schemas are drawn and combined together. The step-by-step instructions in most "how-to-draw" books explicitly spell out the production scripts. For example, most would agree that drawing a stick figure begins with a circle for the head, then a straight line for the body, then either both legs or arms. It would be strange to start with the legs then work upward, or to alternate drawing each leg and arm. This order is not based on the actual schematic elements of the representation, but on the procedure for articulating it. Other schemas may be ad hoc, requiring no intrinsic ordering. For these, drawings might use a default script, perhaps attempting to maintain complete objects throughout production, which results in "ungrammatical" orderings if forms are left unspecified for too long (Willats, 2005).

Production scripts specify how schematic information becomes articulated physically via an interface to the motor system (i.e. how we move our hands). We must remember that drawings are produced because of bodily actions. However, those motions are used to create visible marks, not (usually) for deriving meaning from the bodily motion itself (as in gesture or sign language). This link between bodily action and production scripts is worth remembering, especially in the context of the visual language of comics (and any other images not produced live in front of someone). Comic readers experience printed drawings far removed from an author's actual production of the drawings. Readers have no access to the production script, bodily actions, or temporal process of their creation. As we will see in later chapters, this is not always the case for all visual languages, and such a separation between production and reception may have consequences on the structure and learning of the visual language.

Thus, we create drawings by producing the schemas stored in memory, which are combined through morphological and "photological" rules linked to production scripts. Closing this discussion, it is worth mentioning how this interaction between a graphic lexicon of stored schemas and a system of combinatorial rules allows us to better understand depth and shading. Some aspects of depth can be stored as graphic schemas, such as prototypical patterns for drawing cubes or cylinders (as in Figure 2.5), or as basic rules (like "smaller is further away"). But point perspective cannot be stored in memory as a schema since it must be applied uniquely to each scene using vanishing points. Rather, perspective must be stored as a routinized algorithm that is applied in novel ways to each scene (as in Figure 2.5b).

Aspects of shading can also be stored as schemas, such as drop shadows, cross-hatching, and systematic methods of shading (such as when artists use exactly the same shading pattern every time they draw a backlit ¾ perspective on a face) (as in Figure 2.5c). Yet, "realistic" shading involves light sources and their interactions. This too would involve applying a combinatorial algorithm anew to each scene (as in Figure 2.5d). This

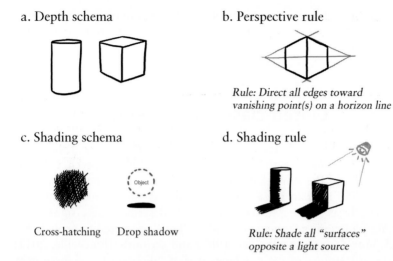

a. Depth schema

b. Perspective rule

*Rule: Direct all edges toward vanishing point(s) on a horizon line*

c. Shading schema

Cross-hatching    Drop shadow

d. Shading rule

*Rule: Shade all "surfaces" opposite a light source*

**FIGURE 2.5** *Aspects of depth and shading that are stored in a graphic lexicon as schemas compared with aspects requiring rules.*

viewpoint on perspective and realistic shading also gives us a cognitive origin for why they are so difficult to learn and need to be invented or discovered: despite being commonplace aspects of visual perception, they cannot be stored easily as graphic schemas, which is how we draw.

## *Conclusion*

In contrast to the viewpoint that drawing is the articulation of perception (be it from the mind or the eye), I have argued that drawing is more like language: it uses schemas that are stored in memory and then combined using rule systems broadly analogous to morphology and phonology in speech. This viewpoint helps explain why many drawers feel frustrated when they cannot "accurately" draw their mental imagery. The perceptual viewpoint of drawing leads people to believe that they should be able to draw their conception of objects. Nevertheless, the "lexicon" of graphic schemas requires schematic patterns for creating representations. Despite believing in a direct link between articulation and conceptualization, drawers must use graphic schemas to represent their intended meanings.

By combining graphic schemas, we can produce novel and unconventionalized images out of systematic parts. Also, the iconic reference between graphic schemas and their meanings allows for the easy creation of new signs. For example, if someone did not know how to draw a dolphin they could either 1) find someone else's schema for this object and copy it, or 2) invent their own schema, either by their own imagination (possibly borrowing from a "fish" or "shark" schema to make a very "unrealistic" dolphin) or by looking at an actual dolphin. Even drawing from perception (looking at a dolphin) would still involve laying the foundation for a schema to be used later. In this way, iconic representations are an open class of the visual lexicon because they readily allow for the creation of new schemas.

# Closed-class lexical items

We now turn to closed-class items of the visual language lexicon. As mentioned, these include things like thought bubbles, speech balloons, motion lines, and the stars that appear above someone's head when they are dizzy. I will refer to these representations as visual "morphemes" or more generally as "signs."[3] McCloud (1993) described these signs as the "vocabulary of comics," and some authors have attempted to provide lists of them, both facetiously (Walker, 1980) and seriously (Forceville, 2011). Like linguistic studies of various languages, a "dictionary" of these items would require extensive corpus analyses across numerous comics within and between cultures. Instead of simply providing a list of signs, here we will focus on the *structure* of visual morphology—the patterned ways in which different types of signs combine together to create an even larger meaning.

Visual languages use the same strategies of morphological combination as verbal languages. In verbal languages, morphemes can attach to each other in any possible relative positioning: a morpheme can appear in front (prefix), at the end (suffix), inside (infix), or surrounding (circumfix) another. Morphemes can also substitute either a part or whole of another word (umlaut/suppletion). A part or whole morpheme might also repeat to create a new meaning too (reduplication). Below, we will see how visual language also uses these same strategies to convey meaning.

Despite these similarities, it is again important to emphasize that this analogy does not draw equivalence between these forms (i.e. affixes in verbal language should not necessarily be assumed to use the same cognitive processes as bound morphemes in visual language). Rather, it may be the case that the human mind generally uses any strategy it can to concatenate meaningful elements, and these strategies extend across domains.

## *Bound morphemes/affixation*

Some visual language signs connect as a whole to other signs. These *bound morphemes*, like affixes, cannot stand alone and have the same meaning. For example, the prefix *un-* cannot exist as a word on its own, although it has a consistent meaning (NOT), and combines with a root word (like *unknown* to mean NOT KNOWN). Several visual signs share this type of bounded relationship.

## Carriers

Perhaps the most recognizable morphemes from comics are thought bubbles and speech balloons. These signs are easily recognizable as bound morphemes because they must attach to whoever/whatever is thinking or speaking. On their own, these signs might convey the idea of thought or speech generally, but to actually convey *someone* thinking or speaking they must attach to a person. This boundedness becomes particularly apparent when a balloon appears at the edge of a panel, where the speaker/thinker is not shown. In this case, a reader would infer that the speaker is still there, just out of sight from the depiction in the panel. Because balloons mandate this inference, it reinforces the bound nature of these signs.

Thought bubbles and speech balloons actually belong to a broader class of "carriers," which all interface between text and image similarly (see Cohn, In Press-a). Carriers function to encapsulate text (or images) that interface with a "root" through a "tail." With speech balloons, like in Figure 2.6, the balloon is the carrier, the speaker is the root, and the tail is the tail of the balloon.

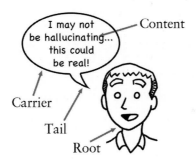

**FIGURE 2.6** *The tripartite structure of carriers.*

Carriers differ in their meaning through two variables: the awareness of the contents of the carrier by the root ("Root Awareness" or RA) or by other characters in a scene ("Adjacent Awareness" or AA). These semantic features vary for each carrier (±RA, ±AA), as in Figure 2.7a. Both a root (the speaker) and other entities in a scene are aware of the contents of a speech balloon (+RA, +AA). These *Public Carriers* do not always look the same (Cohn, In Press-a; Forceville, Veale, and Feyaerts, 2010): squiggles indicate that they come from a TV or radio, scrolls imply something official or old, drippy lines indicate sarcasm, squared carriers come from a robot, and jagged lines suggest loud volume (Figure 2.7b). While these signs differ in their "manner" and representation, they all share a common meaning motivated by these underlying features that both root and other characters know their contents.

a. Underlying features of carriers

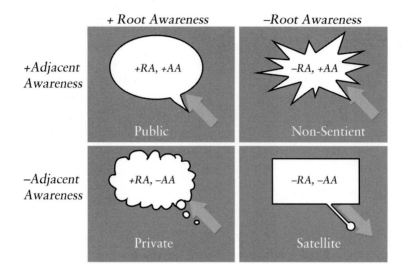

b. Different surface manifestations of carriers

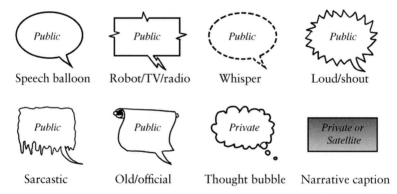

FIGURE 2.7 *Different types of Carriers.*

In contrast, *Private Carriers* like thought bubbles are understood only by their root (the thinker), and not by anyone else (+RA, –AA). These carriers include stereotypical cloud-like thought bubbles, but also narrative captions that might show the thoughts of a narrator in boxes without a physically depicted tail (Figure 2.7b). In these cases, the tail remains implied in the interface from text to image (although it remains there abstractly). Again, these are different surface representations, but ultimately they convey the same underlying meaning.

In *Non-Sentient Carriers*, like sound effects, the root (the sound-maker) is not aware of the contents of the carrier, although it is understandable by everyone else (–RA, +AA). For example, a jagged-edged Non-Sentient Carrier with "BANG!" might be used to show the loud volume of a firing gun. The gun itself does not know the sound, because the gun is not sentient, but everyone else will "hear" the sound. If the gun is anthropomorphized and acts as a character itself, the sound effect might then become a Public Carrier, as a "speech balloon" for Mr. Gun. Notice also that a Non-Sentient Carrier with jagged lines uses the same visual representation to depict loud volume as a jagged-edged Public Carrier. This surface representation uses the same "manner" of the sound (loudness), but the difference in meaning between it being a Public or Non-Sentient Carrier depends on the ±Root Awareness feature.

Finally, neither the root nor adjacent characters know the contents of *Satellite Carriers* (–RA, –AA). These carriers include things like captions, linked to their root by an arrow or line for a tail. They might also include narrative captions for an omniscient narrator in no way directly connected to the depicted image (i.e. the root). Satellite Carriers can also use other visual morphemes, like stars or hearts (content in an undrawn carrier) hovering around an injured (or lustful) body part (root), with or without tail lines running between them.

An interesting feature of carriers as bound morphemes arises because the "flow of the interface" differs depending on their underlying features. Public, Private, and Non-Sentient Carriers all convey the sense that they are *emerging from* their roots. Speech, thoughts, and sounds all *come from* their sources. In contrast, Satellite Carriers imply that they *point towards* their root. They *comment on* whatever they are connected to. In this way, the relationship of bound elements can vary based on their semantic features, despite all using the same general interface.

It is worth noting that carriers of all types are **semiproductive**. A "productive" class of morphological signs means that new forms can easily be invented, in the same way that we can always create new nouns and verbs because they are open-class items. "Semiproductive" means that new forms can be created that use this schema, although they may remain constrained in particular ways. In this case, even though they belong to a closed class, we could invent new types of carriers to provide further surface "manners" for the meanings expressed by the underlying features. For example, a new Public Carrier could have an outer border made of little plus signs (++++++), meaning that a person was lying. This would still have the meaning of a Public Carrier (+RA, +AA), but a new surface form would elaborate on its implications. As we will see, many of the morphological forms used in visual language are semiproductive.

## Indexical lines

Indexical lines are another common bound morpheme that appears in many surface forms. These include lines depicting motion, vision, smells,

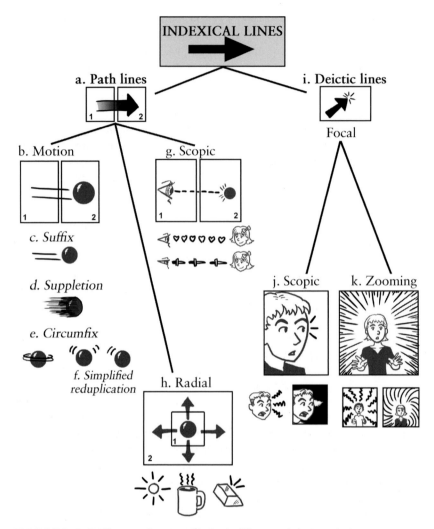

**FIGURE 2.8** *Different subtypes of indexical lines and their variations.*

or lines zooming in to bring focus to an object. Indexical lines are broken up into two subclasses, as Figure 2.8: ***Path lines*** and ***Deictic lines***. Both of these types of lines are highly conventionalized versions of arrows. We will address each type, and their subtypes, in turn.

*Path lines*

Path lines use an arrow to show a *path* moving *from* one state *to* another by affixing to a root morpheme. The most common type of path lines are "motion lines" (also called speed lines or action lines), which show the path of their root morpheme. As in Figure 2.8b, the root object represents the state that the object ends up (TO), while the start of the line represents the (apparent) place where the object began its path (FROM). This path cannot be reversed: it is ungrammatical to have a motion line that precedes the moving object to show what path it *will* be traversing (just like footprints can only show where someone did walk, not where they will walk). This may be why drawings in instruction manuals often look strange when they show an explicit arrow to instruct what action they *should* take, instead of showing an arrow representing the path their hand *would* take.

Motion lines often differ in their surface depiction depending on which country they come from. In some European comics, for example *Tintin*, motion lines are often depicted fairly short and with a minimal number of lines, as in 2.8c (Shipman, 2006). American comics often have larger and longer lines, sometimes giving the space between lines a solid color to make it appear like a ribbon. Japanese manga push this representation even further, with paths being represented by a whole mass of lines (as in Figure 2.8d). Lines might also encircle an object to show it is spinning (see Figure 2.8e), might curve up and down to show bouncing, or might wave back and forth to show a wobbly path (as for a drunk person's stagger). These are all manipulations of the manner of the path of motion, built on the basic structure of the motion path line.

Motion lines might also use other morphological strategies. For example, manga often fully replace the moving object with motion lines, to create a sensation that the object is a blur (see Figure 2.8d). This technique pushes the affixation of motion lines to being more like suppletion—the replacement of one form with another—as we will discuss further in the next section. A similar suppletion occurs with spinning objects—the whole object can become motion lines, to look like a tornado. Motion lines might also run parallel to the moving object, instead of perpendicular (see Figure 2.8f). These cases might be simplified versions of reduplication (again discussed further on), where the object leaves a trace representation behind. This becomes even more apparent when these types of lines appear on either side of the object (as a circumfix), to show shaking. Here the path "bounces" back and forth between the positions on either side of the object to have no defined endpoint.

Another type of path line does not necessarily show movement, but instead shows the path of someone's vision, as in Figure 2.8g. I call these "scopic lines" since they depict the path *from* a person's eyes *to* the object they are looking at. In ancient times people believed that this was the way vision actually worked: our eyes sent out beams called "eidola" to touch what was being looked at (McNeill, 1992). Our folk conception of a path of vision may be related to this belief, even though we know that vision does not actually work in this way. Scopic lines must affix to both the viewer *and* the viewed object. It would be "ungrammatical" if any of these parts were left out. Most often, scopic lines are depicted with a dotted line, but there are several other variants, such as red (or other colored) beams for lasers or white beams for x-ray vision (with an additional component for depicting what is being seen through).

Finally, "radial lines" depict a path that radiates away *from* an object (as in Figure 2.8h). A stereotypical version of this happens in the convention-alized way of drawing the sun: it has a circle surrounded by perpendicular lines representing the path that light travels away from the sun. Unlike motion lines that follow their root, these lines project away from their roots. Other examples of radial lines include lines that radiate from shiny objects, the lines depicting air coming from someone's mouth when they shout, or the often curvy or squiggly lines that emerge away from something if it smells (good or bad) or gives off heat. A similar variant is the "impact lines" that might surround an object that makes impact with a wall or the ground. These lines may be highly conventionalized to represent the rushing of air away from the impact.

### Deictic lines

In contrast to path lines, deictic lines tap into another function of arrows—to point *at* something (Figure 2.8i). These lines primarily function to direct attention or bring focus to something at the endpoint of the arrow. Again, these types of simplified arrows have become highly conventionalized in the visual language lexicon.

Many deictic lines are also "focal lines," which draw attention to what they surround. These might include instances where small lines emerge from a person's eyes to show that they are attentive to something (see Figure 2.8j). These lines do not represent the actual path of a person's vision, as in scopic lines, nor do they show something radiating away from the eye, like radial lines. Rather, they simply draw focus to the eye seeing something, or larger to the whole head being aware of something. Other shapes like curvy or jagged lines can alter the desired emotional quality. For example, jagged versions of focal lines are used to show Spider-Man's "spidey-sense" that represents his clairvoyance when something bad is about to happen.

A more dramatic case of focal lines like this can radiate from the edges of panels toward the object of interest, as in Figure 2.8k. These "zoom lines" dramatically draw attention to a particular object with a sense of "rushing in." Unlike the smaller focal lines, which clearly affix to an object, zoom lines have a more general sense of affixation, often providing a zoom to a whole panel's representation, as opposed to just one object.

As is evident, several examples of deictic lines overlap with radial path lines. The crucial element that distinguishes them is whether they represent a path emanating *from* an object collapsing across two states (FROM→TO), or whether they point *towards* something to bring focus to it. I leave these categorized separately for now, although I am open to a different taxonomy if it is justifiable. However, the important part of this discussion is that all of these cases of indexical lines are bound morphemes that affix a line to another root morpheme.

## Impact stars

"Impact stars" are bound morphemes that often occur in conjunction with motion lines or impact lines. These star-shaped "flashes" show the impact of one object with another. Sometimes, impact stars are only "half-formed," such as when an object strikes the ground or a wall (as in Figure 2.9a). Other times, they are fully formed, such as when one person hits another (Figure 2.9b). Although a person's head might lurch back from the punch, the impact star indicates where the head *once was*. The impact star is bound not only to the head, but to the fist that impacts it. The impact star shows the meeting point for both objects, now separated from that point. Thus, impact stars involve at least three morphemes: 1) the impact star, 2) all colliding objects, and 3) the relationship between them (the impact star serving as a "trace" for the meeting point between the colliding objects).

Impact stars might appear with a path line to show where along a path an object made an impact. For example, a path line with several bumps trails the bouncing ball in Figure 2.9a, while impact stars mark the places where the ball hit the ground and bounced up. In this case, the impact stars are bound to the object via affixing to the path line. The motion line here acts as its own trace for the ball (for where it was along the path), and we infer that this remnant is what actually connects to the impact stars (which are the trace for the meeting of the object with the ground).

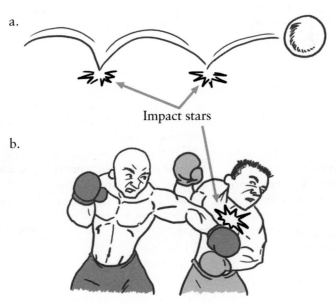

FIGURE 2.9 *Different types of impact stars.*

## Upfixes

Just as "*pre*fixes" appear prior to a root morpheme, another class of bound morphemes in visual languages appears above the head of characters as "*up*fixes," most often to depict emotional or cognitive states. As shown in Figure 2.10a, the space above the head allows several signs including hearts (love), stars (pain), gears (thinking), exclamation marks (surprise),

a. Upfixes

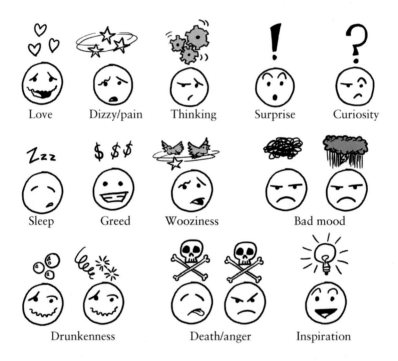

FIGURE 2.10　*Upfixes.*

zzz (sleep), question marks (curiosity), dollar/yen/euro/etc. signs (greed), circling birds (wooziness), dark scribbles or rain clouds (bad mood), bubbles and/or sparks and spirals (drunkenness), skull and crossbones (death or anger), or lightbulbs (inspiration). None of these objects literally float above people's heads, but in this position they convey various conventionalized meanings.

Altogether, these signs use three morphemes, as depicted in Figure 2.10b: 1) the upfix, 2) the root (head), and 3) the relation between them. For example, when hearts appear above a head, it involves 1) the hearts, 2) the lover, and 3) the relationship that the hearts mean that the lover is in love. These signs rely on a schema for using the space above the head to derive their meaning, which "activates" the third morpheme of their relationship. They could not be placed elsewhere, such as next to the head or body, and still derive this meaning. Similarly, in most cases, the same meaning would not arise from these signs if they were not attached to the root. While hearts symbolically stand for love no matter where they appear, gears do not represent thinking and circling birds do not mean wooziness. These meanings arise because of the relationship to the root.

It is worth pointing out that upfixes are *not* simply invisible Private Carriers (i.e. a "thought bubble" without the bubble). The lightbulb makes a good example, as in Figure 2.10c. Sometimes a Private Carrier may be used to further accentuate a lightbulb above the head to mean inspiration, but as soon as that bubble moves away from the head, this associated meaning of the upfix is strained. A lightbulb outside a bubble and not over the head should also feel strange. Nevertheless, the space above the head might also be used to show a person's thoughts, in which case the space simply becomes an extension of a Private Carrier without borders. In the case of rain clouds, this would mean a person is thinking about storms, instead of being a reflection of their mood.

Additionally, the root must *agree* with the upfix. Just as languages like French match feminine or masculine nouns with appropriate articles (*le, la; un, une*), the face of the root must agree with the emotional inference of upfixes. As in Figure 2.10d, a sad or upset face must appear beneath rain clouds; it would look unusual if the face was happy. Similarly, an upset face would look strange under a lightbulb. This correspondence is a type of agreement between root and upfix mandated by the morphological relationship as a bound morpheme.

Like carriers, upfixes are semiproductive. Although they generally belong to a closed class of lexical items, this schema could allow for new upfixes. Again, we can use our example of plus signs (+). A hypothetical upfix could use a swarm of plus signs above someone's head to imply they are lying. Other more complex representations could also appear as upfixes, such as fish swimming above the head (maybe to mean feeling overwhelmed, derived from associations with drowning?). Here as well, these meanings would have to become conventionalized as upfixes to avoid implying that the person is thinking about fish swimming.

## *Suppletion/umlaut*

Morphemes can also replace part or all of another morpheme. *Suppletion* occurs when one morpheme fully replaces another. For example, the plural morpheme in English attaches the suffix *–s* to a root word, as in *dogs* or *metaphors*. In contrast, the plural for *person* uses suppletion to form *people*—a totally different word—since it fully replaces its "root" when the plural is needed. Another replacement occurs in smaller form. For example, the past tense of *jump* uses the suffix *–ed* to create *jumped*. The past tense of the words *run* or *sing* do not use this affix, and instead change a sound inside the word (*ran* and *sang*). This internal change is called **umlaut**.

Visual language also uses this strategy of replacement in several ways, ranging from partial suppletion (umlaut) to full suppletion. For example, as in Figure 2.11a, when someone runs very fast, their legs might be replaced by a several lines in a circle, relying on the association with a wheel rushing around in circles (despite the fact that legs cannot physically do this). Similarly, a tornado-like whirl of lines might replace a whole figure spinning around, as in 2.11b. In this case, no cues signal that the tornado is the same person as the little girl panel-to-panel, yet this suppletion is acceptable as an association between these forms.

Dashed lines also can serve as a suppletive morpheme for invisibility. If the lines of a representation go from being solid to dashed, it means that the object cannot be seen by other characters. This can apply to parts of an object (such as a person's hand, as in 2.11c) or to a whole object (such as a whole person). Suppletion can also occur into other closed-class morphemes. Scopic path lines depicting someone's line of sight usually appear as a dotted line. When replaced by daggers they mean anger (as in "staring daggers at someone") or when replaced by hearts they mean lust

a. Suppletion of     b. Suppletion of whole     c. Suppletion of
legs for running       body for spinning         hand for invisibility

**FIGURE 2.11** *Examples of suppletion.*

(as in Figure 2.8g). This type of suppletion provides further information about the manner of the path line, again in a semiproductive way.

## Eye-umlaut

Another type of morpheme allows for suppletion into the face. An umlaut-style replacement for eyes can use various signs—like upfixes—including hearts (love), Xs (lack of consciousness, pain, or even death), spirals (hypnotism), stars (desire of fame), and dollar/yen/euro/etc. signs (greed), as depicted in Figure 2.12a. Again, these signs use three morphemes: 1) the eye-umlaut, 2) the root (face), and 3) their relationship. Agreement restrictions also exist for eye-umlauts, since a face with Xs for eyes with a giant smile would be unusual.

a. Eye-Umlauts

Love       Death/       Desire for fame       Hypnotized/       Greed
           unconscious                        dizzy/disoriented

b. Suppletion with eye-patch       c. Space constraints for productivity

**FIGURE 2.12** *Eye-umlauts.*

Comparing eye-umlauts with upfixes is particularly insightful. In some cases, these morphemes could be combined together, such as hearts in the eyes and above the head. However, morphemes do not always mean the same thing in upfixes and eye-umlauts—their placement can change their meaning of a sign. While hearts retain the meaning of love or lust no matter where they are placed (due to their fixed symbolic meaning), stars mean different things based on whether they are in the eyes (desirous of fame) or above the head (feeling pain). This would be similar to the difference between the words *recital* and *recitation*—both use the same stem (*recite*) but have different ways of turning it into a noun that yield slight variations in meaning.

Some eye-umlauts may be more entrenched than others. We can test the strength of a sign by doing this suppletion on a face with an eye-patch, as in Figure 2.12b. A heart replacing their good eye works fine to show lust, as does dollar signs (or doubloons!) to show greed. Replacing that eye with a star to show a desire for fame works slightly less well. This constraint may depend on the strength of the association between the eye-umlaut morpheme's meaning independent of its relation to the eye. Hearts and dollar signs have consistent meaning on their own, but the star's meaning relies more on context as an eye-umlaut.

Eye-umlauts are also somewhat semiproductive, and new forms could potentially be created. Again, plus signs (+) could substitute for eyes to mean that a person was lying. This productivity of eye-umlauts is more constrained than in upfixes. Since the space is fairly small, potential eye-umlauts would require a solid shape without much complexity, and could not be circular (to not be confused with an eye). This may be why something like lightbulbs work over the head to show inspiration, but not replacing the eyes, since they would be too visually large and complex.

## Action stars and fight clouds

Another type of suppletion involves blowing up impact stars to a larger size. As mentioned, impact stars affix to objects to show the location of a collision between two objects. This morpheme can also be blown up to a larger size that no longer just shows a specific point of collision, but a consuming representation of action. These "action stars" increase the size of impact stars so large that they omit all or parts of a representation (as in Figure 2.13a). This type of suppletion overlays the action onto the object being affected—we do not suddenly believe that part of the object turns into a star—and we infer the representation of the object underneath.

The "fight cloud" is a similar morpheme which transforms a brawl between two or more people into a cloud, sometimes with legs, arms, and various other objects and signs emerging from it. Fight clouds likely originated from the idea that a cloud of dust is kicked up while people fight, but this sign has become conventionalized as a whole to represent a "fight," but not in any specific way (we do not know who is winning or losing inside the cloud, nor the actual moves being made).

a. Action star

b. Fight cloud

FIGURE 2.13 *Action star and fight cloud.*

## *Reduplication*

Another strategy to create meaning in verbal language is to repeat morphemes or parts of morphemes. For example, the second morpheme in the Hebrew *klavlav* for "puppy" is expanded from repeating the word *kelev* for "dog." In English, this form of ***reduplication*** is found in constructions when someone says, "I'd like a *salad-salad*" to mean a leafy green meal instead of potato- or fruit-salad. This construction uses reduplication of a word to bring focus or clarity to one meaning against other possible meanings (Jackendoff, 2010).

Reduplication also appears graphically in several ways. First, the repetition of whole figures or parts of figures has long been recognized as a way to show movement. For example, if someone wanted to depict a person doing several actions or one full action, they could repeat a character in multiple positions all in a single image (as in Fred the dog's stunt from Figure 1.1). I call this type of reduplication a ***polymorphic*** representation, since it uses "many forms" to convey the whole representation of meaning. In many cases, motion lines use a simplified version of polymorphism in order to show the traces of an object's previous positions along a path. The rough outlines of the object remain following the person. Sometimes, this type of reduplication does not apply to whole figures, but only parts of objects. For instance, in Figure 2.14a, a man is waving his arm, but is drawn to have multiple arms. This "semi-polymorphic" representation consolidates the "partial reduplication" of the moving object while keeping the rest of the figure constant across that span of "time."

Movement can also be shown through reduplication by layering the reduplicated forms on top of each other. In this case, the repetition does not show full actions, but demonstrates shaking, as in 2.14b. This same technique of layering offset lines could also be used to represent double vision, such as the subjective viewpoint of a drunken person. However, double vision would not technically be reduplication, because it does not use a morphological process to create a specific type of meaning. Rather, double vision directly shows the iconic representation of a subjective viewpoint.

a. Partial reduplication          b. Reduplication to
with polymorphic arm                show shaking

**FIGURE 2.14**  *Examples of reduplication.*

Thus, based on context, the same surface graphic structure (offset repeated lines) could be used to show two different meanings (shaking versus double vision) with different underlying morphological structure (reduplication versus iconicity).

# Conclusion

In this chapter, we discussed the open- and closed-class lexical items of visual language that occur at a level smaller than panels. I have described how drawings use simple lines and shapes (graphemes) along with graphic schemas that are stored in memory and recombined into seemingly novel representations. These open-class schemas are highly productive, and can easily add new forms. In contrast, closed-class lexical items use more stringently conventionalized morphemes in specific distributions. Often, these morphemes involve similar strategies of combination as verbal language: affixation, suppletion, reduplication, etc. Together, these forms make up the basic lexicon of visual language, which allows for the creation of an infinite number of seemingly novel expressions constructed from systematic parts.

Again, this chapter does not seek to draw equivalences between the lexical items in verbal language and visual language. The form-meaning pairings in morphemes in verbal languages differ greatly from the ones described here for visual languages. Yet, the connections between these modalities may imply more general cognitive capacities at work in *both* domains. Of the types discussed in this chapter, these would include:

1   The ability to store in memory schematic patterns of sensorial forms (i.e. sound patterns or line patterns) at various sizes of representation (from basic lines/sounds to combinations of those lines/sounds).

2   The ability to create infinite novel expressions by combining finite simple sensorial forms (i.e. sounds or lines, including basic units and schemas).

3   The ability to link sensorial forms (i.e. sounds or lines) to meaning, be it through symbolic, indexical, or iconic reference.

4   The ability to recombine meaningful forms through any feasible strategy possible, including attaching them together (affixation), substituting one for the other (suppletion), altering a portion of one with another (umlaut), or repeating them (reduplication).

Given these overlaps, one could argue that visual language uses these same traits that appear in verbal language. However, it is just as, if not *more* likely that verbal, signed, and visual languages all tap into the same cognitive capacities to accomplish their expressions, but do so in ways unique to each modality. Indeed, these capacities likely appear in other expressive domains as well (such as music, dance, athletics, etc.). We will further explore these types of connections across domains throughout other chapters.

# Notes

1 I realize that there may be some pitfalls with the terms "cartoony" (i.e. an implication of less seriousness or being dumbed down) and "realistic" (i.e. how "real" looking are they?). Given that better alternatives do not exist at this time, I use these terms with intent only for describing stylistic qualities of drawings, and encourage no further implications to be read into this terminology.

2 My personal preference on this terminology is asymmetric, with "photology" to describe the combinatorial principles (as opposed to "graphology," although I don't mind "graphic structure") and "graphemes" for the minimal graphic units (and thus "graphetics" instead of "photetics"). I leave it to future researchers to ultimately make this labeling decision. By comparison, sign language researchers chose to just maintain "phonology" for the structure of the manual modality and its articulation. For the graphic modality this seems inappropriate to me. If the study of a language's modality used a "domain-neutral" term instead of "phon-" referencing sound, differentiating between the actual modalities would likely be unnecessary.

3 These phenomena have been called "pictorial runes" (Forceville, 2005, 2011; Kennedy, 1982) and "emanata" (Walker, 1980). I generally dislike these terms, and previously called them "graphic emblems" (Cohn, 2010b) in line with labeling of conventionalized gestures (like those for "OK" or "thumbs up"). I now believe calling them "signs" or "morphemes" is the easiest and most effective terminology.

# CHAPTER THREE

# The Visual Lexicon, Part 2: Panels and Constructions

As discussed, critics who disagree with the perspective that sequential images could operate like a language worry that panels—the image units of a sequence—are not stored as whole representations. That is, unlike individual words that make up a sentence, no consistent vocabulary of panels appears to exist in graphic communication. For the most part, this is true: panels are often very diverse, even though they are constructed from highly systematic parts (as discussed in the last chapter). Essentially, panels are the most *productive* type of open-class lexical item in visual language. Nevertheless, some systematization exists at the level of whole panels (and sequences), and even seemingly novel panels may be constrained by entrenched cognitive patterns.

In this chapter, we will discuss the systematization found at and above the panel level. We will start by addressing whole panels that are stored in memory, then progress to more abstract templates at the level of panels, whole sequences, and even multimodal interactions.

## Regularity in panels

While most panels are not regularized as whole representations, some panels do appear to be stored in memory as complete units. Many authors consistently use the same panels over and over again, reflecting the storage of these panels in their mental lexicons. For example, in *Peanuts* comic strips, Charles Schulz repeatedly used panels of Snoopy lying on his back on top of his doghouse, Linus sitting holding a blanket while sucking his thumb, or Snoopy walking in front of grass. In many cases, the various instances of these panels look identical between strips, even when they might have appeared months or years apart. Schulz was likely not copying or repeating his own work, but rather the widespread repetition of these panels shows that these representations were part of Schulz's own visual lexicon.

## *Suppletive panels*

Sometimes suppletive morphemes lead to systematic panels. In the previous chapter, we discussed how action stars and fight clouds could replace different types of actions in a representation. In fact, these signs can be enlarged to become regularized panel level units. Both action stars and fight clouds play specific roles as "Peaks" in the narrative structure of sequences—the culmination of actions and events in a visual sequence (discussed further in Chapters 4 and 6). Because action stars show a large "flash" of an event, we know that an action takes place, in particular a violent and sudden action, but we do not know anything more than this. This generalized quality means that this panel can replace nearly any other panel that has some type of full action or culmination of events.

a. Sequence with an action star panel

b. Sequence with an fight cloud panel

c. Sequence using a heart as a panel

d. Sequence using a heart as a panel

**FIGURE 3.1** *Suppletive panels.*

However, because action stars do not show the actual events that take place, this information must be inferred from the contents of the surrounding panels, as in Figure 3.1a. Contrary to theories that focus on the inferences that occur *between* two panels (e.g. McCloud, 1993; Saraceni, 2000, 2003), this type of inference requires a reader to reanalyze the events *in the action star* once they reach the subsequent panel(s).

Similar to action stars, fight clouds can also become whole panels, as in Figure 3.1b. However, fight clouds are far more specific in their meaning: they show a fight between people. Because of this specificity, if these panels were to substitute for another, they could only replace other panels showing a fight. Like action stars, however, these panels do not explicitly show details of the fight (who is punching, kicking, biting, pinching, etc.); rather, they just convey the general concept of fighting.

Despite their similarities, interesting contrasts exist between fight clouds and action stars. The events in a fight cloud must be *durative*: it represents a continuous amount of time in which multiple actions take place. Try to imagine the fight cloud in 3.1b as meaning just *one* punch: it does not work. In contrast, action stars show *punctive* events, which are only a single action in time (like one punch, kick, or explosion). Again, try to imagine the action star in 3.1a covering multiple actions (say, punching *twice* or each boxer punching once), and it will not work. In this way, single morphemes can convey different spans of time and actions, especially if they are conventionalized into whole panels.

It is worth noting that the "panel level suppletion" accomplished by action stars and fight clouds is not a feature of visual language morphemes generally. Not every morpheme can be enlarged to a whole panel to serve as a substitute for representing actions in full. For example, the heart shape commonly means love and can appear in upfixes or eye-umlauts. Yet, this sign cannot conventionally function to *replace* a panel where someone falls in love. In Figure 3.1c, what are we supposed to infer happens at the heart panel? Does one of the boxers fall in love? Similarly, in Figure 3.1d, even when the action fits the context of the heart, we infer the kiss from the context of the rest of the sequence, not this heart panel. The heart panel does not directly imply an action. In both cases, we cannot infer the action because we have not conventionalized this morpheme as a panel-level lexical item in the way that we have for action stars and fight clouds.

## Panel-level templates

Regularity can also be found in various templates for panels. This systematization is most exemplified by "Wally Wood's 22 Panels that Always Work," a "cheat-sheet" of panel compositions created by the legendary comic artist Wally Wood for making "boring" scenes of lengthy dialogue more visually interesting (as in Figure 3.2). Years after its creation, an editor at Marvel

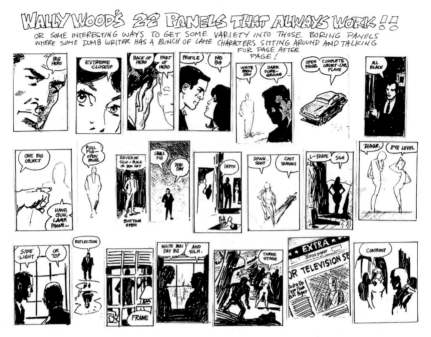

**FIGURE 3.2**  *Panel-level templates from "Wally Wood's 22 Panels that Always Work."*

Comics made a paste-up of Wally Wood's originals to disseminate to other artists, resulting in countless copies floating around the industry (and now the Internet) for several decades.

While no formal studies have confirmed the reach of these schemas, the spread of this cheat-sheet has led to an acknowledged use of various panel compositions across authors' works. For example, Figure 3.3 shows several examples of the "Big Head" schema from four different comics. We should not necessarily assume that these authors consciously thought about this cheat-sheet and decided to deploy this panel from it. Indeed, they may have never seen the cheat-sheet at all. Rather, it is more likely that these templates have become a common part of the visual vocabulary used by comic artists over the past several decades. By virtue of the fact that creators are also readers of comics, they add this template to their own repertoire possibly by repeated exposure alone. In other words, these panel templates have become part of comic creators' visual lexicons, whether they do or do not know their origins.

Several other panel templates are also identifiable. For example, one consistent panel shows the earth hanging in space along the North-South axis, often with the Americas prominently featured (see Figure 3.4a). Long horizontal panels often zoom in specifically on characters' eyes (see Figure 3.4c), while smaller panels hone in on single eyes, often when surprised

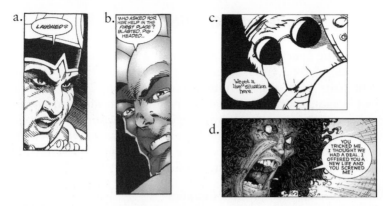

**FIGURE 3.3** *Use of the Big Head schema in panels from various comics. a. Age of Bronze © 2001 Eric Shanower. b. Savage Dragon © 1996 Erik Larsen. c. Replacement God © 1997 Zander Cannon. d. Spawn © 2000 Todd McFarlane Productions.*

(see Figure 3.4d). A common framing may also show a character from the viewpoint between another character's legs (often female), as in Figure 3.4b. These are all common templates for panels. Concerted research could no doubt reveal several other systematic panel-level patterns.

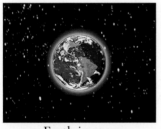

a. Earth in space

b. Through the legs framing

c. Horizontal eyes

d. Single eye

**FIGURE 3.4** *Various conventionalized panels.*

## *Panels as attention units*

Even unsystematic panels can have a degree of abstract regularity. Panels act as a "window" on a visual scene, and thus serve as "attention units" to highlight parts of a scene in different ways (Cohn, 2007). Within a sequence of images, a scene may have two types of elements: *active entities* are those that repeat across panels by engaging in the actions and events of the sequence (i.e. the characters of the scene), while *inactive entities* do not move across panels (i.e. are elements of the "background"). Panels can be categorized by these elements (depicted in Figure 3.5a):

- *Macro*—depicts multiple active entities

- *Mono*—depicts single active entities

- *Micro*—depicts less than one active entity (as in a close-up)

- *Amorphic*—depicts no active entities (i.e. only inactive entities)

These categories are distinguished by the amount of information they contain relative to the meaning of the sequence. This amount decreases successively: Macros contain more active information than Monos, which show more than Micros, which are more than Amorphic panels. These ways of highlighting attention are similar to, although not the same as, types of film shots. Unlike the attentional categories, film shots frame the presentation of objects, as opposed to dividing the amount of information shown, as in Figure 3.5b (Arijon, 1976; Bordwell and Thompson, 1997). In essence, attentional categories frame *meaningful* elements of a scene, while film shots *present* those meaningful elements.

Nevertheless, the correspondences between the attentional categories and film shots should immediately be apparent. For example, a Macro typically involves a long shot to capture the most information possible, but it could tighten on just the specific multiple characters involved in the action. Mono panels show only one character, but that character can be presented in various ways, including full, medium, and close shots. Close-ups may prototypically be Micros, but this varies based on how much information they depict. A panel showing only the hands of individuals exchanging a piece of paper would be a Macro that uses a close-up shot, because it involves multiple characters. Finally, Amorphics have no equivalent category in film shots, since they show a non-active element of the narrative, which can be framed in any number of ways.

The way a scene is "windowed" by a panel can impact the clarity of a sequence. For example, having too many active entities in each panel may strain the reader's working memory across a sequence. Memory would become overloaded by the demand of tracking multiple entities and their

Full scene

a. Attentional panel types

b. Filmic shot type

**FIGURE 3.5** *A single scene framed both by Attentional panel type and Filmic Shot type.*

actions across panels. Figure 3.6a depicts a sequence where each panel is a Macro, with multiple entities engaged in actions (and reactions).

This sequence depicts a shootout in a saloon between a gunman and a victim, while a woman, a man, and a bartender (plus his bird) watch. All six entities' actions need to be followed across panels, and keeping track of it all would require significant attention and effort for a reader. In contrast, Figure 3.6b divides the *same sequence* into panels containing less information. Here, Mono and constrained Macro panels highlight the characters directly, although the same meaning is conveyed across the sequence as 3.6a. This sequence should be easier to comprehend than the one in Figure 3.6a, even though it still requires keeping track of all six characters.

a. Macro representation of a sequence

b. Sequence broken up into panels with less information

c. Sequence highlighting only the most relevant portions of a scene

**FIGURE 3.6** *Several options for framing a scene where multiple entities engage in actions across panels.*

It should be pointed out that a Macro panel also shows you that all the characters belong to the same spatial location, but without that viewpoint you need to *build* that environment in your mind (a process we will call "Environmental-Conjunction" in the next chapter). On the whole, 3.6b is longer than 3.6a, but it more succinctly focuses attention to the different parts of the scene without overloading a reader with too much information.

Consider also Figure 3.6c, which excludes panels that contain less relevant information, focusing directly on the most important parts of its meaning. In this version, the strip focuses on the interactions between the gunman and the victim, with only the bartender (and his bird) playing active roles as bystanders in the final panel. The man and woman are now relegated to inactive entities since they no longer move across panels and appear only in the first panel. In this way, the windowing of attention by panels combines with the selection of what to convey across the sequence.

As discussed, panels have several ways to depict the same scene, solely by modulating the amount of information that they show. This selection of how to present a scene demonstrates panels' roles as attention units. In some sense, this windowing quality reflects a graphic depiction of the "spotlight of attention" that guides our focus to various aspects of perceptual information. When we see the world, our vision takes in information from the whole visual array, but we only focus on the parts of that vision that fall within our "spotlight of attention." Panels serve a similar function for visual narratives, and thereby can simulate what our vision would be like if we were watching a scene in person. This creates a sensation that panels facilitate a "spotlight" that reveals only portions of a larger environment. In actuality, these glimpses *create* the whole view of the environment in the mind of a reader. These various panels represent parts of the scene, which allows us to inferentially *construct* a full understanding of the broader scene.

How can these very abstract categories be considered as systematic parts of the visual language lexicon? First, using panels as "windows" on a scene is a conventional part of the visual language of comics in the mind of a creator, evident because children from graphically enriched cultures draw comic panels using this windowing quality far more often than children from countries with less exposure to graphic images (Wilson and Wilson, 1987).[1] Second, recent studies point to evidence that cultures use these attentional panel types in consistent proportions, and that these proportions differ by culture. For example, American comics seem to use more Macros, while Japanese manga seem to use more Monos (Cohn, 2011; Cohn, Taylor-Weiner, and Grossman, 2012). These trends imply that visual languages consistently frame scenes in different ways (discussed further in Chapters 6 and 7), again reflecting the latent systematicity found in iconic representations.

# Visual language constructions

In language, patterned schemas also exist above the level of individual words. *Constructions* are abstract patterns larger than words, often at the level of phrases or whole sentences, such as the construction *VERB-ing the TIME away*, which appears in phrases like *twistin' the night away* or *drinking my life away*. This pattern is above the level of one word, but is still stored in people's mental vocabularies. Similarly, visual language also uses patterns beyond individual panels, extending into whole sequences. These may be highly abstract, like basic narrative grammatical rules (discussed in the next chapter), or they might be specific instantiations of narrative patterns.

Just as with panels, individual authors may have their own multi-panel constructions in their personal idiolects. For example, I've noticed that Charles Schulz repeatedly used several patterns throughout his *Peanuts* comic strips. One particularly recognizable pattern involved someone playing catch with Snoopy. In the first panel, the person reaches back to throw or kick a ball/stick/etc., while Snoopy stands ready to fetch. In the second panel, the throw/kick occurs and Snoopy runs to chase it. The third panel always just shows the person standing and watching—it *never* shows the retrieval of the object. This absence of substantive information in the third panel allows for the joke in the fourth panel. Here, a punchline confounds the expectations, such as Snoopy amusingly returning the wrong object or someone else returning the object. Schulz used this and other patterns repeatedly in his strips, likely reflecting a systematic pattern stored in his mind.

Other patterns are more recognizable across authors. Consider the sequences in Figure 3.7. In both of these sequences, the panels alternate between characters leading up to the final panel of the sequence where both characters come together. This **Convergence Construction** uses Macro and Micro panels to shift back and forth between characters before finally converging on all the characters in the final panel, represented by a Macro. We can formalize this pattern as:

*Convergence Construction: [Non-MacroA −Non-MacroB]\*—MacroAB*

This rule states that Convergence alternates between panels containing characters A and B. These panels must be less than a Macro (i.e. a Mono or Micro), and this pattern can repeat any number of times (indicated by the asterisk). Finally, both characters are shown together (AB) in a Macro panel. Although the individual panels might vary when it is used, this global pattern is stored as a whole in our memory to guide the production of these types of sequences.

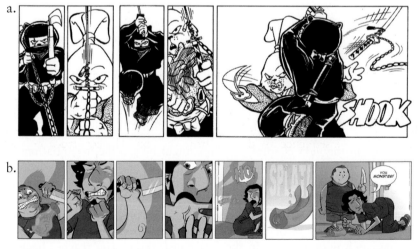

**FIGURE 3.7** *Examples of the Convergence Construction. a. Usagi Yojimbo © 1987 Stan Sakai. b. Butternutsquash © 2004 Ramon Perez and Rob Coughler.*

An important feature of this construction is that we only view the common environment of these characters at the final panel. Before that, we must inferentially build the conception of these characters belonging to a common environment ("Environmental-Conjunction"). As we will see, this capacity is an important part of the broader narrative grammar discussed in the next chapter.

Convergence may actually be one pattern within a broader family of constructions that involve alternating between multiple characters or scenes. This type of alternation has been called "cross-cutting" (Bordwell and Thompson, 1997) or "parallel-cutting" (Carroll, 1980) in film. Other instances of this pattern involve zooming in on information (as in *MonoA – MonoB – MicroA – MicroB*), or simply free-form interleaving between scenes. All of these patterns may be stored in the mental lexicon as ways to solve the issue of how to represent simultaneous events in a *linear* coherent narrative sequence. Regardless, they are all stored as patterns within the minds of creators and consumers of visual narratives.

## *Multimodal constructions*

Finally, some patterns involve the interaction between sequential images and written language. A commonly used pattern places a "silent" or "beat" panel with no text into the narrative sequence. In comic strips, it most often occurs in the next-to-last panel position. This silent penultimate panel is actually part of a larger pattern, coined by artist Neal von Flue (2004) as the "set-up–beat–punchline" pattern (the *SBP construction*). It begins with panels "setting up" the humorous dialogue or situation, only to then give a "beat" or "pause" with a panel that has no text in it. Finally, the last panel delivers the punchline of the joke, as in Figure 3.8a.[2]

Figure 3.8b shows further evidence that this construction is entrenched in people's memory. The "beat" extends across three Mono panels for each of the different characters in the scene. Yet, these panels all belong to the same narrative state, only distributed across several panels (another instance of Environmental-Conjunction). Furthermore, the first, second, and last panels are nearly identical, meaning that most of the narrative qualities of this sequence are derived from the text. The construction itself relies on the text for its effectiveness—the beat being the distinguishing characteristic of the construction and defined by the *absence* of text. Thus, not only are there sequential narrative patterns across sequential images, there are even systematic patterns involving the combinations of text and image.

**FIGURE 3.8** *The Set-up–Beat–Punchline Construction in two comic strips.*
*a. PhD Comics © 2004 Jorge Cham. b. Butternutsquash © 2004 Ramon Perez and
Rob Coughler.*

# Conclusion

In the last two chapters, we have explored the visual language lexicon: the
patterns that are stored in people's minds that allow them to produce and
comprehend images that can be placed into a sequence. We store systematic
patterns in memory across all levels of structure, from the component parts
of individual images, to combinatorial parts of images, to whole panels,
sequences of panels, and multimodal interactions. This shows that, as in
verbal language, various aspects of visual language structure can be stored
in memory, and that the creation and comprehension of individual and
sequential images relies on many interacting parts.

It is worth mentioning that the use of these consistent structures in no way diminishes the creativity or artistry of an author. As we will discuss in depth later on, American and European artistic culture pervasively holds the belief that any imitation or adherence to cultural conventions cedes a person's own personal individuality and creativity. From a linguistic and cognitive perspective, imitation is the manner by which people acquire and adopt their (visual) linguistic system. We do not criticize authors of books in English for sharing the same vocabulary of words, yet this is the way we treat people who may draw in similar ways or use similar conventions in their panels or storytelling. Rather, for verbal language we focus on how authors may *use* those words creatively (or not). Perhaps visual language can be held to a comparable standard.

# Notes

1　Comic industry lore also includes several stories of professionals who drew comics for other countries where the native people could not recognize panels as being a "window" into a fictitious environment. The gist is relatively consistent: panels occlude parts of individuals' bodies and viewers question why those body parts have been severed or are missing. I have heard this story recounted several times by many comic industry professionals, and a variation appears in Walker (1980).

2　For more examples, an Internet search for "silent penultimate panel" will turn up several blogs that chronicle these panels in daily comic strips.

# CHAPTER FOUR

# Visual Language Grammar: Narrative Structure[1]

Moving beyond the visual language lexicon, how is it that people make sense out of a sequence of images? In verbal language, a comparable question would be: How do people make sense out of a sequence of words? Just as syntax is necessary to differentiate random strings of words from coherent sentences, a system of rules and constraints in the visual modality must separate random sequences of panels from coherent sequences. This system is the "grammar" of visual language. Unlike the grammar of words, this grammar of visual language presents meaning at a higher level than that of syntax. As the saying goes, a picture is worth a thousand words, and thus a single image *usually* contains far more information than an individual word. Thus, the combination of images may be closer to the structure used between whole sentences: a *narrative structure*. Indeed, the structure used to understand sequential images may be the same as that for understanding sequences of sentences in discourse and sequences of shots in film.

In this chapter, I will detail the basics of this narrative grammar of sequential images. First, it is worth briefly considering three predominant ideas about the creation of meaning across sequential images (and discourse) that do not use a full grammatical approach.

## Three ideas for sequential image comprehension

Consider a sequence such as in Figure 4.1. This sequence might be interpreted as a man lying awake in bed while a clock ticks away the passage of time, until he talks on the phone (either calling someone or being called).

This sequence is actually fairly complex. We cannot understand it by virtue of the individual events alone, because there are several possible ways

**FIGURE 4.1** *Visual narrative.*

to construe it (Cohn, 2003). Under one interpretation, each panel depicts its own independent time frame. The first and last panels connect as one progression of events, while the succession of the clocks embeds within the progression about the man (as in Figure 4.2a). A second interpretation might be that the juxtaposed pairs of panels of the man and the clock depict the same place *at the same time*. Here, these events occur simultaneously, despite being depicted linearly. Mentally, one must group panel 1 with 2, and panel 4 with 5, which are then connected in a singular shift in time (as in Figure 4.2b).

a. Embedded time shifts

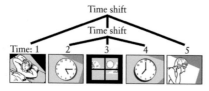

b. Conjoined environments

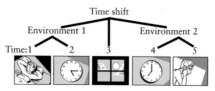

**FIGURE 4.2** *Ambiguity in narrative structure.*

Given this basic analysis of the relationship between time and space in this sequence, how might this example be analyzed by prominent theories of visual narratives? We will address three approaches: 1) panel transitions, 2) "promiscuous" transitions, and 3) general cognitive scripts.

## 1. Panel transitions/linear coherence relationships

The most prominent idea about understanding sequential images posits that people connect the meanings between adjacent panels. This theory most popularly appears in Scott McCloud's (1993) "panel transitions," which characterize various ways that juxtaposed panels shift in meaning across dimensions of time and spatial location. To McCloud, readers comprehend sequences by inferentially "filling in" the information that connects two panels' meaning together. This "panel transition" approach has been operationalized and expanded by several other researchers (Cohn, 2003; Dean, 2000; Saraceni, 2000, 2003; Stainbrook, 2003). Similar notions have described the connections between film shots (Eisenstein, 1942; Kuleshov,

1974), and the "coherence relationships" between sentences in discourse (Halliday and Hasan, 1976; Hobbs, 1985; Kehler, 2002; Zwaan and Radvansky, 1998).

Panel transitions are especially intuitive, since they follow how we experience the reading process: moving from one panel at a time. What might be the problem then? If given *only* the local relationships between panels, the transitions in Figure 4.1 would all be non-sequiturs, or at best transitions between parts of a scene. What relationship does a man lying in bed have to a clock? Clocks to a window? A clock to a man making a phone call? Without a global view of the sequence, there would be no narrative here at all. In fact, without reference to some broader memory for the sequence, we would never know all these panels represent something in the same location, since they are never shown together by one Macro. Rather, our understanding comes entirely from the *global* sequence.

In particular, transitions cannot account for connections between panels that extend beyond adjacent relationships. In Figure 4.1, panel 1 must connect to panel 5, since they both feature the same character (otherwise we would be surprised to see him again!). Meanwhile, panels 2 and 4 show the clock in different states. In order to make these connections, we must have a system that extends beyond linear connections between panels. As will be discussed, studies have shown that people tend to agree on how to intuitively divide a continuous visual narrative into segments, which extend beyond just the linear coherence relationships between panels (Cohn, 2012c; Gernsbacher, 1985). Without such segmentation, we would be unable to resolve or recognize the two different meanings in Figure 4.1.

It is worth noting that the linguist Noam Chomsky (1957) made similar arguments to these for why sentences cannot be structured simply by word-to-word relationships. In fact, Chomsky's arguments for this very issue helped push linguistics and psychology to focus on cognition and the brain, rather than just surface behaviors. Nevertheless, while transitions cannot account for all of sequential image comprehension, particular types of transitions may play important roles in a broader structure, as will be discussed later on.

## *2. Promiscuous transitions*

Another idea expands "transitions" beyond linear relationships between panels, but to relationships between *all* panels in a visual narrative. Comic scholar Thierry Groensteen claims this explicitly, stating that "every panel exists, potentially if not actually, in relation with each of the others" (Groensteen, 2007, p. 146). A similar perspective appears in theories of "causal networks" of discourse, where each sentence potentially connects to any other sentence (Trabasso, Secco, and van den Broek, 1984; Trabasso and van den Broek, 1985). This "promiscuous" approach to transitions addresses the issue of long-distance connections between panels in a visual narrative. For example, the first panel of Figure 4.1 can now transition both with panel 2 *and* panel 5 since all panels have a relationship to each other.

Promiscuous transitions raise other issues, however. Such unrestrained transitions between panels could overload the working memory of the human mind. A five-panel sequence like Figure 4.1 would require just 10 transitions, but an average 24-page monthly comic book with six panels per page would have 144 total panels, yielding 10,296 possible transitions! Although not all pairs may demand an actual transition, all connections would be necessary to confirm or deny an explicit transition. This would overwhelm human working memory without having some underlying system of segmentation. As mentioned, people do break sequences into manageable segments, meaning that sequences are not so unconstrained as promiscuous transitions would suggest.

## 3. General cognitive scripts and schemas

Finally, another approach argues that general cognitive scripts guide sequential image comprehension. Scripts are a kind of template for events and characters in a type of situation (Schank and Abelson, 1977). The classic example is that you know going to a restaurant involves sitting down, ordering, waiting, eating, and paying, but not dancing on tables or taking off your pants (most of the time). This approach has been particularly appealing to theorists from "cognitive narratology" (for review, see Herman, 2003; Jahn, 2005), who often discuss sequential images in their analyses (Bridgeman, 2004, 2005; Herman, 2009; Lefèvre, 2000). This approach has also owed a great deal to the film studies by David Bordwell (1985, 2007), who has eschewed approaches that compare the structure of visual narrative to language. Instead, Bordwell focuses on how people create inferences while watching movies, either drawing upon the basic notion of a narrative sequence, or specific scripts (for example, a narrative about football requires us to know the rules and customs of that game).

Comprehension of a sequence absolutely must engage scripts; however, such general semantic information alone is not enough. For example, theories of scripts only outline prototypical events and the way they normally unfurl. However, events and narratives break these prototypes, have *interruptions*, or involve events that do not cleanly fit into a script. These are all important aspects of understanding both events and narratives. Furthermore, how would inferences alone describe the structural ambiguities in Figure 4.1? Is there a script involved with lying awake in bed before talking on the phone? As mentioned, the first and last pairs of panels can be inferentially grouped into common environments. Yet, this is only one option—each panel could also depict its own unique time frame.

How can a model without an explicit notion of segmentation describe inferences that require grouping panels? Also, how can it differentiate between one interpretation that requires localized *spatial* inference, and another that requires a nested *temporality*? These phenomena require a model of structure that goes beyond general semantic relationships, as important as they may be.

## *Conclusion*

In sum, these previous approaches highlight important observations and insights about the structure of sequential images (and discourse), but each approach is not sufficient on its own. In the rest of this chapter, I will outline a theory that draws upon the insights of these approaches, but proposes a Narrative Grammar (specifically Visual Narrative Grammar for the visual-graphic modality) underlying the comprehension of sequential images. This theory argues that narrative categories organize sequential images into hierarchic constituents, analogous to the organization of grammatical categories in the syntax of sentences. This approach can account for many important attributes of visual narrative, all well highlighted by Figure 4.1. These include:

1 Groupings of panels into constituents (e.g. panels 1 and 2 in Figure 4.2b);

2 Interactions between the "bottom-up" content of panels and the "top-down" narrative schema;

3 Description of narrative pacing through the structure of embedding (e.g. the effect of panel 3);

4 Ability to account for long-distance dependencies between panels (e.g. the relation of panels 1 and 5);

5 Ability to account for structural ambiguities;

6 Ability to account for how the structure of the representation facilitates inferences.

Previous approaches to narrative structure have addressed some—but not all—of these traits. Notably, these traits are not unique to narrative structure, and theories of syntax must address similar issues. The first five traits relate to the *structure* of a narrative, and will be the primary focus of this chapter, largely because little research details them in visual narrative. The sixth trait deals with how structure interacts with meaning, and in fact many approaches to visual narrative have focused on the generation of inferences (e.g. Bordwell, 1985, 2007; Chatman, 1978; Eisenstein, 1942; McCloud, 1993; Saraceni, 2000). In this chapter, I will discuss only some aspects of inferences; further details will appear in future work.

# Basic narrative categories

As discussed at the outset, the function of narrative structure is to order meanings. Observations about a global narrative schema have a long-standing tradition in analyses of plot lines and storytelling, particularly for theatre. Over 2,000 years ago, Aristotle described the *Beginning-Middle-End* schema for plays (Butcher, 1902); in the thirteenth century, Zeami Motokiyo described a similar structure for Japanese Noh drama (Yamazaki, 1984); and in the nineteenth century, Gustav Freytag (1894) outlined the contemporary notion of a narrative arc for five-act plays. More recently, the idea of a canonical narrative schema emerged as central to theories of "story grammars" (Mandler and Johnson, 1977; Rumelhart, 1975; Stein and Glenn, 1979; Thorndyke, 1977).

While "storytelling" is certainly a prototypical case, "narrative structures" here are simply a method of *packaging* and *presenting concepts*, and, as such, they should be applicable beyond just "stories" (which may be an "entertaining" context of narrative broadly). In this context, "stories" are only a prototypical instance of narrative structure, and "good stories" are only a case of rhetorical skill.

Visual Narrative Grammar consists of several core categories:[2]

- *Orienter* (O)—provides superordinate information, such as a setting
- *Establisher* (E)—sets up an interaction without acting upon it
- *Initial* (I)—initiates the tension of the narrative arc
- *Prolongation* (L)—marks a medial state of extension, often the trajectory of a path
- *Peak* (P)—marks the height of narrative tension and point of maximal event structure
- *Release* (R)—releases the tension of the interaction

Together, these categories form *phases*, which are coherent pieces of a constituent structure. Just as phrases make up a sentence in syntax, phases make up an *Arc* in narrative. Each Arc can be considered as a "visual sentence," meaning that a longer comic book or graphic novel may contain many Arcs throughout the whole story. But unlike sentences, Arcs do not overtly mark their beginnings (such as with capital letters) or endings (such as with periods).[3] As we will discuss in Chapter 6, despite this lack of overt markings, readers can intuitively sense where these segments begin and end in an ongoing sequence. The canonical constituent structure and linear order for categories within a phase is:

*Phase* → *(Establisher) – (Initial (Prolongation)) – Peak – (Release)*

This rule states that a phase contains this ordering of narrative categories. In essence, this rule is a type of construction stored in the lexicon. The parentheses indicate optional categories; except for Peaks, they each can be left out of a sequence with no significant structural consequences. Peaks, and to a lesser degree Initials, are the most important components to the structure of narrative. In turn, each category can also serve as a phase. We will address this capacity for expansion in the next section.

First, we must describe these categories in more detail, focusing on the meaningful cues in images that motivate their categorization. An essential trait of this model is that it keeps narrative and meaning separate. Semantic/event structures are aspects of *meaning*—the message conveyed by a sequence of images (or words, sentences, or film shots). Narrative structure is the system by which those meanings are *presented*. This is why the same meaning can be drawn in several possible visual sequences—they convey the same meaning, but have different narrative structures. This same relationship exists between syntax (presentation) and semantics (meaning) in language. For example, "active" sentences (*John kissed Dave*) and "passive" sentences (*Dave was kissed by John*) differ only in syntax; both sentences convey the same meaning in different ways.

Certain semantic meanings prototypically correspond to particular categories, but non-prototypical mappings also occur. In such cases, a panel's context in the sequence may be more influential in determining its category than its content. This is similar to grammatical classes in sentences (like nouns and verbs), which prototypically map to certain semantic features (objects and actions), but ultimately rely on distributional patterns in a sentence (Jackendoff, 1990). For instance, contrary to notions that nouns are "people, places, things, and ideas," words become nouns because of their behavior within a sentence: nouns can be pluralized and, in English, often follow determiners or adjectives, follow prepositions, etc. Comparable patterning applies to other grammatical classes and, by analogy, to narrative categories.

For the sake of simplicity, I will mostly use examples from basic short strips, but as we will see, these structures can be elaborated on to develop far more complex examples. As such, this approach extends beyond short comic strips or isolated visual sequences, although they make for easier examples.

## Peaks

While narratives have many parts, one panel often motivates the meaning of a sequence. Consider Figure 4.3a, which shows a woman smacking a man in the head. The penultimate panel constitutes the **Peak** of the sequence: the location of the primary events of the sequence or phase.

**FIGURE 4.3** *Sequences with narrative structures glossed.*

The Peak is where the most important things in a sequence happen, and it motivates the context for the rest of the sequence. Prototypically, Peaks show the culmination of an event, or the confluence of numerous events. They depict the disruption of narrative equilibrium (Todorov, 1968), and consequently may show the interruption of events, which alters previous expectations. We see this in Figure 4.3b: the soccer players interrupt the dog's chase. In this regard, Peaks best capture the crucial aspect of surprise in many narratives (Brewer and Lichtenstein, 1981; Sternberg, 2001). Indeed, a surprise would be difficult to reveal in a place other than the culmination of a narrative.

When an action involves a trajectory, Peaks prototypically map to the Goal of the Path. For example, when throwing a punch or cutting with a sword, the event is fulfilled at the endpoint of the object's path. The Peak in Figure 4.3d shows this: the paper airplane's endpoint is in the teacher's hair. Such motion also aligns with the endpoint of a transfer of energy (Talmy, 2000).

Similarly, Peaks might contain a change from one state to another, especially in an interruption or termination of a process (as in Figure 4.3b), or the culmination of a growing event. Consider Figure 4.3c, which shows an older man dancing passively until he breaks loose and starts headbanging. The final panel is the Peak, since it shows the events reach their apex (him fully rocking out). Notice also that panels 2 and 3 show virtually the same event, but extending it throughout two panels builds the narrative tension toward the culmination in the Peak. As will be discussed, this is a function of narrative, not just events.

## Initials

Following Peaks, Initials are the second most important part of a phase, because they set the action or event in motion, thereby creating the sense of narrative disequilibrium (Todorov, 1968). Consider the panel just prior to the Peak in Figure 4.3a. The woman reaches back her arm in preparation to smack the man. This panel starts her action, but it does not climax until the next panel. This preparatory event maps to an *Initial* in narrative structure: It *initiates* the primary event of the sequence. Similarly, in Figure 4.3c the Initial shows the man start to groove to the music without yet fully rocking out.

Initials can be related to Peaks in several different ways. The prototypical Initial shows an inception or preparatory action that culminates in the Peak. For example, the woman *prepares* to smack the man by reaching back in Figure 4.3a. Since they contain the start of an action, Initials often mark the Source of a path, as in any event that involves a trajectory (like the Initials in Figures 4.3a and 4.3d). These properties of Initials derive from a panel's content.

Other Initials rely more on a panel's context in the narrative than the depicted events. Consider the Initial in Figure 4.3b. The dog chases a soccer ball prior to being interrupted by the soccer players. This Initial does not show a preparatory action—it shows the dog already chasing the ball. However, this process is interrupted in the Peak. Only after the Peak has been reached can the previous panel be recognized as an Initial. Thus, this type of Initial is defined more by its contextual relationship to the Peak than by its internal content.

## Releases

In Figure 4.3a, the final panel depicts the woman looking angrily at the man—the aftermath of the Peak's action. This panel is a *Release* for the narrative tension of the Peak, which gives a "wrap up" for those events, often as an outcome or resolution. Prototypically, this aftermath involves the coda of an action—such as the retraction after throwing a punch or swinging a sword. Event codas like this often revert to a passive state, such as a person's return to standing *en garde* with their hands or a sword. In Figure 4.3a, the passive state shows that the smack in the Peak had no effect on the man.

Releases also may involve a reaction to the events in the Peak. For example, the final panel in Figure 4.3b shows the dog hiding behind a water-cooler after being assaulted by soccer players. This panel does not relate directly to the actions of the soccer players: a Release of this nature might show the dog flattened on the grass. Rather, this Release provides the dog's reaction of running and hiding.

Finally, many strips are funny *because* of the Release. In Figures 4.3a and 4.3b, the culmination occurs in the Peak, but the actual "punchline" is delivered in the Release. Thus, Releases provide an important panel for humor, perhaps because they convey an aftermath, response, or a (relatively) passive follow-up to the climax of the sequence.

## *Establishers*

The first panel in Figure 4.3a depicts the woman sitting next to the man, not doing anything in particular except looking at him. This *Establisher* provides referential information (characters, objects) without engaging them in the actions or events of a narrative. This most often involves a constant state or process that is changed by the events of the narrative.

Consider the first panel of Figure 4.3b. This Establisher shows the dog watching a soccer ball bounce in front of him. The ball is in a process of bouncing, while the dog is surprised/curious. Despite the high degree of "action" in the panel, it functions to set up the relationship between the dog and the ball. This panel does not just *establish* the relationship narratively to the reader, but also within the strip: the dog discovers the ball, as opposed to already engaging with it. Bordwell (2007) noticed that film scenes often open with characters entering into the shot or moving towards the viewer (as in this panel in Figure 4.3b). This allows the character to enter the scene concurrently with the viewer's entrance into the narrative—an act of Establishment. (The finale of a film often reverses this, with characters leaving a shot or moving away from the viewer—prototypically "off into the sunset.")

Establishers give the first glimpse of a scene and thereby set up the characters. This process provides the building blocks of a narrative; just as the first sentence of a discourse provides new information (Haviland and Clark, 1974), the Establisher lays the foundation of new information for a sequence. In this way, Establishers can also lay the groundwork for a fictitious environment in which a reader can be immersed (Herman, 2009).

Establisher and Release panels are often similar (as are Prolongations, discussed next). Some narratives even make this overt, as in Figure 4.3a, where the first and last panels are identical. "Returning to the start" is a common narrative theme. This is what makes Freytag's (1894) model of plotlines "triangular" in shape: the ending connects back to the beginning. It also appears in Todorov's (1968) notion that narratives return to equilibrium after disruption. Nevertheless, although the first and last panels of Figure 4.3a are identical, they play different functional roles as Establisher and Release. Again, *context* in the sequence interacts with a panel's *content* to determine its narrative role. Even when a sequence begins and ends with the same panel, the Release appears more important to the narrative than the Establisher. Deleting the Establisher in Figure 4.3a would make little impact on the sequence compared with deleting the Release.

Establishers especially connect to several existing notions in discourse and narrative. They function similarly to discourse topics and storytelling prefaces, in addition to upholding the general preference for describing who is doing an action before describing the action itself (Sasse, 1987). Clearly, they relate to "establishing shots" in film (Arijon, 1976; Bordwell and Thompson, 1997; Carroll, 1980) and in comics (Abel and Madden, 2008; McCloud, 2006). However, unlike prototypical establishing shots, Establishers do not necessarily require an expansive long-shot viewpoint highlighting the broader environment, as film and previous comics work suggests.

## *Prolongations*

Consider also the third panel of Figure 4.3d, which shows the paper airplane between going *from* the student (Source/Initial) *to* the teacher's hair (Goal/Peak). We could easily omit this panel with no consequences for the sequence, but, narratively, it holds off the Peak for another panel. This panel is a *Prolongation*, which marks a medial state in the course of an action or event. Prolongations often depict the trajectory between a Source and Goal, sometimes clarifying the manner of the path. They can also function as a narrative "pause" or "beat" for delaying the Peak, adding a sense of atmosphere, and/or building tension before the Peak (as in the third panel of Figure 4.3c, or the central panels in Figure 4.1). When an author wants to draw out a scene, an Initial or Prolongation at the end of a page (or daily episode) can leave readers in suspense until their resolution.

## *Orienters*

An *Orienter* provides superordinate information about the location or context of a sequence, often at its beginning and/or end. The first panel of

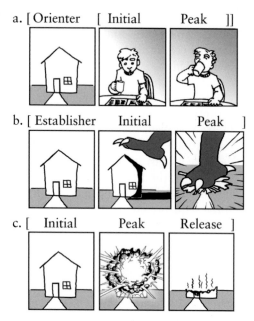

**FIGURE 4.4** *Sequences starting with a place.*

Figure 4.4 is an Orienter, giving the superordinate location for the action of the strip. The person is *inside* the house. Nothing in the subsequent panels shows that the actions of the man take place in the house—the juxtaposition with the first panel alone provides this information.

While Orienters prototypically show places, this is not a rigid mapping. Again, context matters. Although the house panel serves as the Orienter in Figure 4.4a, the same panel sets up the situation as an Establisher in Figure 4.4b rather than an Orienter, because the house itself engages in the actions. As the Establisher, it sets the scene for the Initial and Peak of a Godzilla foot stepping on it. Last, the same panel takes the role of a non-prototypical Initial in Figure 4.4c, providing the nascent state for the house to be blown up in the Peak. In both 4.4b and 4.4c the house actually engages in the interrelation, and thus is not an Orienter.

While Orienters are most often locatives, they can also convey more general superordinate concepts, such as showing an image of a "battle" that frames a sequence about individuals involved in the fray. Like Establishers, Orienters often provide the context for the rest of the sequence. However, unlike Establishers, Orienters provide a *superordinate* framing for the Arc and do not introduce the actual entities involved in the events of the Arc. Because of this context-setting quality, Orienters also relate to the use of extreme long-shots in the "establishing shots" in film that show the broader environment (Arijon, 1976; Bordwell and Thompson, 1997; Carroll, 1980) and to storytelling practices like "Settings" that set the stage for the narrative (i.e. "once upon a time *in a land far away...*"). Because of this, Orienters are placed above an actual phase or Arc, in their own superordinate phase.

## *Summary*

This section has established the basic categories of Visual Narrative Grammar. Peaks, Initials, and Releases function as core categories, while Establishers and Prolongations are more peripheral. These categories fall into a canonical pattern within "phases," and an Orienter may provide a contextual shell for this sequence:

Phase' → (Establisher) – (Initial (Prolongation)) – Peak – (Release)
Phase → (Orienter) Phase' (Orienter)

Finally, any phases that do not play a role in a larger node become Arcs. The categories/functional roles are summarized in Table 4.1.

TABLE 4.1 *Primary correspondences between narrative categories and conceptual structures, in order within a narrative Arc.*

| Narrative Category | Conceptual Structure |
|---|---|
| Orienters | Superordinate context<br>Location of event |
| Establishers | Introduction of referential relationship<br>Passive state of being |
| Initials | Preparatory action<br>Process<br>Departing a Source of a path |
| Prolongations | Position on trajectory of a path<br>Sustainment of a process<br>Passive state (delaying) |
| Peaks | Culmination of event<br>Termination of a process<br>Interruption of event or process<br>Reaching a Goal of a path |
| Releases | Wrap-up of narrative sequence<br>Outcome of an event<br>Reaction to an event<br>Passive state of being |

# Constituent structure in visual narrative

We have now established several categories that serve as the "parts of speech" or "grammatical functions" in Visual Narrative Grammar. So far, these pieces use only a variant of the canonical narrative phase. The implication is that sequences must use this canonical pattern and could not be more than five panels long. Now, consider Figure 4.5.

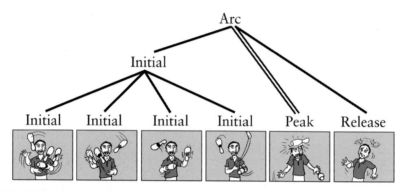

**FIGURE 4.5** *Complicated narrative structure.*

In this example, a man is juggling and then gets hit in the head with his juggling pin. The Peak of this sequence is the penultimate panel, where he gets hit in the head, followed by a Release of him stumbling dizzily. But what exactly is happening in the first four panels? These panels all show roughly the same information: the man juggling. This repetition is a type of **Conjunction**: all four of these panels function as co-Initials of an "Initial Phase" that sets up the Peak. We can formalize Conjunction as:

*A phase uses Conjunction if...*
...that phase consists of multiple panels in the same narrative role. Semantically, this often corresponds with...
1 various parts of an iterative process,
2 various viewpoints of a broader environment or individual, or
3 various images tied through a broader semantic field.

In Figure 4.5, the Conjunction shows an iterative process. Semantically, all these panels contain the same information, which could be achieved with fewer units (indeed, the first panel shows the full event). By extending this action across several panels, *narrative* tension and pacing builds until a culmination in the Peak. This example again highlights how narrative structures differ from events: the event structures constitute the meaning (juggling), while the choice to extend it across four panels involves how the meaning is conveyed, i.e. the narrative structure.

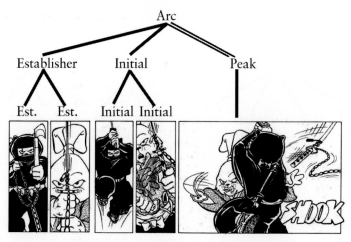

**FIGURE 4.6** *Alternation between characters to build tension. Usagi Yojimbo ©️ 1987 Stan Sakai.*

Consider also the Conjunctive phases in Figure 4.6, where the opening four panels alternate between the characters involved in the interaction. This ***Environmental-Conjunction*** (E-Conjunction) allows Mono panels to each show individual elements of a scene, which together create the sense of an environment in the mind. Essentially, these panels together "add up to" the amount of information that could be depicted by a Macro. However, by showing only parts of the scene, readers must construct the whole environment in their minds.

This sequence uses E-Conjunction in both the Establisher and Initial to create narrative pacing with the Convergence Construction, flipping back and forth between characters to build the tension of the sequence to culminate in the final Peak panel. This sense of narrative pacing would be lost if the Establisher and Initial each used only one panel with both characters together, since all panels would contain the same amount of information. Dividing the scene into parts allows the narrative rhythm to build until a culmination in the Peak.

**FIGURE 4.7** *Short narrative sequence.*

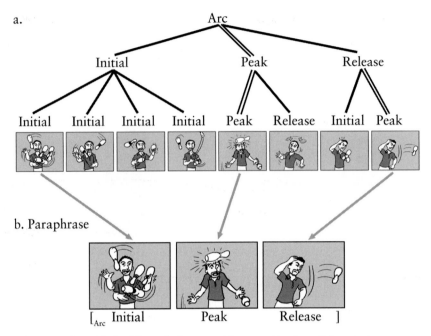

**FIGURE 4.8** *a. Embedding of phases and b. paraphrasing of the whole sequence.*

There is a second way to build larger narrative structures. Consider Figure 4.7. In this sequence, our juggler looks at a pin and then throws it away. On its own, this sequence is a fairly banal narrative with an Initial and Peak. Yet, when added to the end of the sequence in Figure 4.5, additional structure appears, as shown in Figure 4.8a.

By combining these strips, we create a larger narrative structure: the primary events are set up in the first four panels, which culminate in a Peak and have an aftermath in the final two panels. Each grouping forms its own phase. The first four panels create a conjoined Initial, the next two panels constitute a Peak—the main component of the overall narrative—while the final two panels combine as a Release. Each of these phases plays a larger narrative role relative to the others when combined. In this way, narrative categories apply to *sequences* of panels as well as *individual* panels.[4]

The panel that motivates the meaning of a phase can be thought of as the *head* of that node. Normally, Peaks are the default heads of phases. As annotated by double lines in Figure 4.8a, the Peak of the juggler being hit heads the first Peak phase, while the final Peak panel where he throws the pin heads the Release phase. Thus, a Peak provides the key component in its local phase. The other categories simply support, lead up to, or elaborate upon a phase's Peak. In other words, *Peaks drive the narrative sequence.* Because of this importance, deletion of all non-heads from a sequence

a. Left-brancing visual narrative

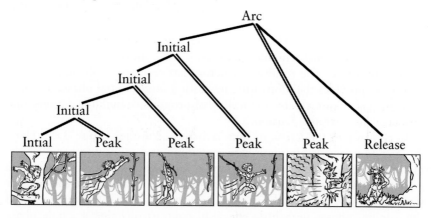

b. Alternating Initials

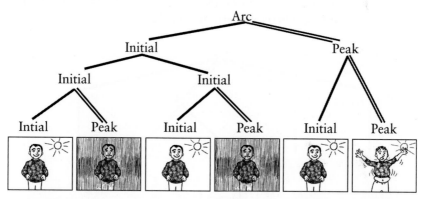

**FIGURE 4.9** *Two examples of narrative structure using different patterns of embedding.*

should adequately paraphrase the sequence's meaning, as in Figure 4.8b (technically, conjoined iterative panels all act as heads, so only the first panel from the Initial is used here).

We see then that sequential images can allow two primary types of elaboration. First, constituents can repeat the same category in a Conjunction that shares their narrative category at the phasal level. Second, a whole phase can play a narrative role in a broader structure, meaning that phases can also embed inside each other. These two strategies create numerous possibilities for sequences to expand to unlimited lengths and narrative patterns.

Consider Figure 4.9a, which has a sequence of Peaks after the first panel. Instead of belonging to a single Conjunction, they create a ***left-branching*** *structure* where each serves as an Initial for the next. It begins with Tarzan preparing to jump, which as an Initial sets up the Peak of his leaping for a vine. Together, these panels act as another Initial for a Peak of him swinging on that vine. These panels then set up a Peak of him reaching for a new vine, which culminates in the main Peak of the strip, where he slams into a tree. The resulting structure has recursive embedding, where each Peak provides the motivating head for a larger Initial phase. The left-branching structure creates the feeling of progressive building actions and/ or increasing narrative tension.

In contrast to the left-branching structure, consider Figure 4.9b. Here, the first four panels alternate between sunny and rainy weather over the man in a sweater. Each pair acts as an Initial phase, and together they form a Conjunction that acts as an Initial for the final Peak, where the sweater shrinks. We can confirm this Conjunction because we can delete either of these Initial phases with little effect. In contrast, deleting a whole phase in the left-branching structures in Figure 4.9a would drastically alter the reading. The embedding of phases also reflects the narrative pacing: the "on-off" pattern of panels (sun-rain-sun-rain-sun…) builds until the final panel (…sun-shrink), where the pattern is broken.

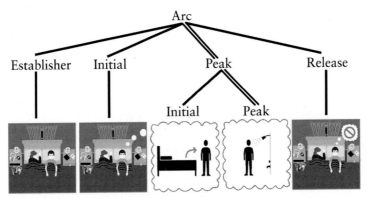

**FIGURE 4.10**  *Center-embedded phase. One Night © 2006 Tym Godek.*

Narrative structure can also use **center-embedded phases,** as in Figure 4.10. This strip shows a man lying in bed. He thinks about going to the bathroom, but decides not to get up. His thoughts stand alone as an embedded phase (here a Peak phase) that we could separate from the rest of the strip. In fact, both the embedded phase and the surrounding "matrix" phase could stand alone as their own independent sequences.

We now have enough machinery to analyze Figure 4.1, the ambiguous sequence of the man and the clock. The sequence opens with two Initial panels, which both show states that undergo a change in the final two Peak panels. The central panel of the windows is a Prolongation, delaying the Peak. As mentioned, this sequence's ambiguity depends on whether

a. Embedded Prolongation phase          b. Conjoined environments

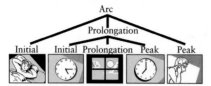
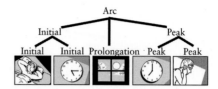

**FIGURE 4.11** *Re-analysis of Figure 4.1.*

the panels of the man and the clock belong to the same time frame. Under one interpretation (see Figure 4.11a), the first and last panels form their own phase. The clocks then form another subordinate Prolongation phase, which delays the final Peak. This structure implies that all of the panels depict different times. A second interpretation (see Figure 4.11b) conjoins the adjacent Initial and Peak panels. Here, the first two panels belong to a single Initial phase, while the last two panels belong to a single Peak phase. Each constituent depicts facets of a broader spatial environment at a single moment in time.[5] Thus, the two rules proposed by this model, for phases and conjunctions, allow us to parse a single ambiguous sequence into multiple interpretations.

An important question worth asking is: How do people know where the boundaries between constituents lie? One possible answer is that people rely on major changes in characters, locations, or causation, like those outlined by McCloud's (1993) panel transitions. Essentially, constituents end when a segment is no longer about particular characters, places, or actions, and thus major breaks in the narrative stream cue a reader that one constituent has ended and the next has begun.

Nevertheless, panel transitions might not always indicate the edge of a boundary. The four opening panels in Figure 4.6 alternate between two characters, yet they do not *all* mark constituent boundaries because they use Conjunction. Conversely, Figure 4.8a has no shifts in characters or locations at all, although narrative constituent breaks still occur. Thus, while they may correlate strongly, transitions between panels do not map one-to-one with phase boundaries and cannot be relied on as the sole indicator of constituents. We will return to this issue in Chapter 6.

## Modification

Beyond the basic categories and structures, additional panels can modify other panels. Consider the sequences in Figure 4.12a, where men are pulling a triceratops skull from a hill. Panels 2 and 3 zoom in on information from the first panel. They cannot be Peaks, because they depict a state prior to the skull being pulled down; and there is no iteration of the Initial action,

a. Sequence with two Refiners modifying a head Establisher

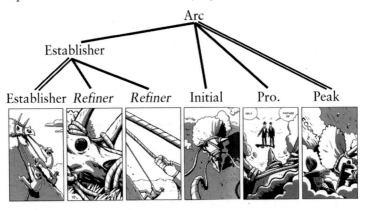

b. Sequence where zooms act as conjoined Establishers

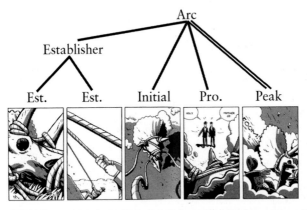

**FIGURE 4.12** *Multiple Refiners modifying Establishers. Bone Sharps and Thunder Lizards © 2005 Jim Ottaviani and Big Time Attic.*

so they cannot be Initials either. Nor do they show medial states between the Initial and Peak, and thus cannot be considered Prolongations. Rather, they only repeat the information shown in the prior panels with a different framing, using Monos and Micros to window attention.

These panels are ***Refiners***, a modifier that hones information also shown in the phase's "head." Here close-ups of the skull and the men provide further detail on the scene. Refiners apply to all types of basic narrative categories, as reflected in the following rule:

*Phase X → (Refiner)\* X (Refiner)\**

This rule stipulates that a phase of category X contains a head of that category (X) that is either preceded or followed by Refiners of the same information. As in the example in Figure 4.12a, Refiners can repeat multiple times (annotated with the asterisks). Because a Refiner focuses on information in another panel, it must have a head to modify. If no head is present, it *becomes* the head. For example, the altered sequence in Figure 4.12b omits the original Establisher (a Macro), and the two remaining Refiners now both take on conjoined Establisher roles. Such absorption of structure may be parallel to constructions like *the poor* to mean *the poor people*. Also, in many languages an adjective can act like a noun, being the sole descriptor for an object, as in *I'd like the red* to mean *red **wine**.*

a. Refiner modifying a Macro head

b. Refiner modifying a Mono head

c. Refiner "projected" away from its head

d. Refiner with ambiguity for its head (projected vs. local)

**FIGURE 4.13** *Refiner Projection.*

Further complexity can arise when Refiners are placed away from their heads. Note the relationships between the starting panels in the sequences in Figure 4.13. We understand the puncher and the victim as belonging to a common environment (E-Conjunction), as evidenced by the panel they share in 4.13a. However, the Refiner of the fist only modifies the puncher. We would assume that heads should stay near their Refiners (as in Figures 4.13a and 4.13b). In contrast, some Refiners can become separated from their heads due to an intervening panel (see Figure 4.13c), as opposed to having the E-Conjunction follow the Refiner (see Figure 4.13b). While both sequences seem grammatical, many respondents report to me that the version where the Refiner is "projected" down the phase (see Figure 4.13c) reads better than the non-projected one (see Figure 4.13b). The challenge here is that the Conjunction of the two characters intervenes between the Refiner and its head.

Another complication arises when we introduce ambiguity for the head of the Refiner, as in the third panel of Figure 4.13d. This Refiner could belong to either character, since their actions are the same and the panel is ambiguously drawn. These sequences illustrate the potential complexity found in sequential images with regard to anaphora, distance dependencies, and ambiguity. Any theory of narrative structure—in sequential images or otherwise—must be prepared to address this type of complexity.

## *Summary*

In this section, we explored how narrative categories extend beyond the panel level in Visual Narrative Grammar. We have described three types of relationships between phases and categories, based on which category assigns a role to the phase (if no assignment, it becomes an Arc). A regular phase elaborates on its Peak as a subordinate narrative Arc, and it plays a narrative role in the larger structure in which it is embedded. A conjunction phase may contain multiple daughters of the same type, which function as co-heads. A modifying phase may also contain a head with Refiners. Thus, only two basic rules are needed to organize numerous narrative categories, along with a single modification rule. This resulting system can generate an infinite array of larger patterns: left-branching trees, center-embedded phases, alternation, etc.

While each of these Arcs can be treated as a "visual sentence," several Arcs may appear in the context of a whole comic book or graphic novel (usually a strip has just one Arc). This requires a system to incorporate smaller Arcs into a larger understanding. Because of the type of recursive embedding allowed by this narrative grammar, "sentence-level" Arcs can play functional roles that build even larger "discourse-level" Arcs. When we speak of "plot lines," we often refer to the structure of these discourse-level Arcs.

# Discourse and film

If narrative structure transcends a single modality, we would expect the same structures to be used in the comprehension of verbal, signed, and filmic narratives. Here, I outline how Narrative Grammar, designed for sequential images, can be adapted to other domains.

Just as panels visually frame a scene, sentences in discourse also package semantic information (Hoey, 1991; Langacker, 2001; Zwaan, 2004), and indeed this comparison has been made in approaches applying discourse theory to visual narrative (Saraceni, 2000; Stainbrook, 2003). Several sentences and phrases exemplify prototypical narrative categories: "There once was an X..." is a prototypical Establisher, providing a frame for referential entities to be introduced. "In a far-off land..." is an Orienter that provides a generic location. "And they all lived happily ever after" is a prototypical Release, a generic aftermath appropriate for all happy endings. These phrases could be added to the beginning or end of nearly any narrative and retain their felicity because of their status as narrative units.

Strings of sentences are used to combine multiple events in discourse much like strings of panels form narrative Arcs in the graphic form. A discourse structure organizes the meanings in individual sentences with respect to each other. We can apply Narrative Grammar to discourse by verbally translating a comic, as in Figure 4.14, which is a verbal version of Figure 4.5.

This narrative conveys the same meaning as Figure 4.5, in the same narrative structure: a series of Initials culminates with the Peak of the juggler being hit in the head. The Peak phase then resolves in the Release phase of him looking at the pin and throwing it away. It is important to note that sometimes a whole sentence can act as a category (as in the first Release), but often a subclause alone can serve as a narrative category.

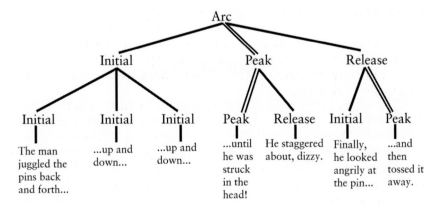

**FIGURE 4.14** *Verbal discourse structure.*

Narratives also appear in the visual modality through film. In film, cameras capture events as they unfold in time—just as in perception. This ongoing temporal progression records a single unbounded stream of events from one camera's viewpoint. Filmmakers then break up this recording into "shots" in the editing process, which combine with other shots to create a novel sequence in which a new temporality emerges, dictated by the shots themselves (Bordwell and Thompson, 1997). Narrative roles are assigned during the process of recombining shots into a novel sequence.

In fact, the filming and editing process often begins with "storyboarding," where shots are drawn out in a form similar to the visual language used in comics. In other words, film uses the same narrative grammar, except the units are not static panels, but moving segments of film. The result is a hybrid: the narrative grammar organizes captured perceptual events in shots. Because film uses motion, this temporality can "gloss over" what in the static form would be individuated narrative units. For example, a single shot may include both a preparatory and completed action, thereby combining what statically would be discrete Initials and Peaks. In fact, because a camera can be left recording, an entire action or even a full scene could be captured in one continuous shot, thereby concatenating what would be a whole Arc or more in drawn form.

Complicating matters further, not only do the elements within a film shot move (i.e. characters and objects move around), but the camera itself can move. Panning and zooming create alterations to a graphic scene that is continuous rather than discrete.

These differences create an area of debate: can non-discrete shots constitute "narrative categories" or not? Most definitely, a continuous single shot would show an *event* structure. However, is narrative dependent upon discrete units that organize those potentially continuous events, or is a continuous representation merely a variation in "performance" but not "competence"? Exploring such questions is important for cross-modality understandings of narrative.

# Conclusion

In this chapter, we explored the question of "how do people make sense out of sequential images?". To answer it, I have outlined a theory of Narrative Grammar for visual language analogous to syntax in sentences. Clearly, syntax operates at a different level of information than found in sequential images: pictures can convey far more information than words. Nevertheless, narrative and syntax *function* as *structures* in much the same way. Like syntax, narrative (presentation) is separate from semantics (meaning), allowing us to convey the same meaning in different surface presentations, as well as the opposite: using a single surface presentation to convey multiple meanings (as in Figure 4.1).

Formally, this grammar uses several core categories that map to proto-typical features of events or play functional roles in a sequence. These categories are organized through a basic canonical pattern similar to traditional notions of narrative. Only here, each category can recursively expand into its own phase. Along with Conjunction and Refiner rules, this recursion allows for complex narrative structures and pacing.

While we have focused on the visual-graphic domain, these structures also appear in verbal/signed discourse and film. Again, this point reiterates our theme that structures involved with sequential images are not unique to the visual-graphic modality. Rather, they cross domains. Thus, exploring visual narratives can not only teach us about the grammar of visual language, but can offer us a better understanding of how narrative structure adapts to the unique properties of each modality, and how its function and structure operates as a general cognitive process.

# Notes

1 Portions of this chapter have appeared previously in Cohn (2010c, 2013a).

2 Many of these categories should be reminiscent of notions from other models of narrative or discourse. For example, the canonical *E-I-P-R* sequence resembles the classic story structure for five-act plays proposed by Freytag (1894): *Set up-Rising Action-Climax-Falling Action-Denouement*. I will discuss some of these connections, but for purposes of space, I will not dwell on them. See Cohn (2013a) for further discussion of these overlaps.

3 Some authors of Japanese manga subtly use larger gaps between panels at places I would identify as breaks between Arcs. Authors sometimes have their own "punctuation" as well. For example, in her manga *Ranma ½*, Rumiko Takahashi often ends an episode with a panel (usually a Release) that has slightly wider margins than the other panels on that page. Further patterns within and between authors would be worth exploring.

4 Note: I offered a slightly different analysis of this sequence in Cohn (2013a) where the Initial phase embeds beneath the Peak phase. Essentially, both interpretations capture the same constituent information, although Figure 4.8 is a simpler embedding structure that further supports a canonical Arc, and better reflects the contributions of each constituent (and their heads) to that superordinate Arc.

5 The middle "window" panel could potentially group in several different patterns. For simplicity, I leave it isolated.

# CHAPTER FIVE

# Navigation of External Compositional Structure

Unlike the temporal unfurling of spoken language, most visual languages have no inherent constraints on how a sequence is received. Since comic pages or strips are presented as whole canvases, how does a reader know where to begin or how to move from one panel to another? While most literate readers of English are familiar with the left-to-right and downward reading orders used in written language (the "Z-path"), comic pages often depart from simple grids in ways that challenge this Z-path of reading. This chapter presents a theory that addresses this issue of *navigating* through the potentially complex *external compositional structure* (ECS) of printed visual language.

## The challenge of page layouts

Naturally, aspects of layout and panels may tie to narrative structures or the creation of the broader meaning of a visual sequence. Panels may take on meaningful shapes that enhance or inherently frame the meaning of the sequence (like a panel in the shape of a heart or the crosshairs of the scope of a gun). Particular narrative categories may end pages (like Initials to create suspense until the page is turned), or may have consistent shapes (like using the same panel shape for all story-ending Releases or story-beginning Establishers). The broader layout may also use decorative functions to enhance a mood. For example, in the comic series I drew as a teenager, gothic statues often held up panels that existed outside the narrative world, yet provided additional decorative aspects of mood or aesthetics to the layout.

Most approaches to layout have discussed these types of meaningful relationships. Several authors have proposed taxonomies of layout types based on how they relate to the content of the narrative (Caldwell, 2012; Groensteen, 2007; Peeters, 1998 [1991]). For example, does the page serve a decorative function or does it just use a standard conventional layout, like a grid? Other conflations of layout and meaning have incorporated aspects of page layout directly into the comprehension of sequential images (Barber, 2002; Drucker, 2008), often grappling with how to resolve the types of non-adjacent connections between panels that we discussed in the last chapter.

While layout and content likely interface in important ways, they are ultimately different structures. This is evident because the same sequence of images can be arranged in multiple ways without impairing meaning. For instance, four-panel comic strips in newspapers commonly appear horizontally, vertically, or stacked in a 2 x 2 grid. In all cases, the content remains the same, while the layout changes. Granted, change in the *order* of panels would result in different meaning, but this still requires a method to explain *why* people read in the sequence they do.

Despite shedding light on the way in which layout may be involved with a narrative, these previous approaches do not address a more basic question: How do people know how to navigate through page layouts? (Or, what constraints motivate authors of comics to design page layouts in the ways they do?) Navigational strategies cannot wholly rely on content, since once a panel is reached, it would require readers to fully engage all possible choices of panels before choosing which one is next. This would place too much burden on the reading process, not to mention working memory. The smooth motions found in eye-tracking studies of comic pages seems to support that expert readers do not explore all options before moving from one panel to the next (Nakazawa, 2002). Moreover, while alterations in panel layouts affect eye movements, they do not appear to significantly impact reading comprehension (Omori, Ishii, and Kurata, 2004).

All of these previous approaches assume that people *do* navigate and understand sequential images, without questioning or offering insight into *how* readers do so. Most authors assume that readers follow the Z-path reading order for written language. Is the navigation of comic pages really this simple? What do readers do when faced with unusual arrangements of panels that seem to flout the expected Z-path of reading? Just what aspects of page layouts might motivate alternative readings besides the Z-path?

## *Variations in ECS*

Page layouts may depart from or manipulate a straightforward grid (Figure 5.1a) in several ways. The borders of panels may become angled, eliminated altogether, or panels might take strange sizes or shapes. These manipulations are relatively superficial since they may not necessarily force a reader to question how to order the panels. More challenging manipulations might vary the *proximity* of the panels with each other, either through **separation** of the panels from each other (Figure 5.1c) or **overlapping** panels on top of each other (Figure 5.1d). This dimension of proximity has been well established as an organizational principle by Gestalt psychologists (e.g. Wertheimer, 1923), who showed that people perceptually group items that are nearest to each other. We might predict, then, that closely grouped panels would be ordered together before those that are further apart. Would such groupings be preferred if they flout the Z-path?

Other orientations between panels create different challenges. On a small scale, this might involve **staggering** panels (Figure 5.1e) so that readers question the expected Z-path because the horizontal gutter no longer runs continuously across the panels. The most extreme example of this type of manipulation occurs when a whole panel "blocks" the horizontal gutter entirely. **Blockage** occurs when several panels are stacked vertically next to a single panel that runs the whole distance of the vertical panels, as in Figure 5.1b.

If the Z-path is used, then panel C will be ordered before panel B. Thus, any subsequent panel (like B) might require backtracking in the opposite direction to the Z-path, thereby passing over the bottom part of panel C. An alternate order would move vertically before horizontally, where panel C "blocks" the Z-path, forcing movement vertically from A to B then horizontally to C. Blockage has often been cited as "problematic" by comic creators and inexperienced comic readers. A study using eye-tracking has further supported this, finding that readers frequently skip over the "B" panels when presented with blockage situations, and that when modified to a horizontal path, the skipping of this panel decreased dramatically (Omori et al., 2004).

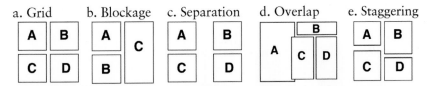

**FIGURE 5.1** *Different manipulations to the external compositional structure of panels.*

Other changes to layout involve where a person starts a page. Conventional wisdom would say that, like reading text, readers of left-to-right writing systems would prefer to start in the upper left-hand corner of a page, while readers of right-to-left writing systems would prefer the upper right corner (such as readers of Japanese manga). Research has supported these preferences by revealing that a person's writing system impacts other aspects of their spatial cognition. For example, readers of left-to-right writing systems are better able to recall elements in the upper left quadrant of an array, while readers of right-to-left systems better remember upper right quadrants (Chan and Bergen, 2005). Such results imply that similar preferences would be maintained for comic pages, while such intuitions would be challenged by layouts where no panel appears in the upper left position, or where this space is split between panels.

## Comprehension of ECS

In order to further investigate how these manipulations impact readers' preferences for navigating through page layouts, I conducted an experiment (Cohn, 2013b). I designed booklets that featured pages with *empty* panels, and then asked participants to number the panels in the order that they would read them. I then examined which orders they chose to navigate through the various manipulations to layout.

Unsurprisingly, participants chose to order the 2 x 3 panel grid in a Z-path at high proportions (94%). I used this finding as a baseline to compare with the other manipulations (see Figure 5.2). Blockage had the largest impact on the Z-path reading order. Only 32% of reading orders maintained the Z-path, meaning that most readers chose to move *vertically* instead of horizontally. What's more, this figure correlated with participants' comic reading expertise: people who had never read comics before used the Z-path more than experienced readers. This goes against the conventional wisdom that says blockage creates navigation problems, since people *en masse* departed from the Z-path for these situations (*if* they had experience reading comics).

Overlap also noticeably impacted the Z-path, with roughly 50% of the paths taken in overlap situations yielding a Z-path order. Closer inspection

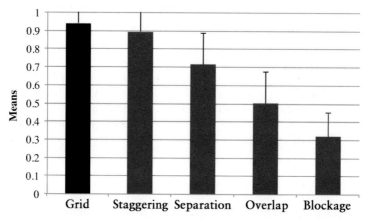

**FIGURE 5.2** *Rates at which readers chose to depart from the Z-path of reading in ordering panels in empty comic panels.*

of the materials showed that this rate was affected more by other factors of the panels' arrangements (like blockage) than the actual overlapping panels themselves. The least impactful manipulations were those using separation (using the Z-path 71% of the time) and staggering (90%). While staggering had almost no impact, the influence of separation was still enough to be statistically significant from the reading of the grid, meaning that separation did influence readers to sometimes take a non-Z-path order, despite it not being a predominant choice.

In addition to these manipulations, I also looked at the "entry point" of a page. Very clearly, participants had difficulty deciding where to start ordering panels when no clear panel appeared in the upper left corner. Nevertheless, participants fairly consistently chose "left-to-right/top-to-bottom" orders over "right-to-left" orders when negotiating the complex aspects of layouts. Interestingly, participants who often read Japanese manga tended to enter pages with more right-to-left orders, despite navigating the remainder of pages in a left-to-right order. Generally, all participants chose orders maintaining a continuous flow of connecting panels over orders where the path would be broken.

These findings raise additional questions: How long does a blocking panel need to be to invoke blockage, since staggering alone created little effect? Why does separation have a significant impact on navigational path, even though the Z-path was still chosen more than any other strategy in these situations? The following section proposes a theoretical model for the navigation of comic pages that incorporates these results. First, I will propose a general principle of navigation based on preference rules for selecting the path of reading. Second, these rules will be situated as part of a broader model for the architecture of external compositional structure.

## Constraints on external compositional structure

The results of my experiments revealed an overarching strategy that expands on the basic principles of the Z-path. By and large, the rightward and downward direction of the Z-path was preferred: participants started in the upper left and progressed to the lower right. However, readers were sensitive to various aspects of panels' relations to each other and the page borders. To negotiate these issues, participants used a general strategy of what I'll call *Assemblage*, which is a principle where a reader or author of layouts seeks *to build successive units of structure based on distance and coherence of composite shapes in as smooth a reading path as possible.* Several general preferences guide Assemblage:

1   Grouped areas > non-grouped areas
2   Smooth paths > broken paths

**3** Do not jump over units

**4** Do not leave gaps

Blockage can provide a good example. Assemblage would predict that readers follow blockage because a horizontal Z-path reading would leave a "gap" in the broader shape of the panels' "additive space," as in Figure 5.3a. In contrast, the preferred reading fills in the whole space in the most economical order possible through an additive process, as in Figure 5.3b. By moving vertically first, the combined space of the stacked panels equals that of the blocking panel to their right. Grouping them first ensures that no excess space remains at any point of the reading process, and that navigation follows a smooth path. This grouping relies on coherence of the lengths of the various panels' borders. Two segments must guide this: the length of the top border, and the length of the inner vertical borders. In blockage, the vertical boundaries guide the navigation before the horizontal border. Meanwhile, the outer horizontal boundary is retained as an overarching space needed to be filled.

Assemblage acts as a general principle to the ECS of page layouts, while a more explicit set of "preference rules" specifies the exact processes of navigation. Like the constraints placed on perception by Gestalt groupings, preference rules specify the "preferred" interpretation out of various possible structural interpretations, and have been used for describing both music cognition (e.g. Lerdahl and Jackendoff, 1982) and language (e.g, Jackendoff, 1983). These "ECS Preference Rules" (ECSPR) state the series of operations that occur when a reader is at one panel and looking to move to a subsequent panel. A navigational choice is determined by moving down

a. Order of reading that does not maintain Assemblage

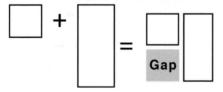

b. Order of reading maintaining Assemblage

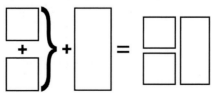

**FIGURE 5.3** *Blockage preferences through Assemblage.*

the list: if a rule is met by all options or if a rule is met by no options, the next rule is invoked, down until a constraint is satisfied. Also, if these rules come in conflict with each other, they must be played off each other to determine the proper path. These constraints will be discussed in turn and then applied to examples.

**Entry Constraints.** Before actually navigating through various panels, readers must first find a starting panel. Thus, the first preference rules outline how a sequence is begun, when faced with an ambiguous page or display (as opposed to a scenario when the first panel is overtly provided, such as a digital comic that forces the reading to begin at a particular panel).

*ECSPR E1: Go to the top left corner:* Readers consistently look for a panel in the top left corner of a page when first entering a "canvas." Note that the directional specifications on this constraint (and all the preference rules) may alter based on cultural experience as indicated by right-to-left preferences from readers of Japanese manga.

*ECSPR E2: If no top left panel, go to either the 1) highest and/or 2) leftmost panel:* When no panel exists in the top left to satisfy the first constraint, this second constraint directs readers to balance either the panel that is most left on the page (so that a rightward reading motion is preserved) or the highest panel on the page (to preserve a continuous path of reading motion).

**Navigational constraints.** Once an entry panel is established, navigational constraints specify how to move through that environment.

*ECSPR 1: Follow the outer border[1] (Assemblage constraint 1):* The first navigational choice seeks a contiguous edge of the outermost borders of the situated panel and its immediate surrounding panels (see Figure 5.4).

*ECSPR 2: Follow the inner border (Assemblage constraint 2):* If contiguous outer borders are available for all paths, the second rule seeks a contiguous border for the inner edges of a panel and its adjacent panels (see Figure 5.4). Rules following outer and inner borders reflect the desire of Assemblage to create groupings out of contiguous motions.

*ECSPR 3: Move to the right (Z-path constraint 1):* When either an outer or inner border can be followed, the first preferred motion goes to the right. In less expert comic readers, this preference may be elevated to the most preferred reading strategy, as acquired by the Z-path. In other words, inexperienced readers ignore Assemblage, seeking only to satisfy a left-to-right reading path.

*ECSPR 4: Move straight down (Z-path constraint 2):* Given the previous constraints, if a rightward movement is unavailable, downward movement is next preferred.

*ECSPR 5: If nothing is to the right, go to the far left and down (Z-path constraint 3):* Sometimes no panel is available to the right, like at the border of a row of panels on a page, forcing the reader to move to the next tier down. This rule specifies the diagonal motion inherent in the Z-path. This rule comes into direct conflict with the previous rule as a separate type of downward movement. In those cases, local context decides which rule wins out.

*ECSPR 6: Go to the panel that has not been read yet:* The final rule provides a general default for reading any panel that has not yet been read. As the terminating constraint, this rule cannot be overridden. When panels are randomly scattered and "floating" on a page, the Z-path rules (3-5) may guide a reader in some semblance of order, while this last rule "sweeps up the remainders."

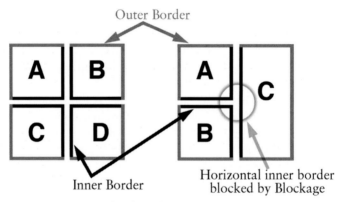

**FIGURE 5.4** *Inner and outer borders of panels in a layout.*

As is labeled, the first two rules satisfy the constraints of Assemblage, while the remaining rules refine the process of the Z-path. Most likely, the default for readers is ECSPR 3-6 acquired by reading text, while experienced comic readers have acquired additional Assemblage constraints that take precedence over this default.

The process of these rules can better be understood through examples. In the case of a grid, as in Figure 5.5a, at panel A both ECSPR requirements for 1 and 2 are met, since both outer and inner borders are contiguous all the way through. This allows ECSPR 3 to be initiated, since a rightward movement can reconcile the ambiguity, resulting in the common left-to-right motion of the Z-path.

When presented with a layout with blockage as Figure 5.5b, ECSPR E1

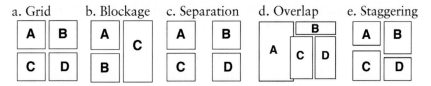

**FIGURE 5.5** *Different manipulations to the external compositional structure of panels.*

is the first engaged by the reader. Since a panel is present at the upper left corner, that constraint is satisfied; a reader first goes to panel A, enabling progression to subsequent navigational constraints. From panel A, per ECSPR 1 the reader checks the outer borders: the contiguity of both outer borders is sustained (A to C and A to B), so this constraint alone cannot determine the path. Moving into ECSPR 2, panel C blocks the contiguity of the inner horizontal border, but the vertical inner border downwards to panel B is not blocked. Since panel C blocks rightward movement necessary for ECSPR 3, the reader initiates ECSPR 4 with movement downward, and the constraints are satisfied reaching panel B. Panel C can then be read afterwards (ECSPR 3).

In situations with separation and staggering, Assemblage competes with Z-path constraints. Once at panel A, ECSPR 1 (and 2) can be satisfied by moving downward, invoking ECSPR 4. If the gap between panels is ignored as a constraining feature, the upper border from panel A can still be perceived as forming a contiguous line with panel B. This may invoke ECSPR 3 for rightward motion prior to ECSPR 4. Such a result is exactly what was observed in the experiment: while readers chose the Z-path (A to B) almost three times as much as the Gestalt grouping (A to C), the vertical path was statistically significant. In this case, both pathways are acceptable, but it appears that the Z-path constraints "win out" over the Assemblage constraints more often.

A similar competition occurs for staggering. The preference rules must weigh the influence of the discontinuous border. If the disruption in the border is perceived as significant (as in blockage), ECSPR 2 will guide the

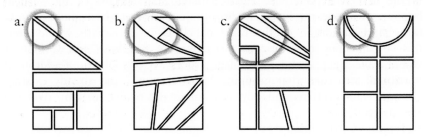

**FIGURE 5.6** *Unusual panel arrangements in the upper left corner of pages.*

reading vertically instead of allowing the Z-path rules to push the motion rightward while following the outer borders.

These preference rules can also account for how readers navigated through the unusual diagonal borders presented in the entry-point pages, as in Figure 5.6. In all but one stimulus (Figure 5.6c), ECSPR E1 is not satisfied, since no panel occupies the upper left corner. In these cases, ECSPR E2 was selected and the reader chose the leftmost panel as the entry point. From here, ECSPR 3 guides the reader in a rightward movement, maintaining general Assemblage principle 3 for a continuous motion to create a grouping out of the whole tier of diagonal panels.

These preference rules and general Assemblage constraints provide an initial foray into describing the governing principles of comic page navigation. In all likelihood, an additional set of constraints must weigh factors like color, panel composition, character's positioning and eye-gaze, and breaking the borders of panels. Further experiments and research can articulate these constraints in more detail, along with the probabilistic weights that readers negotiate in order to determine how one rule is chosen over another.

## Embedding structures

Beyond the navigation that theses preference rules offer, Assemblage creates hierarchically embedded groupings. A simple model of these relations was proposed for converting comic pages into an acceptable format for cell phone and PDA screens (Tanaka, Shoji, Toyama, and Miyamichi, 2007). Their approach divided pages into vertical and horizontal segments that recursively embed into each other. A similar approach will be presented here, with further elaboration.

The ECS preference rules create constituents by forming vertical and horizontal groupings, which concatenate panels additively. For instance, the Assemblage process that guides blockage would be represented on the left of Figure 5.7a, with the illegal order to the right. This organization says that a vertical unit embeds within a larger horizontal composite. This reflects the sensitivities to the contiguity of panel borders set out in the first two preference rules. Satisfying the length of the vertical boundaries allows the broader horizontal structure to be completed only through the addition of the third panel. Using a Z-path would flout this—by finishing the horizontal structure of panels A and C first, it would leave a gap in the Assemblage process. If B is left to an additional horizontal structure, that grouping "runs through" the already existing C panel. This adds redundancy, and forces the reader to jump over the already-read panel.

Typical Z-path orders appear in Figure 5.7b. Under an overarching vertical structure, horizontal segments concatenate various panels in rows,

a. Tree structures for Blockage

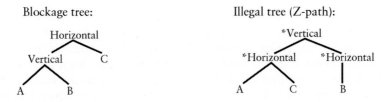

b. Tree structure for Z-path reading of a grid

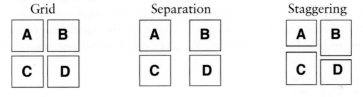

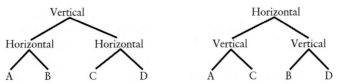

**FIGURE 5.7**  *Tree structures for the reading orders of blockage and grids.*

providing a way to represent successive reading of multiple rows moving downward. Any number of horizontal nodes can be added into this Z-path, as well as any number of panels within each horizontal node. A general rule reflecting the Z-path preference rules could be stated as (with asterisks notating repetition):

Z-path rule: [Vertical [Horizontal * [Unit *]]]

This rule states that an unlimited number of horizontal segments can embed within an overarching vertical unit, into which an unlimited number of units can be placed. In essence, this is the default rule for the alphabetic writing system. Altering it to suit the vertical orders of Japanese or Chinese would merely flip the horizontal and vertical labels. An associated constraint would then specify the direction of motion, moving right, left, up, and/or down.

These groupings further explain why separation could statistically depart from the Z-path yet be numerically chosen less often than the Z-path.

Assemblage works for both routes, allowing for structures to build cleanly using smooth motions, without leaving gaps. As depicted in Figure 5.7b, the tree structure for following separation is very similar to that of the Z-path, only inverting the vertical and horizontal nodes. This same tree would appear for staggering scenarios. Like separation, staggering may push a reader to decide which boundary to complete first: horizontal or vertical. Both the Z-path and vertical orders satisfy Assemblage to be completed without gaps, using a smooth motion. Ultimately, the engagement with the preference rules determines which path will be chosen.

Another important aspect to the ECS system is *recursion*. Any horizontal structure can embed a vertical structure, and vice versa, which means that the embedding can go on infinitely (theoretically speaking). Note also that a node of one type cannot embed a node of the same type (with one exception, to be addressed shortly). We can capture these in a pair of rules:

Horizontal → Vertical*
Vertical → Horizontal*

To summarize, these rules guide the entire embedding process for ECS, with a few exceptions like inset panels, which place panels inside of panels. These rules are emblematic, in that for a 2D space, the grouping rules essentially concatenate elements along X and Y dimensions. These grouping rules are also idealizations in that not all panel groupings involve cleanly rectangular panels (or groupings). Truly, the same rules would apply to panels diagonally arranged or with angled gutters for the overarching grouping patterns, further constrained by the ECS preference rules.

## *Descriptive tree structures*

In addition to reading strategies, this formalism provides a way to describe page layouts. For full pages, a topmost node of "Canvas" covers the maximal space of the ECS. This could be a single page, a two-page spread, or the overall space of a website, wall, piece of pottery, etc. Let's examine a few pages from various comics, starting with Figure 5.8 from *Scott Pilgrim*. This page demonstrates recursive embedding, since each panel is successively embedded within either a horizontal or vertical node. This means that each panel gets progressively smaller, which coincides narratively with the character fading into the distance while riding on a bus.

Consider also a few examples from Mike Mignola's *B.P.R.D.* Figure 5.9a uses a canvas that connects three horizontal rows through an overarching vertical node. Blockage splits the middle horizontal node into a vertical node with two more horizontal sub-streams (3-4-5, 6-7-8) before reaching

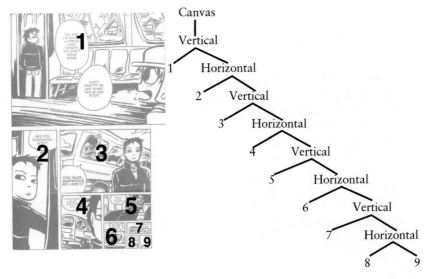

**FIGURE 5.8** *ECS of a comic page. Scott Pilgrim © 2005 Bryan Lee O'Malley.*

panel 9. As long as panel 8 immediately precedes panel 9, the panels within these subordinate rows could be read as vertical columns (with the broader row encapsulating three vertical nodes). However, the rules of Assemblage would guide them to be read horizontally, since no guiding force such as the length of panel 9 dictates a vertical order. So panels 5 and 8 engage in the blockage condition for their respective rows, since only they interact with panel 9.

The next page of the same book (Figure 5.9b) is simpler, with only four panels. The whole page divides into two sections bound through an overarching vertical node. The bottom segment is a horizontal row, but the top half has an inset panel enclosed within another. In tree form, the dominant panel embeds the enclosed panels inside it. Note that the enclosed node could feature multiple panels within it, and also include another "enclosed" node for an inset within an inset (indefinitely, since this too becomes recursive).

a. ECS with blockage

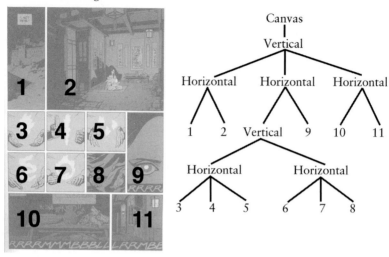

b. Inset panel enclosed by a dominant panel

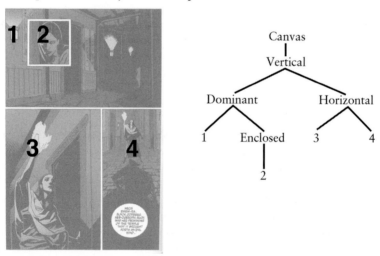

**FIGURE 5.9** *Two page layouts by Mike Mignola and Ryan Sook. B.P.R.D. ©
2003 Mike Mignola.*

By and large, printed books juxtapose pairs of pages, which would
combine two canvas nodes with a broader horizontal node, since pages
are usually read horizontally. This may create the sole exception to the
constraint against embedding a directional node within a like-node. If
adjacent pages feature all vertical columns, the horizontal order of panels
would be embedded within the horizontal progression of the pages, as in
Figure 5.10.

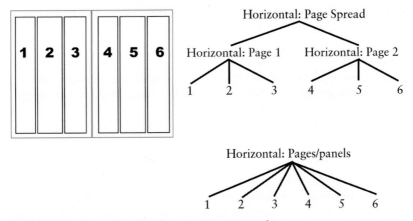

**FIGURE 5.10** *Tree structures for a two-page spread.*

This scenario then raises a theoretical question: To what extent would such an example be considered two individual pages each with their own directions, and to what extent would they be a singular "two-page spread" governed by one horizontal reading? Both interpretations yield the same equally valid reading, however, if only one page featured columns of panels and the other page had a different layout, the ambiguity would be immediately resolved.

## *The infinite canvas*

Before concluding, a brief discussion should be made about layouts outside of books, especially given the thrust of digital publishing. Given that any website can use scrolling to move through a page, physical boundaries do not restrict the size and shape of a canvas on a computer screen. This "Infinite Canvas" allows for a multitude of creative and dynamic layouts, along with novel navigational methods (McCloud, 2000b). In some online comics, panels merely follow a consistent path guided by local proximity of continuous panels. They may also use "trails"—lines or images that connect one panel to another (McCloud, 2000a)—which order panels through local connections without needing to retain close proximity. Trails create a simple preference rule that says, "Follow Trail," an instantiation of the Gestalt principle of Connection (Palmer and Rock, 1994). Such a basic command lends simplicity to a reading that might otherwise be very difficult.

Animation can also provide further constraint. A screen can act as a window to show the reader only a selection of the overall comic page, with animation moving the viewpoint either across the page or zooming directly *into* the panel along a Z-axis to reveal the subsequent panel (as in

McCloud's *The Right Number*). Instigated by clicking on the screen, the animation only allows the reader to move to the intended subsequent panel. This prevents any navigation that flouts the intents of the author. By virtue of its unrestrained boundaries, the Infinite Canvas allows layouts to bypass ECS preference rules and constraints like Assemblage, instead relying on simple Gestalt groupings, trails, or animated routes forced by the interface.

## Conclusion

This chapter explored the question of how readers progress through visual language's external compositional structure, and provided a theory of navigational structure to account for this ability. This structure is separate from meaning and the narrative grammar. Of course, this does not mean that ECS and meaning cannot or do not interact. The tree structures presented here for ECS interface with the tree structures for visual narrative grammar presented in the previous chapter. Having shown that readers *do* have a system for navigating layouts outside content, it is an open question as to what happens when the content defies these principles. Do readers face difficulties in these mismatches? Does the content override the external compositional structures? Does this create costs in processing? With these foundations in place, future studies can probe these and other concerns more deeply, particularly with the use of eye-tracking that can pinpoint the online strategies of reading pages of visual language.

It is also worth noting that this structure is almost wholly an artifact of book-formatted pages for visual language. As technology grows, we may see these types of rules become less necessary because the format for conveying the visual language changes (as in digital comics). Furthermore, visual languages outside the context of books do not need such rules in the first place (as in the sand drawings discussed in Chapter 9). The lexicon and grammar of visual language described in earlier chapters tap into facets of how languages in general are structured. However, while general cognitive traits like Gestalt groupings are engaged, this navigational structure deals with how visual language appears in *our* cultural context.

## Note

1 "Border" in this case may be considered as an abstract. Panels often do not have drawn geometric borders. My guess is that borderless panels would obey the same principles sensitive to borders, but this would require further testing.

# CHAPTER SIX

# Cognition of Visual Language

Thus far, we have described the *structure* of visual language—the representations in the minds of individuals that allow them to read and create sequences of images. We now turn from structure to *processing*—what happens in people's minds/brains while they *comprehend* or *produce* a sequence of images. Framed another way: to what degree do people actually use the representations posited in the previous chapters as they read/draw sequential images? Are these constructs psychologically real? If any theory of the structure of sequential images is "valid," then it must reflect how people actually comprehend sequences of narrative images. To address this question, we must move beyond theory and address research based on experimentation. Most of this discussion will focus on sequences of images, but first we begin with a brief look at graphic morphology.

## Graphic morphology

While ample research has looked at the visual perception of images, only limited studies have looked at how people comprehend the morphology in visual language. On the more banal side, gestures made by characters in comics have been found to be interpreted the same as real-life gestures, no matter the content of the text (Fein and Kasher, 1996). More unusual however, the upfix of lightbulbs above the head to mean inspiration can translate to real life: bright lightbulbs were found to give people more "inspiration" to complete logic puzzles than general ambient light (Slepian, Weisbuch, Rutchick, Newman, and Ambady, 2010).

Generally, closed-class morphology has been examined through the lens of development: how do children progress to understand these signs? The most consistent finding is that the comprehension of closed-class morphology gets better with age (for review, see Nakazawa, 2005). For example, children around kindergarten ages (~5 years old) often have difficulty interpreting morphemes like motion lines, changes in facial expression, and abstract marks expressed in the backgrounds of panels. By eighth grade (~13 years old) these signs are almost fully understood (Nakazawa, 1998). Below, we look closer at research that has explored two of the most prominent graphic morphemes: motion lines and carriers.

## *Motion lines*

As discussed, motion lines commonly depict the path of a moving object. Previous studies on the psychology of motion lines support that they aid the understanding of events and motion. In general, images with motion lines are considered as depicting more motion than those that rely on only the postures of characters (Brooks, 1977; Friedman and Stevenson, 1975; Gross et al., 1991; Ito, Seno, and Yamanaka, 2010; Kawabe and Miura, 2006), although the combination of motion lines and postural cues synergistically clarifies the expected path of an action more than is offered by each of these components alone (Kawabe and Miura, 2006). Furthermore, motion lines trailing an object are comprehended more easily and are rated as more effective at depicting motion than an absence of lines, background lines, or lines moving in the wrong direction (Ito et al., 2010). Motion lines facilitate comprehension and memory of depicted events more than when those same images lack motion lines because they help clarify the interaction between entities that otherwise may remain underspecified (Brooks, 1977).

Since they relate to the interpretation of actual movement, motion lines also facilitate understanding about the direction and speed of a moving object. For example, they may bias an expectation for the direction of moving objects (Kawabe, Yamada, and Miura, 2007; Kim and Francis, 1998). Furthermore, the number and length of lines used in a representation both have an influence on the perceived speed that they convey: more lines and longer lines lead to participants interpreting faster movement (Hayashi, Matsuda, Tamamiya, and Hiraki, 2012).

Some researchers have claimed that the comprehension of motion lines ties directly to biological foundations of vision. Moving objects leave behind "streaks" in the visual system when a viewer tracks an object (similar to a slow shutter speed of a camera), and thus this residual could form the basis of our understanding about motion lines (Burr and Ross, 2002). However, tying motion lines to a biological basis of vision has several limitations. First, motion lines are understood by blind people comparably to sighted people when presented using raised-line pictures (Kennedy, Gabias, and Piertantoni, 1990). Second, motion lines do not always appear as trailing linear streaks, as stressed by the diversity of types discussed in Chapter 2 (a point many researchers in this vein neglect to realize).

Third, motion lines are diverse across cultures, as is their understanding. People of cultures unfamiliar with this style of drawing have trouble understanding that these lines depict motion, although they do understand the meaning of accompanying iconic representations (Duncan, Gourlay, and Hudson, 1973; Kennedy and Ross, 1975; Winter, 1963). These studies indicate that motion lines as found in the visual languages used in comics may not be universal graphic signs. However, drawing systems of native peoples often use their own conventionalized motion lines, such as in the sand drawings used by indigenous communities of Central Australia (Munn, 1962, 1986; Wilkins, 1997), as will be discussed in Chapter 9.

Fourth, the interpretation of motion lines appears to change as people age. Experiments generally support that younger children (5 years and younger) have difficulty recognizing that these signs specifically represent motion, although by around age 12 children have no trouble understanding their meaning (Carello, Rosenblum, and Grosofsky, 1986; Friedman and Stevenson, 1975; Gross et al., 1991; Mori, 1995; Nakazawa, 1998). Younger children often interpret these lines as invisible yet iconic physical forces, such as wind or air moving; they are only recognized as symbolic conventions of paths as people age (Gross et al., 1991). As children accept this as a conventional sign, they also decrease in reliance on characters' postures to signify movement, which they do understand even at younger ages.

Altogether, this research implies that motion lines are conventional signs that become more understood as people age. Yet, once understood, their presence helps facilitate memory and comprehension for images of moving objects. While some researchers view this understanding as a metaphor for physical motion (Kennedy, Green, and Vervaeke, 1993), a simpler interpretation is that paths are a basic part of conceptual understanding (Jackendoff, 1990; Talmy, 2000), and motion lines graphically represent one type of path (with some others described in Chapter 2). Thus, the variability in comprehending motion lines (and the development of that comprehension) emerges from the conventionalized mappings that are made between this conceptual knowledge of paths and depictions in graphic structure.

## Carriers

Carriers have also been looked at experimentally, particularly in developmental psychology. In one study, preliterate Greek children looked at carriers from *Asterix* comics and, despite being unable to read the words in the carriers, the children understood several of their attributes (Yannicopoulou, 2004). They had extremely high recognition that angled edges on a balloon meant anger (87%) and that a flowery border meant politeness (83.7%). Many also recognized that the size of the text correlated with the volume of the utterance (78.7%)—even though they could not understand its meaning! Despite this, only half of these children recognized the primary distinction between speech balloons (49.7%) and thought bubbles (47.5%), which is fundamental to the core knowledge of a carrier's meaning (i.e. Root Awareness and Adjacent Awareness).

This knowledge of "awareness" relates to the concepts of "Theory of Mind" that have emerged in the past several decades of psychological research (Premack and Woodruff, 1978). The Theory of Mind focuses on humans' ability to recognize the existence of mental states in other people. We know that other people have thoughts, and we interact with them on the basis of that knowledge. In a sense, we are mind-readers! Typically, children around age 4 begin to understand the difference between their own mental states and those of others. It is significant to note that this coincides with the recognition that one's perceptions do not always equate to reality, and that some beliefs may be false. Impairments in the development of Theory of Mind have most often been associated with individuals with autism, who have difficulty with tasks requiring the representation of mental states. As discussed in Chapter 2, the Adjacent Awareness feature underlying the understanding of carriers relates to Theory of Mind quite clearly, and helps motivate the comprehension of Private carriers (i.e. "thought bubbles"), which directly depict the mental states of a character.

Some evidence has suggested that the understanding of thought bubbles coincides with the understanding of Theory of Mind. Children as young as 3 years can understand that thought bubbles contain intangible mental contents if they are first told the conventional meanings (Wellman, Hollander, and Schult, 1996). Without instruction, substantial advancement in recognizing that these morphemes depict thoughts seems to occur between the ages of 4 and 5 (Takashima, 2002). Some experiments have actually used thought bubbles as an intervention with autistic children, who often have difficulty with Theory of Mind. Autistic children can possibly learn that thought bubbles can represent an unknown reality related to people's thoughts (Kerr and Durkin, 2004; Parsons and Mitchell, 1999). Thought bubbles have thereby proven to be an effective technique for teaching autistic children about other people's thoughts, and this intervention technique has enhanced performance on other diagnostic tests for Theory of Mind (Parsons and Mitchell, 1999; Wellman et al., 2002). Thus, like motion lines, the knowledge that is required to understand carriers—especially Private carriers—links to very basic aspects of cognition.

# Narrative grammar

Beyond the comprehension of the graphic morphology, what are the processes that go into understanding a sequence of images? While some researchers have examined the comprehension of sequential images directly, others have used sequential images alongside verbal stories as a way to understand narrative more generally. We will focus here on studies directly related to sequential images, referencing a few important studies of verbal narrative.

In general, the ability to comprehend and recall the narrative of a sequence of images gets better from childhood to adulthood (Nakazawa and Nakazawa, 1993a, 1993b), while regular comic reading increases these abilities beyond those who do not read comics (Nakazawa, 1997). A series of studies by Japanese psychologist Jun Nakazawa and colleagues examined the influence of age and experience on sequential image comprehension (for review, see Nakazawa, 2005). Participants were asked to reconstruct unordered panels into their original order and to identify the contents of a panel that had been deleted from the sequence. Across age groups, no children in kindergarten or first grade could accurately determine what was missing and had difficulty reconstructing strips into correct orders; older children did progressively better at these tasks (Nakazawa and Nakazawa, 1993b). College-aged adults, who read comics more often, were the most accurate in inferring missing contents, better than younger children and older adults (Nakazawa, 2004). These results suggest that the ability to infer missing content and reconstruct the order of sequences increases with age and with increased experience reading comics.

In another study, Nakazawa (2002) tracked the eye-movements of an experienced comic reader and a novice comic reader as they interacted with a comic page. He found that the novice reader had more erratic eye-movements across the page, tended to focus more on the text than the images, and took longer to read the page. But the experienced reader had smoother fixations and tended to skip over panels and carriers more often. In addition, the expert reader also had better comprehension and recall for aspects of the story than the novice reader, despite having skipped over more elements. In other words, a reader's expertise directly impacts their eye-movements across a comic page.

Some researchers have described a more explicit development of visual narrative understanding. Trabasso and Nickels (1992) found that children pass through several distinct stages in comprehending sequential images, similar to those in understanding narratives in the verbal domain (Stein, 1988). Children at age 3 only recognize referential information like objects and characters, but by age 4 can recognize relationships between characters and can describe actions in single images. By age 5, children can identify the goals and intentions motivating those actions and begin to tie the content of images together. These abilities may be connected with Theory of Mind, which also begins to mature at this age (Trabasso and Stein, 1994). Altogether, these findings emphasize that comprehension of sequential images progresses in stages of development that move from the establishment of referential information through the understanding of actions, events, and their motivating causes (see also Pallenik, 1986).

## *Narrative categories*

Beyond this basic knowledge of visual narratives, what evidence do we have that people understand the specific type of narrative grammar outlined in Chapter 4? In Visual Narrative Grammar, a canonical narrative arc uses specific categories as a basis for a complex hierarchic structure. Several studies from the late 1970s and early 1980s looking at "story grammars" of verbal and written narratives have supported that people use a canonical narrative structure in their comprehension of stories.

After reading or hearing stories, participants remembered stories following the canonical structure with better accuracy than narratives with changes in temporal order (Mandler and Johnson, 1977), inversion of sentence order (Mandler, 1978, 1984; Mandler and DeForest, 1979), or fully scrambled sentences (Mandler, 1984). The further a structure departed from the canonical order, the harder it was to comprehend (Stein and Nezworski, 1978). Furthermore, adults recalled the surface structure of altered stories more accurately than children, who were more likely to reconstruct altered stories back into their canonical patterns (Mandler, 1978; Mandler and DeForest, 1979). Altogether, these studies established that the canonical narrative pattern is entrenched in people's memory.

Nevertheless, individual narrative categories play functional roles in Visual Narrative Grammar beyond just belonging to a canonical arc. How might we show evidence that panels play narrative roles that are not solely defined by the context of a global canonical pattern? In linguistics, various diagnostics have been developed for recognizing the category of a structure—be it phonemes, words, or phrases—as well as the constituents of that structure. These techniques include substitution, alteration, deletion, or reordering of a word or phrase. By analogy, similar diagnostics can be used to identify narrative categories, and my colleagues and I designed several experiments that draw upon these types of manipulations (for further discussion of these diagnostics, see Cohn, 2013a).

## Substitution

In verbal language, syntactic noun phrases can be replaced by a pronoun. For example, we know that *The politician* is a noun phrase in the sentence *The politician delivered a speech* because it can be replaced by *he* or *she*: *She delivered a speech*. Similarly, some narrative categories can be replaced with another panel. Consider the action star in the fifth panel of Figure 6.1 (where the security guard gets hit by the tossed backpack).

As discussed, action stars indicate the culmination of an event (characteristic of a Peak), without revealing what it actually is. Action stars thus allow narrative structure to be retained without being specific about its content, thereby forcing a reader to infer a "hidden" event. This makes an

**FIGURE 6.1** *Action star in a visual sequence. Grrl Scouts © 2002 Jim Mahfood.*

action star almost like a "pro-Peak," comparable to a pronoun (*he, she, it*) or other pro-forms (*here, there*, etc.) that have a grammatical category but minimal semantics. Thus, just as a pro-form can replace its corresponding grammatical category, substituting an action star for a panel serves as a diagnostic test for Peaks.

An action star can replace nearly any Peak panel, especially one with some sort of impact, but it cannot replace any other category.[1] Consider the sequences in Figure 6.2, which insert action stars into Figure 4.3b.

a. Action star replacing a Peak

b. Action star replacing an Initial

**FIGURE 6.2** *Action stars substituting for narrative roles.*

When the action star replaces the Peak (Figure 6.2a), the sequence reads acceptably, but when moved to the Initial (Figure 6.2b), the sequence worsens. Also, in Figure 6.2a, we no longer see the soccer players—we only know that something frightened the dog (perhaps the ball exploded?). In other words, an action star demands that the reader infer the missing event.

We designed an experiment to test the structural and inferential role that action stars play with regard to narrative sequences by replacing normal Peak panels with either action stars, blank panels, or semantically anomalous Peaks taken from other strips (Cohn, 2009). Participants read anomalous Peak panels slower than normal Peaks, because the anomalies were strange in context, but action stars and blank panels were read faster. Both of these panels had far less visual information in them than panels with figures; however, action stars were read *faster* than blank panels. This suggested that action stars facilitated processing about narrative in the Peak position beyond the fairly impoverished visual surface. Nevertheless, people read the panel *after* the Peak much slower in both of these cases than following normal Peaks, suggesting that both action stars and blank panels forced readers to make inferences about their content. This supports that action stars play a role as Peaks, but have an impoverished semantic structure.

## Deletion

Deletion can also be used as a diagnostic. For example, as discussed, deletion of non-Peak panels from a phase results in a narrative Arc with about the same sense. As a result, a simple diagnostic for Peaks is that they are the only panels capable of paraphrasing the meaning of the entire phase, as in the paraphrase of Figure 4.8a with Figure 4.8b in Chapter 4.

Deletion of other categories offers insight both into the characteristics of those panels and into the inference created by their omission. First, because Peaks are so important for the sequence, their deletion creates large inferential demands. Take for example Figure 6.3.

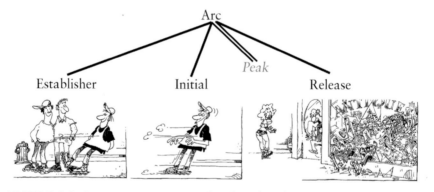

**FIGURE 6.3** *Sequence requiring a Peak to be inferred. Actions Speak* © 2002 *Sergio Aragonés.*

The first panel shows a man skating backward past two spectators; it's an Establisher that sets up the scenario. The skater then opens his eyes and notices something in the second panel, an Initial. The final panel, a Release, shows his legs sticking out of a broken window of an antique store, while a sexy woman looks on. The primary action (the Peak) of the sequence is missing: we never see him crash into the window. We only infer this event by seeing its aftermath in the Release. Furthermore, depicting the woman in the Release reveals that she distracted the skater in the Initial. The final panel demands that the *given* graphic sequence be reanalyzed and the unseen information inferred. Thus, because Peaks hold the main events of a sequence, omitting them creates a significant inferential demand on a reader.

In a series of experiments (Cohn, In Press-b), we tested the distributional tendencies of narrative categories in various ways. One task presented participants with a three-panel comic strip where a panel had been omitted. We then asked them to rate how much the sequence made sense and identify the location of the deleted panel. Another task gave them four randomly ordered panels: they arranged three into a strip, and chose one to delete. These tasks gave us insight on which panels might be more or less essential to the narrative sequence.

Figure 6.4a shows a sequence where the Peak has been deleted from Figure 4.3b. It no longer makes sense without the Peak. Why is the dog suddenly scared? Inference alone cannot fill in this information, since the Peak was an unexpected interruption. By and large, deletion of Peaks damages how much a sequence makes sense. This was also the intuition of the participants who saw similar sequences: when participants were

a. Deletion of Peak

b. Deletion of Initial

c. Deletion of Release

d. Deletion of Establisher

**FIGURE 6.4** *Sequences with deleted narrative categories.*

presented with a three-panel strip and asked to identify the location of a deleted panel, Peaks were the category most recognized when missing. These strips were also rated as highly incoherent. Furthermore, when participants were given four panels and asked to arrange three but delete one, Peaks were the least deleted narrative category. All of this points to Peaks holding the primary information of a sequence.

Information is noticeably missing when the Initial is deleted, as in 6.4b; it jumps from an established relationship to a culminating event. This is particularly pronounced where the Peak is an interruption. Studies of verbal narrative echo this feeling: the deletion of initiating actions in a discourse creates a more "surprising" narrative (Brewer and Lichtenstein, 1981). Like Peaks, deletion of Initials often strains the comprehension of sequences. In our experiment, Initials were second only to Peaks as the category most recognized when missing and as the least chosen to delete. Despite this, strips with missing Initials were rated as fairly coherent.

In contrast, the deleted Release in 6.4c renders the events of the sequence fairly complete, with less indication that something is missing. Yet, the sequence ends abruptly and leaves the reader expecting that something should come next. Unlike Initials, the aftermath in a Release may not be inferable from other panels' content. In our experiment, Releases were deemed fairly expendable. Participants often deleted Releases and had trouble recognizing when they were missing. However, strips with missing Releases received among the lowest ratings of coherence of all omitted categories. This suggests that, while Releases' content do not appear as central to the core events of the sequence (and thus are willingly deleted), a sequence feels substantially worse to the reader when they are missing because of the lack of narrative resolution.

Finally, 6.4d shows a sequence without its Establisher. This alteration has almost no impact on the sequence—you can hardly tell that the panel is missing! In our study, Establishers were the most deleted and least recognized when missing. Furthermore, strips with missing Establishers were rated as the most coherent of all sequences—their absence made little impact on the sequence. Studies of film have shown similar results when establishing shots are deleted—they have almost no effect on the overall comprehension of the film (Kraft, Cantor, and Gottdiener, 1991). Because Establishers set up characters and interactions, this information is often redundant with subsequent panels, where those characters engage in the actions of the sequence. So, deleting Establishers should make little difference to the sequence's meaning. However, it can impact the narrative *pacing*. By leaving out an Establisher, the actions immediately appear at the first panel. This leaves no "lead-in" time for the reader to be acclimated to the elements involved prior to their events.

In sum, deletion—and recognition of deletion—can reveal the characteristics of categories and the inferences that omissions create. The generation of inference is *not* the same across all panels in a sequence (as posited by theories of "panel transitions"), and greatly depends on the content of what is deleted as well as the surrounding context. That is, the understanding of inference benefits from detailing the formal properties of a narrative.

## Reordering and alteration

Categories can also be distinguished through reordering. An additional task in our experiments presented participants with four randomly ordered panels from a comic strip and asked them to arrange them in an order that made sense (Cohn, In Press-b). This type of "reconstruction" task is common in studies of sequential image comprehension (Bresman, 2004; Huber and Gleber, 1982; Nakazawa, 2004; Nakazawa and Nakazawa, 1993b), and is used as a measure of "logical/sequential reasoning" in

**FIGURE 6.5** *Reordering of categories to other places in a sequence.*

non-verbal IQ tests (Kaufman and Lichtenberger, 2006). We reasoned that categories misplaced from their original orders would reveal tendencies about their preferences for distributions in a sequence.

In our study, a distinct separation emerged between "core" and "peripheral" categories. Peaks and Initials were rarely misplaced in the sequence. As discussed before, these panels should be more important to the meaning of the sequence, and their tendency to not be misplaced supports this. For example, bringing a Peak to the front worsens the sequence, since the culmination then precedes its lead-up. Figure 6.5c should feel weird because of this, since the Peak makes no sense out of context. A sequence-final Initial also feels unusual. In Figure 6.5d, the dog's enjoyment for chasing the ball seems odd given the prior context.

In contrast, Establishers and Releases were put into the wrong positions far more frequently. Indeed, Establishers and Releases were most consist-ently misplaced at the end or beginning of the sequence respectively, and, in certain sequence patterns, sometimes exchanged positions. This supports the previous hypothesis that a panel acting as a Release could potentially start a sequence as an Establisher, as depicted in Figure 6.5a. The dog starts off scared, only then becomes curious about the ball and chases it. The reverse should be just as good: an Establisher can be reordered to the end of a sequence, to where it acts as a Release. In Figure 6.5b, a panel that once introduced the dog and the ball as an Establisher now shows the dog's frightened response to an object that earlier led to danger.

In humorous contexts, Releases can often be identified by their punch-lines. Bresman (2004) used a similar reconstruction task, and found that panels with a punchline were consistently put at the end of sequences—even if they were for the wrong strip! This effect of a punchline may be wrapped up in the knowledge that Releases give a response to the events in the Peak. This quality can be playfully highlighted by the fact that a word balloon saying "Jeez, what a jerk!" can be added to the final panel of nearly any comic strip without it losing its felicity (Sinclair, 2011).[2] More specifically, such a balloon can be attached to any *Release*, not to any final panel. It works because this phrase pragmatically responds to an action, and thus only makes sense in panels that share this context.

Altogether, these tests—substitution, deletion, reordering, and alter-ation—all provide ways to assess the attributes of different panels. They create several diagnostic questions that can be asked to determine each narrative category:

*Establishers*—Can it be deleted with little effect? Can it possibly be reordered to the end of a sequence and function as a Release?

*Initials*—Does its deletion affect felicity (although its absence may be inferred by the content of a Peak)? Is it impossible to reorder it in the sequence without disrupting felicity?

*Prolongations*—Can it be deleted with little effect?

*Peaks*—Can this panel paraphrase a sequence? Can an action star replace it? Does its deletion make large inferential demands and adversely affect felicity?

*Releases*—When a sequence's Release is deleted, can it still show a coherent event, yet be an infelicitous narrative? Does the panel carry a punchline? Can you insert the phrase "Jeez, what a jerk!" as a speech balloon?

## *Separation of structure and meaning*

It is important to emphasize that these narrative categories are not based solely on meaning. Rather, narrative grammar and meaning both contribute to the structure and comprehension of a sequence of images. This type of division has appeared throughout many previous theories of both written and filmed narratives (Bordwell, 1985; Bordwell and Thompson, 1997; Brewer and Lichtenstein, 1981, 1982; Chatman, 1978; Genette, 1980; van Dijk, 1977). Nevertheless, very few of those previous studies contained experimental evidence of this separation (although, see Brewer, 1985; Brewer and Lichtenstein, 1981, 1982; Ohtsuka and Brewer, 1992).

In recent studies, my colleagues and I have looked specifically at the separation of narrative and semantic association predicted by my theory of Visual Narrative Grammar. Our experiments have used a variety of measurements, including analyzing reaction times (e.g. how long a panel stays on a screen while being read), or analyzing "event-related potentials" (ERPs), which record the electrical activity of the human brain coinciding in time with certain stimuli (such as the onset of a panel on a screen). Since much of this section will discuss ERP research, it is worth detailing this technique further.

Within the brain, the electrical signal of synchronously firing groups of neurons can be measured using external electrodes. We can present participants with some form of stimulus (like viewing a panel) and measure their brainwaves for this particular "event" in time. Thus, we record the brain "potential" that is *related* to this "event"—an "event-related potential." This electrical signal has fairly small voltage, and must be amplified and digitized to be analyzable (see Figure 6.6a). This initial recording of brainwaves from the scalp (using EEG) renders an electrical signal that is too noisy to discern much about specific functioning (see Figure 6.6b). We thus filter out this noise by averaging across numerous participants and trials, thereby resulting in brainwaves that can inform us about the function of processing whatever kinds of stimuli are being tested (see Figure 6.6c). A

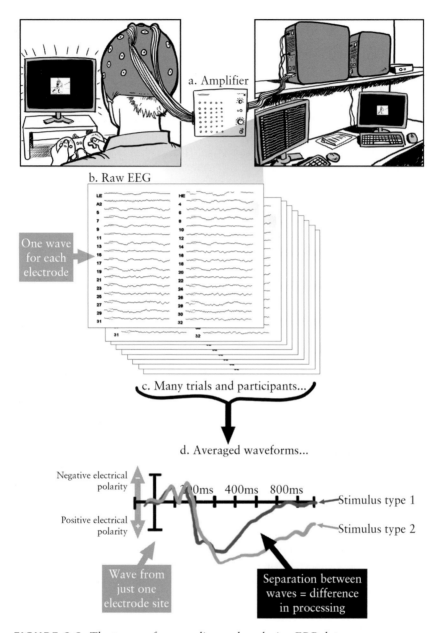

**FIGURE 6.6** *The process for recording and analyzing ERP data.*

separation between these "smoothed out" waveforms can indicate departures in the processing of different stimuli (see Figure 6.6d).

For those unfamiliar with this technique, it is important to stress that ERPs do not inform us much about *where* something in a brain is processed. The electrodes can provide us with an idea of the positive or negative electrical distribution across the outside of the scalp. However, these signals could be coming from any number of locations in the brain. Just because a positive electrical signal appears in the back of the scalp, it does not necessarily mean that neurons in the back of the brain produced that signal. Think about each neuron being like a person in the audience of a sporting event. If you are listening to a particular section of people cheering *together* from outside the stadium, you may know the volume or sound of their cheer, but you probably won't know their exact seating location very well.

So, what *does* this technique tell us? While brain scans from fMRI give us pretty pictures about where processing might happen in the brain, they are limited in terms of telling us how fast that processing takes place. Often, fMRI recordings observe activation whole seconds after a stimulus appears. ERPs give us a much faster recording, down to milliseconds. Not only does this tell us how fast comprehension might take place, but in research of language and other domains (like visual perception or music), several patterns of divergences between waveforms have become well established and they often correlate with particular types of processing. Thus, waveforms can tell us about the functional nature of processing.

One waveform identified in language research is called the "N400 effect," which is a negative deflection that peaks roughly 400 milliseconds after the onset of a stimulus (Kutas and Hillyard, 1980). This waveform has been associated with the processing of meaning (semantics), and was first found to be larger in response to sentence-ending words that were incongruous to their preceding context compared to congruous words, such as *He spread the bread with **butter**/**socks*** (Kutas and Hillyard, 1980). This effect has been found to the processing of meaning across domains, be it words, images, film clips, etc. (Kutas and Federmeier, 2011). Overall, the N400 is thought to reflect the brain's activation of meaningful information in relation to their preceding context. In general, amplitudes increase when a stimulus has a less transparent connection to its context, as in unpredictable or incongruous phenomena (for further detail, see Kuperberg, 2007; Kutas and Federmeier, 2011; Lau, Phillips, and Poeppel, 2008).

Just as with sentences, the first studies looking at sequential images using this ERP technique focused on sequence-ending panels that were incongruous to the context of a sequence. As expected, a larger N400 effect appeared in response to panels incongruous to the prior context than to normal panels ending the sequence (West and Holcomb, 2002). Similar results have been found with incongruous movie clips at the end of filmed scenes (Sitnikova, Holcomb, and Kuperberg, 2008). An additional study showed that the N400 does not just appear in response to incongruities in sequential images. Larger N400 effects have been found to be evoked by images that are unexpected—but still congruous—to the context of a sequence than by predictable images (Reid et al., 2009). These studies set the stage to show that N400 effects appear in response to images that are unpredictable or incongruous to their context in a sequence of images, just like words in sentences.

With this information, we decided to directly test the separation of narrative grammar and meaning predicted by my theory. In our initial study, we presented participants with four types of sequences constructed using the criteria from Visual Narrative Grammar (Cohn, Paczynski, Jackendoff, Holcomb, and Kuperberg, 2012). Our "normal" sequences had both a coherent narrative and meaningful relationships between panels (see Figure 6.7ai). "Scrambled" sequences were the exact opposite, with neither narrative nor meaningful relations between panels; they were sequences of random panels (see Figure 6.7aiv). Other sequences had *either* narrative or meaningful relations. "Semantic only" sequences shared a common meaningful theme across panels, such as random panels about baseball, but no coherent narrative arc tying them together (see Figure 6.7aii). Finally, our crucial manipulation was the creation of sequences that had a coherent narrative structure, but lacked meaningful ties between panels.

These sequences were analogous to Noam Chomsky's (1965) famous sentence *Colorless green ideas sleep furiously*, which has a grammatical syntactic structure, but lacks any coherent meaning. In our "structural only" sequences, we combined prototypical panels of various narrative categories into a sequence that created a grammatical narrative structure. However, these panels originally came from various unconnected strips, so their combination did not make sense meaningfully (see Figure 6.7aiii).

In our first experiment with these sequence types, each trial began by showing participants a single panel from a sequence, followed by the full sequence shown one panel at a time that contained that original panel somewhere in it. When they again saw the original panel in the context of the sequence, they pressed a button. We found that reaction times to "target" panels in the normal strips were the fastest, because participants could rely on the context of both the narrative and meaning (see Figure 6.7b). Conversely, reaction times to panels in the scrambled strips were the slowest, because a random sequence of panels allowed for no context. Finally, reaction times to panels in semantic-only and structural-only sequences were roughly the same, falling directly between the fast times for panels in normal sequences and the slow times for scrambled sequences. Thus we demonstrated that the presence of either narrative *or* meaning gave an advantage in processing, but not as much as their combination.

We then looked at the brain's response by measuring ERPs while participants viewed each panel of these sequences (see Figure 6.7c). We found that normal sequences had the lowest amplitude of the N400, indicating that it

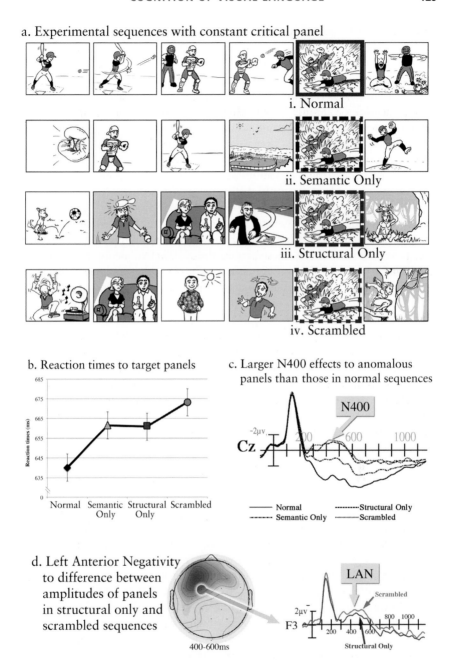

FIGURE 6.7 *Experimental stimuli and results examining the separation of narrative grammar and meaning using reaction times and ERPs.*

was the easiest sequence to process. Next, semantic-only sequences had a slightly larger amplitude N400, suggesting that they were harder to process than normal sequences, because they lacked a narrative structure. Despite this, the meaningful relationships between these panels made them easier to process than panels in scrambled or structural-only sequences. These latter sequences had the largest N400 effects, suggesting that participants had a harder time integrating meaning across these sequences.

A significant finding was that no difference appeared in the N400 effect between scrambled and structural-only sequences. Since the N400 effect indexes the processing of meaning, and since the N400 was the same in these sequences where the only difference was the presence of a narrative structure (in structural-only sequences), this supports that narrative and meaning are different structures that combine in the comprehension of sequential images. Additionally, when we looked at the amplitudes for panels at each position of the sequence, the N400 effect decreased with each subsequent panel in normal sequences, but the other sequence types did not. This decrease in amplitude suggests that each subsequent panel became easier to understand given the context of the normal sequences, but only with the combination of both narrative and meaning.

One additional finding from this study provided further support for the presence of a narrative grammar. Even though we found no difference in the N400 effect for scrambled and structural-only sequences, we did find a slight difference between the amplitudes of these sequences localized to the left anterior region (front) of the scalp. This placement on the scalp was distinct from the more widespread anterior distribution of the N400 effect (see Figure 6.7d). This effect was consistent with another waveform called a "left anterior negativity" or "LAN" which often appears in response to violations of syntactic structure in sentences, including phrase structure violations, agreement violations between noun phrases and verbs, and long-distance dependencies (Friederici, 2002; Neville, Nicol, Barss, Forster, and Garrett, 1991).

Again, since structural-only sequences differed from scrambled sequences only with regard to the *presence of narrative*, we interpreted this left-lateralized negativity as possibly being a LAN, supporting the theory that participants used a narrative grammar in the processing of these sequences. Even more interesting, the amplitude of this effect correlated with participants' expertise in reading comics: the more often they read comics, the larger the difference between these brainwaves (i.e. the more these stimuli were distinguished from each other in the brain).

This study provided initial evidence that people use separate systems for narrative and meaning to process sequential images. We had manipulated the entire sequence—they either did or did not have narrative or meaning. However, we did not necessarily violate the narrative grammar, which usually gives different types of brain responses than the N400 effect, indexing the processing of meaning. One such waveform is the "P600 effect," a positive deflection that peaks roughly 600 milliseconds after the onset of a stimulus (i.e. a word in a sentence) and is distributed towards the back of the scalp. This waveform appears in response to numerous types of violations of grammar (Hagoort, Brown, and Groothusen, 1993; Osterhout and Holcomb, 1992). For example, in comparison to the sentence *The cat ate the food*, a violation of meaning like *The cat **baked** the food* evokes

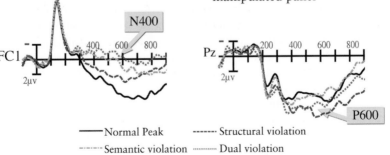

**FIGURE 6.8** *Stimuli and ERP results for an experiment that introduced violations of narrative grammar and/or meaning into sequences.*

an N400 effect (since cats don't bake), but a violation of syntax like *The cat **eating** the food* evokes a P600 effect (Osterhout and Nicol, 1999). A violation of both meaning and syntax like *The cat **baking** the food* evokes both N400 and P600 effects. Functionally, this P600 effect has been associated with a process of continued analysis or reanalysis, attempting to integrate grammar and meaning (Kuperberg, 2007).

Thus, in a subsequent study we violated sequences with panels that were anomalous to the narrative grammar and/or the semantic associations between panels. We reasoned that, if an N400 effect could be evoked by violations of meaning, a P600 effect could be evoked by violations of narrative grammar. Such results would provide further evidence for a separation between these structures, since each manipulation would yield a different waveform. Furthermore, it would support my theory that similar cognitive processes guide the comprehension of syntax in sentences and narrative in sequential images.

Therefore, in this study, we substituted panels into the "Peak" position of a narrative sequence, where they either violated the meaning, the narrative grammar, or both (Cohn, 2012c). For example, our "normal" sequences had regular Peak panels that fit their context in the sequence (see Figure 6.8ai). In "semantic violations" we inserted Peaks from a different sequence. They were still Peaks narratively—showing culmination of the strip—but the meaning no longer matched the context of the sequence (see Figure 6.8aii). In "structural violations," we replaced the original Peak panel with an Initial panel (prototypically a preparatory action), so that it violated the narrative structure (see Figure 6.8aiii). However, this panel still retained the thematic relationship to the context of the strip. So, a strip about baseball still retained a violation about baseball, only it was no longer a Peak, but an Initial. Finally, in "dual violations," critical panels violated both the narrative (they were Initials instead of Peaks) and the meaning (they no longer retained the theme of the strip), as in Figure 6.8aiv.

People read these sequences panel-by-panel while we measured their brainwaves. At the critical panels, all of the violations evoked larger N400 effects than the normal Peak panels (see Figure 6.8b). The largest N400 effects appeared in response to semantic violations and dual violations, showing that, as expected, violations of *meaning* required the most effort in semantic processing. Still, a slightly larger N400 effect appeared in response to structural violations than normal Peaks. Even though these sequences maintained the theme of the sequence, the actions that take place in an Initial are unexpected enough to cause some difficulty in processing their meaning (Reid et al., 2009).

Next we looked beyond the manipulated panel to the *subsequent* panel, to see if violations caused additional effects further along in the sequence. At the panel *after* the critical panel, we found evidence of the grammatical violation. Here, structural violations and dual violations both showed a larger P600 effect than normal or semantic violations (see Figure 6.8c). In

a. Comprehension of normal sequence

Semantics: Preparation √ ➝ Completion √ ➝ Coda √

Narrative: Initial √ Peak √ Release √

b. Comprehension of sequence with unexpected Peak

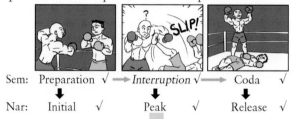

Sem: Preparation √ ➝ *Interruption* √ ➝ Coda √

Nar: Initial √ Peak √ Release √

*Unexpected =*
N400

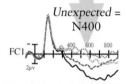

c. Comprehension of sequence with ungrammatical panel in place of Peak

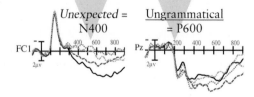

Sem: Preparation √ ➝ *Passive* ? ➝ Coda X

Nar: Initial √ Establisher ? Release X

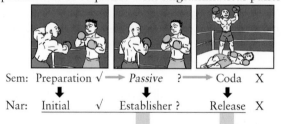

*Unexpected =*
N400

Ungrammatical
= P600

**FIGURE 6.9** *Panel-by-panel comprehension of sequential images.*

fact, the panels after semantic violations—which had no violation of the narrative grammar—did not differ in amplitude from panels after normal Peaks. This suggested that only panels that violate the narrative (structural or dual violations) evoke this P600 effect, providing further evidence for the psychological validity of this narrative grammar.

Why might the violations of the narrative grammar—as evidenced by the P600 effect—only appear in response to the panel *after* the violations? Why don't structural violations become recognized at the panel themselves? These results give us further clues about the panel-by-panel comprehension of a sequence of images. When first reaching a panel, a person assesses the "morphological" meaning of its content (i.e. the depicted characters and events). This information is then used to assess its narrative category. For example, if a panel shows a preparatory action, then the narrative structure guesses that the panel will be an Initial. At the next panel, this assessment of meaning again takes place. Now, if the events or characters (the properties of meaning) in this subsequent panel do not match the *meaningful* expectations of the prior panel, that meaning becomes harder to integrate, as indexed by the N400 effect (Figure 6.9b). For example, it may be harder to process a panel where characters change or an unexpected action occurs. These types of changes in semantic continuity may be characterized by the linear "panel transitions" outlined by McCloud (1993) and others.

Recall that at the first panel, a guess was made using its meaningful content about what narrative category it might be. Let's say it was an Initial. This process repeats at each subsequent panel. However, the narrative structure now has its own expectations to sustain (separate from the continuity of meaning), for instance that an Initial will be followed by a Prolongation or a Peak (but not an Establisher or Orienter). If the *previous panel* does not match the narrative expectations of this subsequent panel, the narrative structure recognizes something is awry, resulting in the P600 effect (Figure 6.9c).

In other words, if the first panel showed a preparatory action for an Initial, the second panel showed an Establisher, and the third panel shows a Release, the sequence may be deemed ungrammatical since *Initial-Establisher-Release* is not a coherent narrative pattern. Thus, a panel's role in a narrative is determined both by its content—the meaning it conveys—as well as its context in the sequence—how it relates to both previous and subsequent panels.

Of course, these studies just provide first steps toward understanding the processing of sequential images. As mentioned in Chapter 4, complex sequences manipulate the structure of narrative grammar beyond simple canonical sequences, and connections between adjacent panels alone are not enough to explain the structure of a sequence. What happens when narrative categories have non-prototypical mappings to meaning (i.e. when Initials are not just preparatory actions)? What happens when panels must connect across distances in the sequence or when complex embedding breaks the canonical pattern (as in center-embedded phases)? These simple questions require additional experimentation. Our initial studies provide support that two systems complement each other in the comprehension of sequential images: a narrative grammar *and* a system of semantic meaning. Additional research has already begun to further explore the complex mappings between these structures.

## *Constituent structure*

As discussed in Chapter 4, the comprehension of sequential images must extend beyond linear relationships between panels, and also beyond just narrative categories. Visual Narrative Grammar also organizes sequences of images into constituents—groupings of panels that can be embedded within other groupings. Remember, the existence of such groupings makes it difficult to give much credence to panel transitions or promiscuous transitions as the motivators of sequential image comprehension. So, what evidence do we have for their psychological validity?

The first evidence came from studies using "picture stories," where psychologist Morton Ann Gernsbacher (1985) found that, when presented with seemingly continuous sequences of images in a story, participants agreed on where episode boundaries began and ended. These boundaries divided the overall graphic discourse into sub-episodes and consistently parsed whole segments of sequential images within a story. Comparable segmentation has been found for episodes made up of sentences within verbal stories (Mandler, 1984).

Beyond just showing that people can locate boundaries for graphic constituents, Gernsbacher (1985) also found evidence for such divisions through people's memory. Participants were asked to remember the visual composition of particular images within a picture story (normal versus horizontally flipped), and they had a harder time remembering images that appeared after, as opposed to before, the segment boundary. Because recall of the visual composition was more difficult after a boundary, it implied that readers build up a structure across the course of a segment, and then start a new build-up after crossing the boundary. Similar results have been found for the recall of manipulated film shots at the boundaries of segments in a film (Carroll and Bever, 1976). As in the picture stories, film research showed a build-up of structure throughout the sequence until viewers reach a boundary, at which point the segmentation begins anew with the next constituent.

It is important to note that similar segmentation has also been examined by looking at videos of real-life events—not narratives. In a series of studies, psychologist Jeffrey Zacks and his colleagues showed that people agree upon how to break apart events into segments at both coarse- and fine-grained levels (Zacks et al., 2001a; Zacks and Tversky, 2001b; Zacks,

Tversky, and Iyer, 2001c). In these studies, participants watched videos of actions and tapped a button when they thought one action ended and another began. On the whole, segmentation between participants was highly consistent. Zacks and colleagues also showed these videos to people while scanning their brain activity using fMRI as participants either actively parsed the events or passively just watched actions unfold (Zacks et al., 2001a). They found that the same brain areas became activated in both the parsing and observing tasks. Additionally, activation in certain areas occurred *prior* to the actual boundaries between events, indicating that the brain may be anticipating the segmentation before it actually occurs. Taken together, these studies show that people are sensitive to the boundaries of visual events and their internal structure.

These previous studies contain some evidence that a constituent structure exists in sequential images, be they pictorial or filmed. This raises the question: How might readers know the borders of these segments? Unlike sentences, we do not use punctuation like periods or commas in visual sequences to give cues about boundaries of phases or Arcs. As mentioned above, readers do notice major changes that occur in the meaning of panels' relations to each other. As proposed by Visual Narrative Grammar, it may be the case that people use the most significant changes in space, characters, and/or causation as cues for the constituent boundaries. Indeed, these types of linear changes often coincide with breaks between event segments (Newtson and Engquist, 1976; Zacks and Magliano, 2011; Zacks, Speer, Swallow, and Maley, 2010). It may be that major "panel transitions" provide cues for the boundaries between constituents.

Given these precedents, my colleagues and I sought further evidence for constituent structure, looking especially at its interaction with panel transitions (Cohn, 2012c). We followed the logic of classic psycholinguistic studies (Fodor and Bever, 1965; Garrett and Bever, 1974) that investigated constituent structure in sentences. These studies introduced disruptions of white noise ("clicks") either within constituents (in the first or second constituents) or between constituents. We reasoned that, as in these studies, if participants use a constituent structure, processing should be easier for sequences where the disruption cleanly divides constituents than when the disruption interrupts a whole complete constituent.

We designed sequences that had only two constituents using my theory of narrative grammar. We confirmed the location of the boundary between constituents using a "segmentation task" like Gernsbacher's; people actively chose locations that would best divide a sequence into two parts, and we only used sequences with the highest agreement for these segmentations. Also, prior to experimentation, we coded our sequences for their linear panel transitions. As predicted, we found that changes in spatial location and characters were far more likely to occur at the boundaries between constituents than within the constituents by a huge margin. However, this created a quandary—we needed to make sure that any effects could

a. Experimental sequences with disruptions

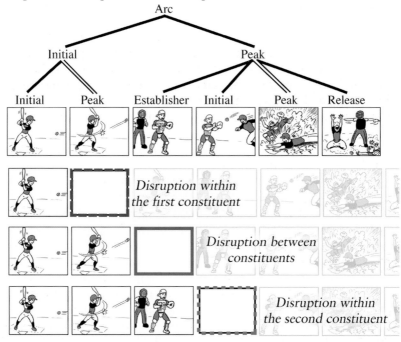

b. Larger LAN effect to disruptions within constituents than between them

c. Larger P600 to disruptions in the second constituent than before it

FIGURE 6.10 *Example stimuli and ERP results for sequences where disruptions were placed within or between narrative constituents.*

not simply be attributed to these changes in meaning, instead of actual constituent structure.

With these sequences, we then created three types of manipulations (see Figure 6.10a) by introducing blank white "disruption panels" either within the constituents—either inside the first or second constituent—or between the two constituents. Like our previous studies, we presented these sequences one panel at a time to people on a computer screen while we measured their brainwaves. We predicted that brainwave effects associated with grammatical processing, such as the P600 or the LAN, should be more severe for disruptions within constituents than between them. In contrast, if people only attend to the transitions between panels, we should see a larger N400 in response to disruptions between constituents than within them, since that is where the largest meaningful changes in space and characters occur.

Our most interesting results occurred at the disruption panel itself (see Figure 6.10c). First, we found a P600 effect that was larger in response to disruptions appearing within the second constituent than those between constituents or within the first constituent. Why might processing within a second constituent evoke a P600 effect compared with those in the first constituent or between constituents? We believe that the break provided by the disruption forces people to question whether *all* of the preceding panels form a grammatical constituent. When participants reached the disruption in the second constituent, they had already been presented with a whole constituent plus one additional panel. Thus, this P600 reflects the *reanalysis* of unsuccessfully integrating the panel following the first constituent into that grouping. This result could be likened to the effect of a comma placed in the wrong location in a sentence, which would create a grouping of words that cannot be parsed grammatically.

Even more telling than the P600, we also found a leftward anterior negativity. This LAN was larger in response to disruptions appearing within constituents than between constituents, as in Figure 6.10b. It is important to note that the amplitudes of disruptions within the first constituent and between constituents were different. Participants could not have relied on panel transitions to figure out these constituents, since both of these disruptions *preceded* the panel following the constituent boundary. Nevertheless, a greater negativity appeared in response to disruptions within the first constituent than between constituents, suggesting that people recognized that violations were worse within that constituent than following its completion. This implies that people do not solely rely on linear relationships, like changes in space or characters, as cues for constituent structure, since they *have not yet reached* the panel that signals this transition. Rather, even though constituent boundaries co-occur with panel transitions, this provides evidence that people make *predictions* about constituent structure from the *content* of images as they read a sequence of images panel-by-panel.

With these results, we suggest that participants do indeed use a constituent structure in the processing of sequential images. Although we previously saw that linear panel-to-panel changes in meaning can have an effect on the processing of sequential images (with the N400), this experiment shows that they do not necessarily impact the structures guiding the grouping of panels into constituents.

## Visual narratives and brains

Altogether, this research provided us with evidence supporting several of the predictions in the theory of Visual Narrative Grammar. Narrative categories are influenced by an interaction between content and context, and have distributional tendencies in a sequence. Narrative structure is a distinct system that interacts with meaning throughout comprehension, and this narrative grammar organizes units into constituents beyond mere panel-to-panel relationships. This research is only an initial foray that sets up potential further research on narrative comprehension in sequential images and other domains.

It is important to discuss the similarities in the neurocognitive effects we found in our ERP studies of sequential images with those of other domains. All of the effects that we have found—the N400, the P600, and the LAN—have appeared previously in manipulations of sentences. It has been well established that the N400 appears in response to the processing of meaning across all domains, ranging from language to vision (Kutas and Federmeier, 2011). Furthermore, the P600 and an analogue of the LAN on the right side of the scalp have also appeared in response to violations of "syntax" in music (Koelsch and Siebel, 2005; Patel, 2003; Patel, Gibson, Ratner, Besson, and Holcomb, 1998).

Now, we could say that the presence of these waveforms shows that visual narratives and music use the *same* grammar as language. However, this is probably incorrect. The system of syntax that uses nouns and verbs has a very different nature from the narrative grammar in visual language; it is even more different than the grammar that governs music. Rather, it is more likely that general neurocognitive functions permeate across different domains, such as the activation of meaningful information or the building of hierarchic constituent structures. Notice that this maintains the theme of the overarching theory of the mind in which visual language is embedded, as described in Chapter 1: different domains make use of the same cognitive resources (meaning, grammar), but do so in ways that are unique to their particular modalities.

# Fluency

Across this research, we find a common theme: we acquire the understanding of many parts of visual language through exposure and experience. Conventional representations like motion lines and carriers are all understood better with age and more experience reading comics. Furthermore, effects of expertise appear across many measurements of the comprehension of the narrative grammar in sequential images, including people's memory for narratives, the speed at which they read panels, their eye-movements across pages, and even directly in the brainwaves evoked while they read a sequence of images.

Altogether, these findings suggest that the comprehension of visual language requires a certain degree of *fluency* for various levels of structure. This may seem like an odd notion, since the iconicity of images makes them seem fairly universal. The idea of "fluency" in a cognitive sense is the proficiency a person has with producing or comprehending a particular system: to what extent do the structures in a person's head allow for them to understand some external phenomena "in the world"? In terms of comprehension, iconicity makes graphic representation much more accessible. By and large, people across the globe understand that images of objects mean what they represent. Nevertheless, this iconicity does not make ease of comprehension inevitable, and various factors can inhibit or alter understanding. As we will see in a few chapters, familiarity with a different kind of visual language may actually cause disparate interpretations of what would otherwise appear to be simple images.

Fluency with *sequential* images requires yet another layer of proficiency. We cannot assume that the ability to understand a sequence of images inevitably comes from understanding how events operate in the world alone. Rather, through this research we find evidence that comprehension of sequential images requires a degree of expertise that goes beyond knowledge of events. This may be why some people struggle to understand or appreciate comics: they simply never gained fluency in a visual language.

Such a notion raises some questions with regards to our use of sequential images in assessments of intelligence. For example, one section of the standard IQ test asks people to arrange randomly ordered images into a coherent sequence, similar to the "reconstruction task" we discussed. Given the type of research described here, it is important to ask whether this test truly assesses a facet of "intelligence," or does it just measure the degree of fluency in a visual language? An important goal for future research is to try to disentangle such notions and to develop reliable assessments for what it means to be fluent in a visual language.

# Notes

1 Fight clouds can also serve this purpose, but only for fights, not more generally like action stars.

2 The original contents of the balloon used by Sinclair were a bit more risqué!

# SECTION 2

# Visual language across the world

So far, we have discussed the basic foundations of the structure of visual language: the lexicon and grammar of sequential images. While the capacity for "Language" is an innate and universal part of being human, specific *languages* are not universal. Japanese, English, Swedish, and Warlpiri all differ as cultural manifestations of the larger capacity for "Spoken Language" shared by all humans. These languages use varying lexicons and grammars, but they share basic underlying principles. In the following chapters, we extend this observation to visual language as well. While the broad idea of "Visual Language" transcends culture as a property of human cognition generally, it manifests in different visual languages across the world in culturally diverse ways.

Why has the graphic style in Japanese manga traditionally looked different from that in mainstream American comics? Are there visual languages outside the context of comics? How might the visual narrative grammar change within and between different cultures? Do different dialects of visual language exist within and between cultures?

In this section, we start addressing these questions by discussing the properties of three visual languages of the world. Two come from "comic" cultures: American Visual Language and Japanese Visual Language. The third details a visual language outside the context of comics, found in the sand narratives of Aboriginal communities in Central Australia. Clearly, visual languages exist in many other cultures both within the context of "comics" (various European countries, China, India, etc.) and outside of it (for example, the "instruction manual" dialect). Technically, *all* drawing systems in the world and throughout history are covered (and can be studied) by the theory of visual language. We focus here on these three systems to frame this branch of research. Hopefully, future research can take aim at other systems of the world.

At the outset, I should note that explicit research looking at the properties of these visual languages remains limited. These chapters aim to educate the reader about what these systems look like through the lens of visual language theory. Further, these chapters illustrate how this theory extends beyond broad generalizations and hopefully can serve to inspire additional cultural and cross-cultural research along these lines.

Elaborating on the notion of visual languages in the world underscores an important aspect of language: its interface with culture. Cultural influence ranges from attitudes about the nature and development of drawing to the broader ecology of the environment in which visual languages are used. Some of these differences have profound effects on the nature and usage of visual languages. The following chapters attempt to outline these close relationships binding together culture, cognition, and the structure of visual languages.

Finally, the ties between a language and its community create a sense of identity for speakers, which in turn frame their assumptions about other language users. People from one part of America may have accents that grate on the ears of those from another region (and vice versa). Similarly, some people often dislike one set of comics, while having a strong liking for others. It may be that people prefer their "in-group's" drawings while disliking those outside of it. For example, some fans of Japanese manga greatly dislike mainstream American superhero comics (and vice versa). While "taste" may be one factor, so too may be the cognitive preferences for patterns that conform to one's own visual language identity. These preferences may also surface in critiques by older generations that younger artists are horrible at drawing or storytelling. Like the persistent (and erroneous) belief of every generation that "kids today are ruining the language," this same sort of idea may be why older readers of comics sometimes find younger artists' creations harder to understand (or at least, more distasteful). All these socio-cultural factors relate to (visual) linguistic identities.

While these sociocultural factors will not be addressed directly here, the idea of diverse visual languages in the world opens the door to research of "visual sociolinguistics" akin to those found in verbal and signed languages. Among the questions that can be asked are: Why do people dislike some styles, while liking others? Why do readers of one type of visual language hold particular stereotypes about other visual languages? Are people who can draw in more than one style "visual language bilingual"? These are all basic questions yet to be explored, but all hinge first on the recognition that manners of drawing originate as different visual languages found in the minds of disparate people of the world.

# CHAPTER SEVEN

# American Visual Language

A defining feature of visual language in America is the vast diversity: people draw in ways very different from each other. Variation in spoken languages most often reflects the geographic differences between populations. One group of people speaks differently from another because they live in a different place. However, visual languages appear in a print culture, which does not constrain them to any particular geographic location, especially in this digital age. Rather, diversity in the print form emerges through different *genres*—which often delimit the boundaries between different populations of authors and readers. While overlap does exist, mainstream authors draw differently from newspaper cartoonists, with yet further variation from more artsy independent authors. We will focus on these three "dialects" of American Visual Language, while consistently questioning how appropriate such classifications may be.

## Graphic structure

### *Mainstream American VL: "Kirbyan"*

The "mainstream" style of American Visual Language appears most prevalently in superhero comics (and other related genres) found in the mainstream comic industry. I will refer to this dialect as "Kirbyan," in honor of the historical influence of Jack "King" Kirby in defining this style (Duncan and Smith, 2009; Hatfield, 2012). Other significant influences on this style were Steve Ditko, Neal Adams, John Byrne, and many others. During the 1990s, Kirbyan was heavily influenced by Jim Lee, and further influenced by Japanese manga (discussed in the next chapter).

Of course, the graphic structure of a visual language does not rest in one person's idiolect—these are merely prototypical authors. Rather, the language itself is an abstract "average" of the "speakers" of that language group—the style attributable to no person in particular, but to the generic look of stereotyped American comic authors. We might think of this as the "Standard" dialect of Kirbyan AVL. Often, the basic schemas of a dialect can be found in "how-to-draw" books and lessons. Essentially, lessons on "how to draw superhero comics" instruct how to draw Kirbyan AVL. Of course, not all authors of comics in America use this dialect, and many have other influences (some also conventionalized, others less so). The validation of this style as a visual language comes from enough consistency in patterns across authors to make it recognizable at a glance as indicative of "American superhero comics," not just individual authors.

How people are drawn often exemplifies a visual language's graphic structure. In Kirbyan AVL, bodies are often physically exaggerated—men are more muscular, women are more curvy. Stereotypically, all figures look

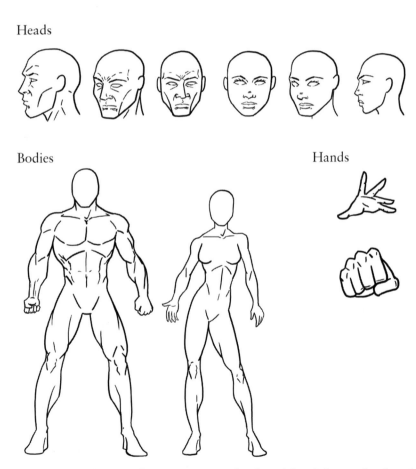

Heads

Bodies                                             Hands

**FIGURE 7.1** *Schematized representations of male and female human heads and body in Kirbyan American Visual Language.*

like athletes or models. As depicted in Figure 7.1, the conventionalized face in Kirbyan AVL has an angular jaw, pronounced cheekbones, and distinct eyebrow muscles, especially in men (exemplified also by the schemas from Erik Larsen in Chapter 2). Often, lines from the eye socket might stretch across the upper cheek, while lines highlight the upper lip from the sides of the nose. Crosshatching often varies densities to show volume.

When figures perform actions in Kirbyan AVL, they often appear in "dramatic" and "dynamic" poses that stretch slightly beyond the full point of action. In many cases, figures and poses are highly unrealistic. Few people actually look like the drawings in mainstream American comics, and their poses would be near impossible (or at least uncomfortable) for actual human bodies. Some authors even represent figures in ways that are not anatomically "correct."

It is important to remember that—given their basis as *cognitive schemas*—these drawings do not or should not necessarily represent the way things actually exist "in the world." At their basis, these are patterns in the minds of their creators, and need only correspond loosely to "reality." Put another way, "speakers" of AVL have learned to draw things in certain ways, just as people learn to say certain things in particular nomenclatures. Authors could certainly learn a different way to draw things, just as people learn new words and phrases. Yet for now, these are the characteristics of Kirbyan AVL in the minds of comic creators.

## Cartoony American VL: "Barksian"

Cartoony styles make up a second dialect in American Visual Language, which we will call "Barksian," after Carl Barks who most famously drew the Scrooge McDuck comics. This dialect is probably the most far-reaching in American representation, since it extends across comic books, comic strips, and cartoons. This dialect has diverse and varied origins, but the styles found in animation like those of Walt Disney and his animators are obvious influences, as are early authors of comic strips like Rudolph Dirks, Carl Barks, Charles Schulz, Walt Kelly, and many others.

Considerable diversity exists between authors of Barksian AVL. If one opens a newspaper comic page (to the extent that they persist), most of the strips will be drawn in a "cartoony" style, yet few will share schematic patterns with each other (see Figure 7.2). However, some consistent patterns do exist. On the whole, Barksian uses what McCloud (1993) has called an "amplification of simplification"—the highlighting of a few features while downplaying others. That is, cartoony images simplify images to their essential components while exaggerating the remaining features. Often, this emphasizes the basic geometric shapes that underlie figures, in many cases resulting in a pronounced roundedness or angularity to the figures. Because some features are heightened at the expense of others, many features of

Heads

Eyes

Nose/Mouth

Hands

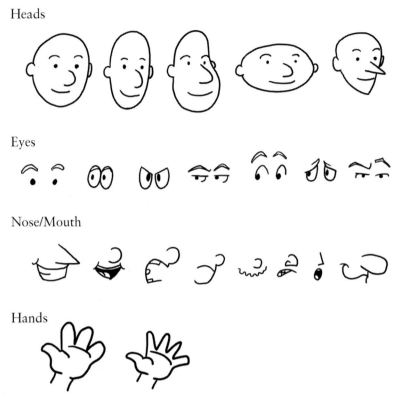

**FIGURE 7.2** *Some conventional features of Barksian American Visual Language.*

anatomy are often downplayed, altered, or omitted. Characters may not have elbows or knees, or at least their joints only appear when bent, while muscles are only drawn when emphasized (like when flexing).

A common trend among many authors is to draw characters with only three fingers plus a thumb on each hand, an influence attributed to Walt Disney's early drawings of Mickey Mouse. Mice do only have three fingers/claws, but this anthropomorphized representation quickly became conventionalized to any Barksian hand. It has been said that this may relate to efficiency: it is easier to squeeze three fatter and larger cartoony fingers onto a hand than four.

It's interesting to note that while people often critique "incorrect anatomy" in various authors of Kirbyan AVL, rarely do people complain about figures having only three fingers, lack of joints, strange geometrically shaped body parts of odd proportions, or other anatomical irregularities in Barksian AVL. One reason for such disparity may relate to an "attempted realism" by Kirbyan AVL. The more "realistic" that authors "try" to be, the more harshly irregularities may be judged (by some). Another related alternative is that cartoony images are immediately recognized as conventional, while more "realistic" images are not (thereby falling prey to the erroneous "perceptual viewpoint" that believes drawings function to represent the way things look rather than concepts in the mind), despite having the same cognitive status as schematic representations.

If a "language" is a cognitive system reflecting similar patterns in the heads of various "speakers," then to what extent "Barksian" is an actual dialect remains an important question. Are the similarities between authors enough to warrant being included as a whole dialect? Or, are these merely commonalities between diverse idiolects belonging to individuals? This will be a theme as we discuss American Visual Language generally.

## Independent American VL

The label of "Independent" books covers a broad swath of topics outside mainstream comics and may constitute another dialect. A separate, yet related category is the "Alternative" or underground genre of comix (Duncan and Smith, 2009). Together, these genres thematically differ from mainstream comics, often addressing mature, serious, visceral, or realistic topics (although not exclusively). Collectively, I will group all of these authors under the broad umbrella as the "Indy" dialect. Nevertheless, the diversity of graphic structure across authors brings into question whether there is any consistent dialect at all, despite loosely belonging to similar genres or traditions outside the mainstream.

Similar to Barksian AVL, vast diversity exists between styles in the "Indy" dialect. First, "alternative" or "underground" comix from the 1960s shared a fairly recognizable graphic structure. Authors of these works, like Harvey Kurtzman, Robert Crumb, Harvey Pekar, and Art Spiegelman, sought an "authentic" and idiosyncratic style in contrast to the mainstream styles of superhero comics. This graphic style often uses thicker lines and cartoony— yet deformed and lumpy—figures. Again, while some similarities persist across authors, others still differ widely.

A second thread of the Indy dialect varies even more. In recent years, several authors have become associated with a more serious genre of comics independent from the mainstream. Some common features persist in these styles, such as simple, yet straightforwardly realistic drawings, as with Adrian Tomine, Daniel Clowes, and the Hernandez brothers, Jaime and Gilbert. Figures in these drawings often retain proportions close to realistic bodies, even accentuating the plainness of people. These drawings are the antithesis of the fantastical bodies in Kirbyan AVL. Poses in this dialect are often underemphasized in events, such as prior to the maximum point of depiction (as opposed to beyond it in Kirbyan AVL).

Finally, a thread of highly stylized "cartoony" representations also exists. As in Barksian AVL, authors like Ivan Brunetti and Chris Ware use clean and geometric cartoony representations. If we go by graphic structure alone, it may be more appropriate to include these authors within the Barksian AVL dialect, although they are separated by the topics and subject matter appropriate to the Independent genre. This crosscutting of schematic patterning and sociocultural context creates an interesting challenge to delineating clear-cut dialects in AVL (see Witek, 2012 on this topic).

## Art versus language

If drawing is cognitively language-like, why is there so much diversity in the graphic structure of American visual languages? Remember, a language as a cognitive system reflects the patterns in an individual's brain, but a language as a sociocultural system reflects patterns shared by the brains of people in a community. What in America then disconnects the patterns used by individuals and those of a community?

One reason may be a predominant idea about art and art education within American and European culture that focuses on individuality and innovation in each person's drawing style. Over the past hundred-plus years, art education in this tradition has generally admonished children against imitating others' drawings (Cižek, 1927; Richardson, 1937; Viola, 1936). This emphasis originated with the Austrian educator Franz Cižek (1865–1946), whose theories in the late 1800s promoted the belief that children had an innate "artistic ability" that could only develop naturally without influence from external forces (Cižek, 1927). Imitation of other people's drawing styles, and any explicit instruction by a teacher, stifled a child's innate creative potential because it reflected cultural influence over subconscious instincts (Cižek, 1927; Richardson, 1937; Viola, 1936). Cižek and later proponents went so far as to claim that imitation not only limited creativity, but was a detriment to a child's mental health (Arnheim, 1978; Lowenfeld, 1947), comparing it to child slavery, prostitution, and even murder (Costall, 1997).

These anti-imitation ideas actually trace to the eighteenth-century philosophy of Jean-Jacques Rousseau (Paine, 1992), who viewed children's development as a ripening process of innate capacities. Such trends in art education began emerging in the mid-1800s in the writings of Rodolphe Töpffer, who was not only experimenting with sequential art, but was also an influential Swiss educator (Wilson, 1992). With the publication of Charles Darwin's evolutionary theories looming large over the scientific community in the 1800s, people seized on comparing "primitive" drawings with children's drawings as a theory of recapitulation, thus viewing children as "noble savages" who needed to be shielded from external influence. Despite some pushback in the early twentieth century, this emphasis on individual creativity—and against imitation—quickly spread to become the dominant paradigm in art education around the world, and continues to frame notions of drawing and art today in our broader culture (an excellent review of this ideology of education can be found in Willats, 2005).

This ideology has formed the core of cultural assumptions about drawing in the United States and Europe. I refer to this set of assumptions as the "Art Frame" and contrast it against the "Language Frame," which focuses on drawing as similar to other aspects of conceptual expression (namely speech and gesture). A "frame" in this sense is a collection of ideas and conceptions within a cultural setting that act as a filter that enables people to make sense of the world (Goffman, 1974). The Art Frame includes the various beliefs of drawing that we have discussed so far: that drawing is rooted in the presentation of perceptual information found in either the world ("life drawing") or the mind ("drawing from memory"), and that those images reflect an individual's unique creativity and conceptualization of the world. The development of this ability should be left unsullied by outside influence; imitation is thus frowned on because it could limit the fruition of an individual's innate creative style.

**TABLE 7.1** *Contrasting viewpoints of the Art Frame and Language Frame*

|  | Art Frame | Language Frame |
| --- | --- | --- |
| **Function** | Drawings are for re-presenting perception (either through vision or visual memory) | Drawings are for expressing concepts visually |
|  |  | Focus on communication and contextual functionality |
|  | Focus on performance or aesthetic, and personal expression of creativity as part of the signs | Aesthetic is an interpretive layer (i.e. Rhetoric) |
| **Learning** | Fruition of individualistic creativity and talent, or skill learned through explicit instruction | Innate ability naturally learned through exposure and practice to external schema |
|  | Individuality and innovation are stressed as good while imitation is bad | Communally used schemas are learned through imitation |
| **Images** | Drawings reflect perception (either from vision or from visual memory) | Drawings reflect the patterned mental schema conventional to one's culture |
|  | Drawings are universal | Drawings are culturally diverse patterns in individuals' minds/brains |

In contrast, the Language Frame—as outlined throughout this book—considers drawing to have a cognitive structure similar to other aspects of conceptual expression, particularly language and gesture. This view sees drawing as the expression of concepts via the visual-graphic modality by means of patterned schematic knowledge stored in long-term memory. Thus, development of drawing ability is the acquisition of these schemas through exposure and practice. This set of conceptions frames the natural inclination of the drawing system. The contrasts between the Art and Language Frames are summarized in Table 7.1.

These Frames offer us a way to understand the diversity of graphic structure in American visual languages. These two Frames vie for influence over people learning to draw in America and Europe. Because it reflects similar operations to other domains of cognition, the Language Frame outlines the *natural inclination of the mind/brain for the structure of drawing*. If drawings are structured like language—as has been argued in Chapter 2—then learning how to draw involves imitating the schemas in a person's environment (for further detail, see Cohn, 2012b).

Transmission of cultural conventions through imitation has long been recognized as a spontaneous and common trait of child development (Piaget, 1951). Copying drawings benefits learning a great deal (Gardner, 1980; Wilson and Wilson, 1982) and imitation of external graphic sources is largely motivated through observation and modeling, not necessarily explicit art instruction (Lamme and Thompson, 1994; Wilkins, 1997; Wilson, 1997; Wilson and Wilson, 1977). This benefit is enhanced when a learner interacts with the process of drawing (the production script), and not just the end result (Pemberton and Nelson, 1987).

Also, contrary to the traditional belief that imitation limits children's creativity, recent work suggests that imitation actually *fosters* creativity for drawing (Huntsinger, Jose, Krieg, and Luo, 2011; Ishibashi and Okado, 2004). Finally, imitation is important for socialization (Korzenik, 1979), which thereby facilitates drawing ability (Callaghan, 1999). While younger children copy as a means of acquiring knowledge, older children do so to adapt to the conventions of their culture (Smith, 1985). In sum, imitation appears central to children's natural development of drawing ability.

Given these natural inclinations for learning to draw, the Art Frame acts as a cultural force that encourages people to *not* learn schemas through exposure and imitation. If individuals do not imitate external sources, they neither partake in nor contribute to a conventionalized system of signs across individuals. This yields a culture that lacks (or lacks the desire for) a conventionalized system. As a result, learners do not have a system to acquire from, thereby creating a vicious circle for lack of a system to be *exposed to*. An Art Frame-dominated society will thus lack a conventional representational system, and/or contain highly diverse styles based on the idiolects of each individual drawer, since each person must invent their own system.

Of course, even with the heavy influence of the Art Frame, the natural inclinations to imitate may persist. For example, many mainstream comic artists draw similarly to each other, all sharing common influences of particular artists. There would not be "styles" to speak of without imitation. Further, artists belonging to a similar studio naturally gravitate towards each other's styles. This similarity may not be conscious. Individually, they might be trying to uphold their own unique styles, although the communal influence of being surrounded by a particular dialect of visual language no doubt has an influence.[1]

It should be no surprise, then, that the most diversity in graphic structure comes in the "Indy dialect," which most significantly values the individualism of the Art Frame. Case in point: no books instruct "how to draw" the Indy dialect. Thus, the diversity of graphic structure in America can be viewed as a negotiation between Nature (Language Frame) and Nurture (Art Frame), the interplay between natural inclinations for imitation and cultural inclinations for individuality.

## Morphology

While their graphic structure may differ, dialects of American Visual Language share a lot of closed-class morphology. Especially in the more cartoony dialects, authors use both the conventionalized morphology discussed in Chapter 2 and more creative instances of visual metaphor. On the whole, more "realistic" graphic styles rely less on closed-class graphic morphology, favoring morphology that is subtler and fits within the constraints of a more "realistically" depicted world. For example, Kirbyan AVL rarely uses upfixes, eye-umlauts, or fight clouds, yet there is an abundant use of impact/action stars, motion lines, and variations on scopic lines (i.e. x-ray or laser vision). Independent and Barksian AVL tend to make more creative and prevalent uses of closed-class morphology. These dialects also make greater use of overt visual metaphors, such as the

**FIGURE 7.3** *Visual metaphor of a head as a pressurized container/machine. Journal Comic* © 2002 Drew Weing.

one in Figure 7.3, where the head/brain is viewed as a pressurized container or machine that explodes when overworked (Forceville, 2005; Lakoff and Johnson, 1979).

# Narrative grammar

Given the diversity in graphic structure, is there evidence that these authors share a common narrative structure in their visual language grammar? In other words, are these dialects completely unconnected to each other, and comprise an "American Visual Language" simply through the coincidence of belonging to the same geo-political culture? Or, do these diverse graphic styles actually mask a common underlying grammar?

In *Understanding Comics*, Scott McCloud (1993) looked at the distribution of "panel transitions"—the linear relationships between panels—in a variety of comics from America, Europe, and Japan. He found that American comics used a common pattern of transitions across genres. Transitions mostly shifted between actions (~65%), with some shifts between characters (~20%), and even less shifts between scenes (~14%). Almost no transitions between panels highlighted aspects of the broader environment, such as background elements of the scene. As he noted, these patterns draw focus to the actions and events in the narrative, using other transitions for shifting to new characters and scenes. For our purposes, McCloud's findings imply that, despite very different graphic styles, the underlying grammar of American Visual Language remains consistent across dialects.

In Chapter 4, I presented an alternative approach to panel transitions that instead uses a narrative grammar. What might this grammatical approach tell us about differences between dialects in AVL? Rather than focusing on the relationship between panels, here focus shifts to the representations within panels and their relationship to the broader sequence. Such an approach has precedents in an early dissertation by Neff (1977), in which he found that panels use types of film shots differently between genres of American comics. Wide shots (long and medium) far outnumbered close shots (close and close-ups) in panels for all genres. Still, far fewer panels used close shots in Adventure and Romance comics than in Mystery and Alien Beings comics. These findings imply that genres of American comics do represent scenes differently.

Beyond types of filmic shots, panels frame "attention" on a visual scene in various ways, as we discussed in Chapter 3. Recall that Macros show multiple characters, Monos show a single character, Micros show less than a full character, and Amorphic panels show no characters at all, only aspects of the environment. By looking at these types of categories, we can characterize how various authors highlight aspects of a scene, thereby converging on McCloud's panel transitions.

In an initial study (Cohn, 2011), I found that American comics from the 1980s through early 2000s generally used far more Macros than Monos. In fact, Macros comprised nearly 60% of all panels, while Monos were only half that (30%). Meanwhile, Micros consisted of around 7% (Figure 7.4a).[2] The results of this study suggested that American authors depict the whole scene twice as much as they show a scene's component parts. These results

a. Study 1: American comics

b. Study 2: Attentional categories and filmic shots for American

**FIGURE 7.4** *Attentional panel categories and filmic shot types in American comic panels.*

somewhat resemble McCloud's: more Macros suggest that authors depict a whole scene (and the actions occurring within it), while fewer Monos suggest shifts between individual characters. While this study cast light on the general tendencies of American comics, it did not distinguish between books of different genres.

Thus, in a second study, we compared the attentional categories in Mainstream comics and Independent graphic novels from the 1990s and 2000s (Cohn, Taylor-Weiner, and Grossman, 2012). In this case, we coded attentional types as well as filmic shots (Figure 7.4b). We found that Macro panels and Mono panels dominated both genres to near equal amounts (~45%), while Micro and Amorphic panels fell under 10% each. Between genres, proportions of attentional types did not differ, but filmic shot types varied somewhat. While Mainstream comics used slightly more close shots and slightly fewer close-ups, they maintained almost the same amount of long, full, and medium shots. In contrast, Independent comics used more medium and close shots, moderate amounts of long and full shots, and very few close-ups. Thus, while attentional types did not differ between genres, the proportion of filmic shots did.

These results are consistent with both McCloud's findings that panel transitions *did not differ* between genres and Neff's findings that filmic shots of panels *do differ* between genres. Attentional categories frame the depiction of the meaning of a scene and can inferentially lead to predictions about the grammatical structure. For example, a high proportion of Macros suggests that E-Conjunction is used less frequently, since it requires using portions of a scene (Monos) to build the larger conception of the environment. Rather, it seems common in AVL to show the whole scene more often with a Macro, thereby including its parts upfront. Such results maintain McCloud's findings that American comics do not use as many transitions between characters and aspects of a scene.

Nevertheless, differences between genres did arise with regard to how authors chose to show the elements within a panel. A Mono panel of a single character can be shown as a full body (full shot), waist up (medium shot), a whole head (close), or zooming into a body part (close-up). These categories do not emphasize *what* is shown in a scene, but *how* it is shown. Despite Mainstream and Independent comics using similar attentional categories, they differed in how those categories are presented in filmic shots types. The results of these studies thus imply that both dialects use a similar underlying AVL grammar. However, their presentation of scenes differs, at least to some degree (as do their graphic structures). Thus, as we might expect, different dialects of AVL seem to share some structure, while differing in others.

# Languages versus dialects

The diversity of graphic styles between the visual languages in the United States raises several questions related to the interface between culture and cognition, and how we identify a "language" socioculturally. For example, authors like Chris Ware and Ivan Brunetti draw with a highly refined, cartoony style. Is it more appropriate to say that they belong to the Barksian dialect (reflecting their patterns), or does their association with an Independent genre of comics with regard to content warrant inclusion in an Indy dialect?

An even more challenging issue is whether we can identify one broader system as "American Visual Language" at all, or if this is simply the collection of many unique and diverse systems in a common geopolitical setting. An analogy to this issue comes from the conception of a "Chinese" spoken language. In actuality, there is no language called "Chinese." Rather, several hundred languages are spoken in the country of China, the most prominent being Mandarin and Cantonese. Yet, the languages in China vary so much that many are not mutually intelligible (despite sharing a common written language).

Is the notion of an "American Visual Language" similar to "Chinese"? Is each diverse drawing style actually its own unique visual language, or does the diversity in graphic structure betray a shared grammar of several dialects? In addition to sharing many aspects of visual morphology, we have at least some hints that consistent trends in the narrative grammar might underlie these different systems. These are questions that can only be answered by further research in the visual language paradigm.

# Notes

1  An anecdotal example: When I was 15, mainstream superhero comics inspired most of my drawings. Before the mass translation of manga into English, I received several volumes of a series from a friend who lived in Japan. I did not want to draw in the style of manga, nor did I ever directly imitate them. However, the eyes of my characters steadily grew larger and their chins grew pointier. This influence arose solely because of my constant reading and rereading of these books, making the properties of the Japanese VL more normalized in my mind. This trend persisted until I consciously halted it and once again pressed for a more individualistic, Art Frame-inspired style.

2  Other panels were ambiguous. Amorphic panels had not yet been theorized in this study and were likely incorporated into the Mono or Micro categories.

# CHAPTER EIGHT

# Japanese Visual Language[1]

Over the past several decades, Japanese Visual Language (JVL)—the system of graphic representation used in Japanese "manga"—has become one of the most recognizable styles of representation in the world. In Japan, manga are far more popular than comics in any other culture. They are read by people of all ages, cover innumerable genres, and ubiquitously appear throughout the country. Indeed, manga constitute nearly one-third of all printed material (Gravett, 2004; Schodt, 1983, 1996). Even more important for the conception of drawing as a visual language, the stereotypic style of JVL extends beyond manga into nearly all aspects of visual culture, such as animation and advertising. Mass exportation of manga into the United States has been relatively recent, but this style has permeated the visual languages of most other Asian countries, including Korea, China, and Malaysia, among others.

The term "manga" originates from the nineteenth-century artist of woodblock prints, Katsushika Hokusai (1760–1849), to mean "whimsical drawings"—a description mostly of caricature. Japanese history also abounds with narratives told through sequential images, in particular *emaki*—illustrated "picture scrolls" that told stories—which date back to the twelfth century (Schodt, 1983).

Despite this, little evidence supports that drawing styles and techniques from traditional Japanese artwork influenced the structure of contemporary Japanese Visual Language, especially when considering a language as a set of cognitive patterns. Granted, a cultural familiarity with sequential images may have facilitated the growth of modern sequential image storytelling. However, contemporary manga have little in common structurally with the visual styles (i.e. graphic structure/morphology) or storytelling (i.e. grammar) of emaki or woodblock prints. Rather, authors of Japanese manga found greater inspiration from imported American comics and animation throughout the early twentieth century (Gravett, 2004). By the 1950s, the Japanese manga industry was flourishing and the properties of JVL developed with little outside influence, resulting in many unique conventions differing from other visual languages of the world.

# Graphic Structure

Most people can identify Japanese Visual Language by the most salient feature of its graphic structure: the stereotypical way that people are drawn with big eyes, big hair, small mouths, and pointed chins (see Figure 8.1). This "style" is so schematized that often characters' faces cannot be distinguished from each other, leading authors to use other features to differentiate them (Natsume, 1998; Rommens, 2000), such as hair styles or hair color (Levi, 1996).

Heads

Eyes

Nose/Mouth

Hair

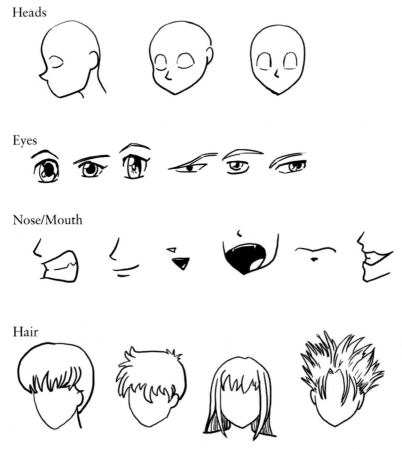

**FIGURE 8.1** *A sampling of the stereotypical schema for heads and faces in Japanese Visual Language.*

Eyes are one of the most noticeable traits about figures in JVL, and their features imply different things about the characters (Brenner, 2007). The stereotypically large, round eyes are most prominent in women, children, and some men. More masculine men often have narrower eyes. Larger, rounder eyes generally correlate with innocence and purity, while narrower eyes indicate more seriousness or amorality. Evil characters often have very narrow, squinty eyes, no matter their gender. Irises also have meaning: larger irises indicate that a character is good, while smaller or absent irises indicate that a character is bad.

Consistent patterns also underlie other parts of faces. Chins of characters are most often pointed, although rounder and squarer variations exist for some male jaws (rounder jaws for less serious characters, squarer jaws for older or more grizzled characters). Noses are typically underemphasized, formed by a simple L-shape, a single horizontal line, a small triangle, or are omitted altogether. Mouths are also simplified, rarely appear with lips, and vary depending on the emotion. Hair is often very large, and has several conventionalized styles, including parted in the middle with pigtails, ponytails, a large wispy mop of spiky hair, and long bangs covering a single eye. Together, these and other facial features can combine to form a variety of different characters.

Often, these varieties join with other templates, depending on what type of person is being drawn. For instance, a stereotypical "big strong male" has a consistent conventional style different from the pointy chin pattern. Again, "how to draw manga" lessons outline templates for this visual language.

Naturally, not everyone in Japan uses this conventionalized style. Others have been inspired by alternative visual styles, like *Akira* creator Katsuhiro Ōtomo, who drew greatly from French artists (Schodt, 1996). Many manga use diverse and varying styles, especially in the "artistic" or *garo* genre (as would be predicted by the Art Frame). While diversity clearly exists across all genres of manga and warrants interesting discussion, we will focus on the conventionalized manner of drawing as most representative of the visual language of Japan. Similar to the way that the Tokyo dialect is considered the "standard" dialect of spoken Japanese, this stereotypical "manga style" can be considered the "standard" dialect of Japanese Visual Language, since it uses schemas shared by a broad range of authors.

The overarching schemas in JVL are commonly attributed to Osamu Tezuka, who was himself greatly influenced by the drawing styles of Walt Disney animated films and American comics while growing up in the 1930s (Gravett, 2004; Schodt, 1996). So, just like most other languages in the world, JVL's graphic vocabulary did not appear out of nowhere, but has been tempered and transmitted from other sources (the same way that spoken "Chinese" influenced spoken Japanese).

No matter his own inspirations, Tezuka's impact is hard to deny. Due to his unprecedented popularity at the birth of the contemporary Japanese manga industry, many other authors imitated his style. Most manga today do not directly mimic Tezuka's drawing style, but various graphic dialects have developed from Tezuka's influence and that of other subsequent influential authors. At this point, people around the globe can easily identify Standard JVL unconnected to any particular author's manner of drawing. The "style" has transcended individuals to become a visual vocabulary representative of Japan as a whole. Indeed, JVL is not constrained to manga, and recurs ubiquitously in cartoons, advertisements, emoticons, and visual culture generally. One is pressed in Japan to *not* find this style in graphic representations.

Nevertheless, proficient readers can easily tell the difference between Standard JVL and the diverse variants from various genres of manga. *Shojo* (girls) manga feature a more rounded and "soft" style of representation, while *shonen* (boys) manga often use more angular lines. *Chibi* styles are easily distinguished by their short and cute figures, while various other styles play off the abstract schema of Standard JVL in a variety of ways. To the extent that the representations from genres can be grouped into recognizable "styles," each constitutes a sub-variety of JVL.

Compared to the dialects of American Visual Language, which feature vastly different styles, variations in JVL remain subtler. We might liken these differences to "accents" rather than full-blown "dialects," since they all play off the same general template from Standard JVL in unique and specific ways. Of course, in cognitive terms, the difference between accents and dialects is merely one of degree, reflecting the extent to which a population of people share a common set of patterns in their minds.

# Morphology

While Japanese Visual Language uses many of the same elements of visual morphology as AVL, it also has many unique and culturally specific signs. Like AVL, some signs are non-conventional visual symbols and metaphors. Shojo (girls) manga often make emotional use of non-narrative signs in the backgrounds of their panels, using pastiches of flowers or sparkling lights to set a mood or hint at underlying meaning (Sakurai, Narumi, Tanikawa, and Hirose, 2011; Shinohara and Matsunaka, 2009). Sex especially is often depicted using crashing surf, blossoming (or wilting) flowers, or far more suggestive metaphors in erotic comics in lieu of the forbidden depiction of genitalia (Schodt, 1983).

Other visual metaphors are more overt, such as a scene in Osamu Tezuka's *Buddha* where arrows pierce through the Buddha's belly to show the agonizing pain of being poisoned. A similar metaphor appears in Rumiko Takahashi's *Maisson Ikkoku*, where an arrow shoots out of a gossipy speech balloon to stab a character in the heart (Ceglia and Caldesi

Valeri, 2002). In most cases, visual metaphors like these heighten the emotional impact of the representations, or creatively adapt them to better suit the graphic form.

Conventional closed-class morphology in manga varies in their transparency of meaning. In addition to the eye-umlauts used in AVL, JVL also uses suppletions like an X or >< covering across both eyes to represent nervousness or excitement. In conventional depictions of rage or anger,

| | | | |
|---|---|---|---|
| Lust | Sleep | Anger or Irritation | Dirty Thoughts |
| Shock or Exasperation | Anger | Relief | Excitement |
| Mischief | Begging | Glaring | Crying |
| Shock | Loss of control | Shock | Super-deformation (Chibi) |

**FIGURE 8.2** *Various morphology found in Japanese Visual Language.*

characters grow sharp fangs and pointy claws while fire erupts behind them, or possibly show an exaggerated vein popping out of their head (Shinohara and Matsunaka, 2009). These representations require little decoding and seem to have conceptual underpinnings similar to depictions of anger in other visual languages (Eerden, 2009; Forceville, 2005; Shinohara and Matsunaka, 2009).

Other morphemes are more opaque to those who have not learned their symbolic meaning, such as gigantic sweat drops conveying embarrassment or nervousness, glowing eyes for glaring, bloody noses depicting lust, bubbles from the nose to depict sleep (Brenner, 2007; McCloud, 1993), or the lengthening of the area between the nose and lips to indicate sexual thoughts (Schodt, 1983). Animal imagery also abounds, with mischief or feistiness represented by characters growing a single fang or having mouths shaped like the number "3" sideways (like a cat) along with big eyes. Wolf ears and a tail may appear when a character is leering, and dog ears, a wagging tail, and curled paws may appear when a character is begging (Brenner, 2007). A mushroom shape emerges from characters' mouths when they exhale to represent a sigh of relief or depression. Blackened eyes may represent a vengeful personality or anger, small bubbles in the corners of eyes suggest that a character is starting to cry, or vertical lines along the cheeks show pouring tears. Characters may take on certain poses for different emotions, like a twisted-up position for shock. A small sampling of these morphemes and their meanings are depicted in Figure 8.2, yet no studies have yet attempted to catalogue a "dictionary" of these signs.

Some morphemes in JVL use even more extreme manipulations, particularly suppletion. Among the more unusual, some characters will suddenly become "super-deformed"—taking on a hyper-cartoony or "deformed" style—to show a spontaneous general lack of seriousness or exaggerated emotion (especially anger, joy, or surprise). Super-deformed bodies are usually far smaller than the normal size of the character, with the head of the character one-half to one-third the size of the body. Full suppletion like this also arises when characters make the pose of Edvard Munch's painting *The Scream* when they are screaming or surprised. Another conventionalized suppletion deletes or omits parts of bodies in extreme emotional states. In particular, hands transform into stumps to metaphorically represent the emotional loss of control, although other instances include feet turning to stumps in extreme happiness, and the shrinking of a whole body to convey humiliation (Abbott and Forceville, 2011).

Another ubiquitous element of JVL's closed-class morphology is the use of motion lines, which have historically differed between American and Japanese visual languages, at least until the 1990s. Rather than showing lines trailing the moving object (as in Figures 8.3a and 8.3b), manga often showed the moving object statically with streaming background lines, as in Figure 8.3c (McCloud, 1993, 1996). These lines are no longer affixing or suppletive path lines because they do not actually attach to the moving

a. "Objective" affixing lines

b. "Objective" suppletive lines

c. "Subjective" background lines

d. Subjective viewpoint

**FIGURE 8.3** *Objective and subjective conventions in motion lines and framing.*

object (the lines are set behind the object) and they no longer show an explicit path (FROM→TO). Rather, these lines give the illusion that the viewer moves at the same speed as the object, resulting in a "blurred" background. This is one of numerous techniques that McCloud (1993, 1996) claims manga use to give a more *subjective* viewpoint.

Motion lines as a whole appear different in manga than in older American comics. Lines commonly substitute for the object itself to show a blurred motion, or surround an object in a flurry of background lines. These distinctly different strategies for depicting motion were amongst the first characteristics appropriated by English-speaking comic authors as manga increased in readership in America throughout the 1980s and 1990s (McCloud, 1996).

# Narrative grammar

We now turn to the grammar of JVL by considering whether it is substantially different from that of AVL. We again start with McCloud's (1993) study of panel transitions, which also compared American comics and Japanese manga. He found that while American comic panels consistently shifted between actions, characters, and scenes, Japanese books introduced some fine-grained temporal shifts between moments and high numbers of "aspect transitions" showing elements of the surrounding environment that were otherwise absent in American comics. These aspect transitions increased the proportion of panels that set a "wandering eye around the scene," and similar effects have been reported in Japanese animation and film (Shamoon, 2011). Along with the more "subjective" types of motion lines, this greater focus on environmental aspects in storytelling led McCloud (1993, 1996) to propose that manga allow a reader to take more of a "subjective" viewpoint on a story than American comics. He also based this proposal on the subjective viewpoints in panels, which show the viewpoint of a character in the narrative, as in Figure 8.3d.

How might we account for McCloud's observations with a narrative grammar? Again, panel transitions look solely at the difference *between* panels, while the narrative grammar places focus on how the *content* of panels fits into a broader architecture. One place to start is by looking at McCloud's claim about subjectivity. In order to test this claim directly, I coded a corpus of comics and manga for panels depicting the viewpoint of a character in the narrative (Cohn, 2011). Overall, subjective panels only comprised about 1% of all panels in both samples—a relatively small amount—although more subjective panels were used in Japanese manga than American comics to a statistically significant degree. These subjective panels positively correlated with Monos but negatively correlated with Macros, meaning that subjective viewpoints in Japanese panels look at parts of scenes, not whole scenes. This provided evidence that manga do indeed use more subjective viewpoints, at least across one measurable dimension.

A second focus has been on coding the attentional categories found in various books: Macros, Monos, Micros, and Amorphic panels. Last chapter, I reported results for American comics, but these panels were also compared with those from Japanese manga. My first study revealed that American comics used almost twice as many Macros as Mono panels, with very few Micros, as in Figure 8.4a (Cohn, 2011). In other words, American comics showed a whole scene in panels twice as much as the individuated parts of the scene. In contrast, Japanese manga used only slightly fewer Monos than Macros, with a higher proportion of Micros. That is, manga depicted whole scenes as much as they showed the parts of scenes.

Again, our follow-up study compared American Mainstream and Independent comics along with Japanese manga (Cohn, Taylor-Weiner, and Grossman, 2012). As discussed in the previous chapter, no statistical differences appeared between attentional panels types in American genres: they both featured near equal amounts of Macros and Monos, which far exceeded Micros and Amorphic panels. Again, panels from Japanese manga

■Macro        ■Mono    ■Micro        □Amorphic

a. Study 1: American comics vs. Japanese Manga

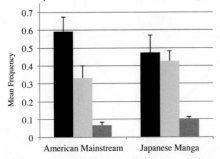

b. Study 2: American comics of different genres vs. Japanese

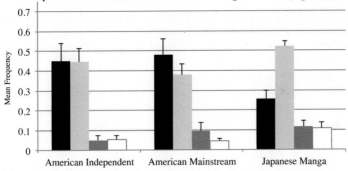

**FIGURE 8.4** *Comparison of attentional panel categories in American VL and Japanese VL.*

differed from these. Manga used almost twice as many Mono panels as Macros, again with higher proportions of Micros and Amorphics than either American genre.

Like McCloud's findings, these studies suggest that Japanese panels place a greater emphasis on the parts of a scene (through Monos, Micros, and Amorphics) than on the whole scene (Macros). American comics seem to show a different trend—they focus on whole scenes as much if not more than the elements within those environments. Thus, by focusing on the content of individual panels, we can account for the differences that McCloud found in relationships between panels.

What might these proportions of panels tell us about differences between the actual narrative grammars used in JVL and AVL? The increased number of panels in JVL *not* showing whole scenes (Monos, Micros, Amorphics) implies that readers may need to infer these whole environments. This would suggest that JVL uses E-Conjunction more often than AVL. Similarly, the increased number of Micros implies that focus directs to parts of individuals and scenes more than in AVL, likely with a greater use of Refiners. This can be seen clearly in Figure 8.5.

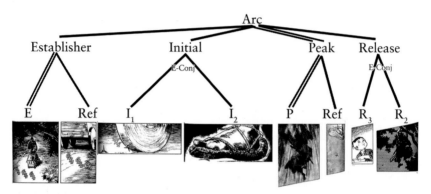

**FIGURE 8.5** *Typical manga sequence using E-Conjunction and Refiners. Lone Wolf and Cub* © *1995 Kazuo Koike and Goseki Kojima.*

This example from the manga *Kozure Okami [Lone Wolf and Cub]* shows a samurai pushing his child in a cart. He then steps on *makibishi* nails, placed on the ground by ninja, which causes him to leap in the air and grab a branch of a tree to avoid any further dangerous missteps. The sequence opens with an Establisher setting up the scene of the samurai and his child walking. A Refiner in the second panel then draws attention to the ground and the cart's wheels. The third and fourth panels, both Initials, show close-up views of the wheel and foot both stepping on nails. These panels depict similar narrative events, and thus unite via E-Conjunction as part of a larger Initial phase. The samurai then jumps away in the Peak, the culmination of the sequence. A Refiner again shows us more detail in this action: the nail drops out of his foot while in mid-air. The sequence concludes with Releases, as the child looks up at his father hanging from a branch, united again by E-Conjunction into a common narrative state.

As should be evident, this sequence uses a lot of modifying functions in the narrative grammar, with only the first Macro panel showing more than an individual character. This use of E-Conjunction forces a reader to inferentially construct the spatial relationships between elements out of the depicted parts of the scene. Similarly, the Refiners allow focus to shift to the specific parts of the scene most relevant to the intended meaning, while implying the rest of the scene (for example, we know that the foot in panel

4 belongs to a whole person). Since the corpus analyses showed that AVL uses Macros at a much higher proportion, it implies that American readers are not forced to make these sorts of constant inferences while reading AVL.

It is important to note that neither strategy is inherently "better" or "worse" than the other, just different. Showing full scenes, as in AVL, likely requires less cognitive processing than extensive use of modifiers, as in JVL. Using more Macros also allows sequences to be shorter, since more information can be encapsulated in each panel, versus letting a scene extend across multiple Mono or Micro panels. In contrast, a larger use of inference in this way allows the images to draw focus to parts of a scene in specific and creative ways.

## Differences in visual language grammars

Why might Japanese Visual Language place more emphasis on the parts of a scene than the whole scene, like American Visual Language? One possible explanation is fairly banal: these are simply different languages. Spoken languages differ across the world in diverse ways, yet we do not point towards anything more than historical development for these differences. Thus, it should not be unusual that visual languages vary simply because of differences in population either (such as the clear differences between AVL and JVL closed-class morphology). Nevertheless, there may be justification for arguing that these differences in grammatical structure actually connect with deeper cognitive differences between authors in American and Japanese cultures.

First, the focus on surrounding aspects of a scene (in Amorphics) may not have originated in manga. Shamoon (2011) argued that these techniques were not present in manga from the early 1950s, and they likely emerged from the *gekiga* movement of manga creators who wrote about more mature and serious topics. These authors sought a more "cinematic" style of manga and thereby imitated the "wandering eye" technique used by Japanese filmmakers. Following their lead, this technique quickly spread as a common manga convention. Yet, even if this technique's origins lie in cinema and it is simply conventional, the question remains: why does it appear so prevalently and naturally in Japanese visual narrative compared to American storytelling?

In his observations of panel transitions, McCloud offered two explanations. First, he hypothesized that the increase in viewpoints of characters and background elements may be due to the format of manga versus comics. In contrast to the small pamphlet-style monthly comics in America, he hypothesized that manga's anthology and *tankōbon* formats allows authors to devote more panels to drawing out scenes and focusing on the setting or mood, a sentiment also echoed by Rommens (2000). A second, more radical explanation looks to cultural motivations. McCloud proposed that Asian culture is less "goal-oriented" than Western culture, and that "Japanese comics... often emphasize *being there* over *getting there*" (McCloud, 1993, p. 81, emphasis in original).

McCloud's first hypothesis—that differences are due to format—is supported by these patterns of attentional and narrative structure. The expansion of information across several panels using Monos and Micros suggests that manga draw out the representations of events instead of simply showing the actions in the setting outright. However, no data outright supports that this is due to format alone. Just because manga authors have more pages at their disposal does not insinuate that they "decompress" their scenes (and indeed, their anthologies are first serialized in episodes, just like in American comics). They could just as easily fill that space with compact narrative and even *more* plot.

Rather, we might say that they use the visual language *as a language*— allowing the visuals to express meaning through their own capacities and thus require more length to do so. In fact, Osamu Tezuka intended his first hit, *Shin-Takarajima [New Treasure Island]*, to open with a 31-panel sequence, which was *shortened* to only four panels, despite launching a new, longer format of manga (Gravett, 2004). Both the published and unpublished versions of this sequence rely almost solely on visual information. Placing focus on the visuals at the expense of the verbal is consistent with other research suggesting that when the verbal form does not dominate meaning, other modalities become more complex (e.g. Goldin-Meadow, 2006; Wilkins, 1997).

Another possibility is that these differences in attentional panel types reflect the expertise of each culture's readers. Manga are far more prevalent in Japan than in the United States, and the Japanese on average have a greater expertise in reading sequential images than Americans (Nakazawa and Shwalb, 2012). This argument might go...: American comics may be geared towards less experienced readers, and thus they need to be constantly reminded of the elements in a scene with more Macros. Meanwhile, the more experienced Japanese readers may be able to retain or construct the whole scene without being presented with it. This explanation is likely also unfeasible. Manga do indeed have wider readership across the country of Japan compared with the readership of comics across America. Why should this mean that American comic authors simplify their sequences for a more general readership? Regular American comic readers are often serious and devout fans, and would have as much if not greater fluency in their visual language than casual manga readers in Japan. Thus, attributing these findings to expertise alone seems unlikely.

Finally, a compelling origin for the difference between AVL and JVL narrative structure might come from deeper aspects of cognition. Ultimately, these patterns in framing capture ways in which attention focuses on different parts of a scene. In a sense, a sequence of narrative images acts as a *simulation* of how an individual might view a fictitious visual scene (a similar argument for film shots is made by Levin and Simons, 2000). Cross-cultural research has shown that Asians and Americans direct their perception to aspects of visual scenes in different ways (Nisbett, 2003; Nisbett and Miyamoto, 2005). On the whole, Americans focus more on focal objects and characters with agency than aspects of the background, while Asians attend to aspects of the whole environment or to how characters relate to the contextual environment. These findings were initially based on studies of general visual perception analyzing participants' eye movements while they looked at visual scenes. Additional analysis of artwork and photographs has further supported this distinction: Western paintings emphasize the focal objects and figures, while East Asian paintings emphasize the broader context and environment (Masuda, Gonzalez, Kwan, and Nisbett, 2008; Nisbett and Masuda, 2003).

As with attention, readers of sequential images must track only the most important aspects of a sequence to establish the continuity of the narrative. Non-relevant information may then go unattended by the "spotlight of attention" across panels (just like in "change blindness" paradigms of the study of attention [Levin and Simons, 2000]). Thus, authors can use two strategies when drawing a sequence of images. They can either show a full scene (Macro) while relying on the reader's attentional intuitions to discern the most important parts (Figure 8.6a), or they can use panels to directly highlight only those salient parts, omitting unimportant portions altogether (Figure 8.6b). This latter use of panels would heighten the "subjective viewpoint" of panels simulating attention.

The results of our corpus analyses suggest that American comics more consistently use the first option: letting the reader direct their own attention across panels to find the most relevant aspects of continuity, while allowing

a. Sequence with panels depicting full scenes in an "objective" viewpoint

b. Sequence with panels focusing on parts of a scene to create a "subjective viewpoint"

**FIGURE 8.6** *Different strategies for depicting events across a sequence of images.*

less important elements to simply go unattended. This is suggested by the larger number of Macros found in American comics. In contrast, Japanese manga do more to simulate a subjective viewpoint of a reader's attention, evident in greater use of Monos, Micros, and Amorphic panels. That Japanese manga use a more subjective strategy for directing attention is consistent with McCloud's (1993, 1996) claim that manga allow a reader to take more of a subjective viewpoint on a story. This interpretation is also supported by the finding that "subjective panels"—which directly show the viewpoint of a character in a narrative—are more plentiful in Japanese manga than American comics (Cohn, 2011). The positive correlation found between subjective panels and Monos is also telling—they show a subjective viewpoint on the parts of a scene, not whole scenes, just as the eye might focus on parts of a scene.

These different strategies of depicting actions by simulating attention reflect how attention may differ between American and Japanese readers. Manga panels highlight elements of a scene or environment because that would be how Japanese readers' attention would fall on elements of a visual array, and out of this information would need to integrate these parts into a coherent whole. In contrast, because American readers will naturally pick out the focal characters of the scene, American comics can use more Macros, assuming that attention will be directed to the important elements of interest automatically. In this way, panels from comics and manga may reflect how Japanese or American readers might look at a visual scene if the whole array were in front of them, thereby echoing the differences in cultural windowing of attention.

## Influence in Japan and abroad

Compared to the limited influence and spread of AVL through American comics, it is amazing to consider the influence of JVL both in Japan and abroad. Researchers who specialize in drawing have marveled at the proficiency of Japanese children's drawing skills compared to their relatively unskilled counterparts in other countries like America or in Europe (Cox et al., 2001; Wilson, 1999). Much of this proficiency is attributed to the influence and pervasiveness of manga (Cox et al., 2001; Toku, 1998, 2001b; Wilson, 1988, 1997, 1999). Studies have found that over two-thirds of children's drawings imitate manga (Wilson, 1999), which may be a conservative estimate. Not only do Japanese children imitate the graphic structure of JVL, but they also appropriate their methods of spatial representation, such as alternative viewpoints to the predominant lateral viewpoints like aerial and close-up views (Toku, 2001, 2002).

The imitation of manga has also affected Japanese children's creation of narrative sequences. Nearly all Japanese 6-year-olds can draw complex narrative sequences, yet fewer than half of 12-year-olds of other countries have this proficiency (Wilson, 1988). One cross-cultural study showed that two-thirds of Egyptian children, who have little exposure to comics, could not create narratives where the contents of one frame related to the next frame. In contrast, all Japanese children studied were able to create coherent narratives, often using sophisticated techniques like Refiners and subjective viewpoints (Wilson and Wilson, 1987). For example, Figure 8.7 is a sequence drawn by a 7-year-old Japanese boy, in which he used clearly identifiable narrative categories, a Refiner in the second panel to modify the first, and subjective viewpoints in the first two panels depicting a character's viewpoint through a camera.[2]

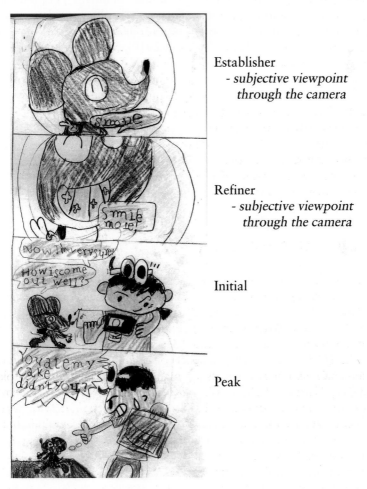

**FIGURE 8.7** *Narrative sequence drawn by a 7-year-old Japanese boy using complex aspects of narrative grammar.*

Children in Japan acquire JVL through their own exposure to and imitation of manga. Institutional art classes in Japanese schools focus mostly on the same Art Frame ideals heralded by Western art education and on the whole do not promote or practice drawing manga (Wilson, 1997). Japanese children spend their own time reading and drawing manga—often with their peers—leading to fluency that is acquired informally and spontaneously through their own actions (Nakazawa, 2005). This activity is not necessarily tied to the manga industry or fan culture. Rather, in most cases, it is simply children drawing—actively participating in their society's visual language.

Japanese Visual Language has also had a far-reaching influence outside of Japan. The visual languages used by authors in Korea, the Philippines, and several other Asian countries heavily imitate Standard JVL, although they sometimes make subtle variations. For example, the visual language in Korea has been claimed to have softer, more rounded lines than the more stereotypically angular Standard JVL (Lent, 2010). In the United States and Australia, many authors of "Original English Language" (OEL) manga (Brenner, 2007) have emerged (along with fans' homemade manga), which are essentially works drawn in JVL by English-speaking non-Japanese individuals. These works ostensibly appear to be written in the same Japanese Visual Language, but they are produced by authors outside the context and industry of manga in Japan.

Even outside the creation of full-blown non-Japanese "manga," the structure of JVL has heavily influenced authors in other countries. American comic authors in the late 1990s began incorporating slightly larger eyes and features of the basic graphic structure, changing their depiction of motion lines (Horn, 1996; McCloud, 1996), and "decompressing" their storytelling—letting actions stretch out for longer sequences of panels. These changes did not lead to mainstream American comics predominantly transforming to look completely like manga, but many authors did fuse elements of JVL with their native Kirbyan AVL.

## Transmission of visual language

Why might the Japanese Visual Language found in manga so readily spread across the world? And why do fans latch onto this style so vehemently? Is this something special about the visual language? Several possible factors may explain why, ranging from the sociocultural to the structural.[3] One simple reason might be because of manga as a literary form. Manga often feature a large range of genres and topics that appeal to wide audiences, especially with types of plot lines and characters not often found in comics from other countries (particularly in the United States). The fact that these stories have different emphases, and appeal to different people, might be an important factor in their spread.

The actual structure of the visual language may also influence its widespread transmission. JVL is highly consistent in its standard features—people easily identify that the regularized patterns do not belong just to an individual author, but to a broader population. This consistency of the visual language across authors makes it easier to learn as a set of cognitive patterns. Think about this as if it were a spoken language. In which scenario would language would be easier for a child to learn: growing up in a town where everyone spoke the same language, or growing up in a town where everyone had very different languages, each unique to themselves or at least to their own family? The inconsistency of visual styles in comics across America and Europe (as per the Art Frame) means that learners of those systems have a harder time imitating and acquiring a specific graphic system, as opposed to learning from the consistent visual language provided by manga.

While conventionalization does exist between American comic authors (especially within Kirbyan AVL), great diversity exists between the visual dialects throughout the culture. Comics, cartoons, advertisements, etc., all use vastly different graphic styles, and this stylistic diversity is something our culture revels in (per the Art Frame). Without a ubiquitous consistent style, American children face a harder choice for acquiring an external system of schemas—which style, if any, do they choose? Comparatively, the consistency of JVL provides a readily accessible structure for imitation.

As discussed, this view of drawing also conforms to the expectations of the Language Frame, as opposed to the Art Frame that focuses on individuals creating their own style. Viewed from the Language Frame, the beliefs of the Art Frame would be akin to pushing a child to make up their own language with its own vocabulary and grammar, and to actively pressure them *not* to imitate the language of their community and peers. If we did this with spoken language, it would be considered inhumane. However, it is the norm for learning to draw, despite substantial evidence that imitation facilitates proficient drawing skills (Gardner, 1980; Huntsinger et al., 2011; Wilson and Wilson, 1982) and actually leads to more creativity, not less (Huntsinger et al., 2011; Ishibashi and Okado, 2004). Thus, if learning to draw involves the acquisition of schemas through imitation, we now have a way to understand the difference between the development of drawing skills in children in America and Japan: Japanese children receive the requisite practice of and exposure to a visual vocabulary, but American children do not (for further detail, see Cohn, 2012b).

Finally, social motivation may also play a role in the transmission of JVL. Individuals have a social identity wrapped up in the language that they speak. Accents from places like Texas or Boston mark people from those regions, and often provide a badge of pride representing a person's geographical roots and inclusion in a social group. Likewise, copying JVL from manga does not just mean imitating an individual, but entering into a visual language community sharing a common visual vocabulary. Through such imitation a person acquires a social identity as a "speaker" of JVL, which they may value for its entrance into a broader community of like-minded people (Bouissou et al., 2010).

By imitating the visual language from manga, Japanese children participate in the visual language native to their culture. In contrast, without a consistent style that reflects the social community writ large, American and European children do not have such a social motivation to imitate (although motivation may come if they expressly value a subculture that has a visual language, such as Kirbyan AVL).[4] This same appeal of JVL applies to non-Japanese readers of manga as well. They want to acquire this visual language because they feel they belong to a broader community of manga readers, and thereby identify with becoming a speaker of Japanese Visual Language (Sell, 2011).

## *Language contact*

The dispersion of JVL around the globe also raises several important questions regarding the interaction between (visual) language, culture, and cross-cultural cognition. For example, the transmission of signs from JVL into Kirbyan AVL illustrates how "language contact" can initiate changes in a system graphically the same way it can verbally. Languages only remain bound by borders that limit their transmission. Since manga have transcended their geographic borders to a dramatic extent in the past decades, JVL has unsurprisingly influenced drawers in America and Europe (Horn, 1996; Rommens, 2000).

This influence manifests in a variety of ways. The appropriation of morphemes like motion lines appears among the smallest instances of this influence—akin to how English has borrowed the words *tycoon* and *karaoke* from Japanese with no overarching change to English grammar. The graphic structure of American comic authors has also changed under influence of JVL. In certain authors, eyes have become larger, chins pointier, and bodies lankier. We would expect that a longitudinal study of American comics that looks at morphemes and graphic structure would show fairly consistent trends until the 1990s, at which point the influence of manga would make the trends look more like JVL. Does this influence go deeper? Has the influence of manga led authors to actually frame scenes in different ways and convey meaning across sequences of images differently? If we were to code the attentional panel categories across the decades, would we see an increased usage of Monos and decreased use of Macros in American comics starting in the 1990s?

More significant questions relate to the structures used by authors of OEL manga. We have yet to study the degree to which the grammar of OEL manga truly reflects that of Japanese manga or is merely the JVL vocabulary painted over AVL grammar. Will the underlying grammar of OEL manga—the system guiding the sequence of images—look like AVL or JVL? Would the coding of attentional categories yield patterns that reflect the differences between Asian and American direction of attention (i.e. more Macros in AVL and Monos in JVL), or do authors of OEL manga actually acquire these patterns as conventionalized traits of the visual language?

I have raised the possibility that the framing of panels reflects cultural tendencies of attention in visual perception. By this account, we would expect the attentional categories used by OEL manga authors from America to be more similar to those of other American authors. If their trends for using attentional categories resemble those of authors from Japan, it would support the idea that they acquired the conventionalized system of JVL by reading manga. Even more interesting would be the possibility that such conventions might actually change the way these authors (and readers?) focus their attention in visual perception more generally. If this were true, it would provide an interesting case of a visual language actually shaping people's cognition away from that of their predominant culture. Now, I should stress that these latter ideas are purely speculative and actual research must provide us evidence one way or the other. Nevertheless, these questions are significant in that they illustrate how studying visual language can address deeper issues related to cross-cultural cognition.

# Notes

1  Parts of this chapter appeared previously in Cohn (2010b).

2  Some context: This and other strips were given to me as gifts for doing some outreach at this child's elementary school in Tsuru-shi, Japan in 2001 while I was an exchange student. I never instructed the class about manga nor did any related activities. Thus, this seemed to be a reflection of his regular drawing practice. Notice that, though the strip uses JVL, the text is in English, which relates to the language exercises I did with the class.

3  Sociocultural factors might include aspects of fandom, pricing of the books, the sense that manga are "cool" compared to native comics (Bouissou, Pellitteri, Dolle-Weinkauff, and Beldi, 2010), or the promotion of popular culture by the Japanese government (Lent, 2010), among others. Since these factors relate to the sociocultural phenomena of "manga" and not Japanese Visual Language, I will not address them further in this discussion.

4  *Rejecting* imitation may allow American or European learners to feel part of a community as well, since they thereby reinforce their identity within their cultural Art Frame, despite it not providing them actual stimulus to become proficient at drawing.

# CHAPTER NINE

# Central Australian Visual Language

As was stressed from the outset, the notion of "visual language" goes beyond comics to describe the human capacity for creating sequential images. Visual languages most often appear in comics in *our* industrialized societies, as in AVL and JVL. Though these systems appear to have clear cross-cultural variations, the differences between AVL and JVL may be marginal when compared to visual languages outside the context of comics or manga. In Central Australia, several Aboriginal communities actively use a system of sand drawings for narratives and even casual conversation. In this chapter, I will argue that this system of sand drawings is a visual language comparable in cognitive status to the visual languages found in the context of comics in other parts of the world. Because of the vast differences in culture and ecology, the structure of this visual language manifests in very different ways. Thus, detailing this system serves as an important contrast to the previously discussed visual languages, and its study offers further questions about aspects of universality and diversity in the visual-graphic modality.

Sand drawings are used by several Aboriginal communities in Australia, especially those in Central Australia surrounding the Alice Springs area (Dubinskas and Traweek, 1984; Green, 2009, In Press; Munn, 1962, 1966, 1986; Strehlow, 1951, 1964; Wilkins, 1997). Most scholarly works focus on the sand narratives found in neighboring regions with common cultural traditions: the Warlpiri region, Arandic region, and the Western Desert (particularly speakers of Pitjantjatjara and Kukatja, as well as the Balgo community). However, systems of sand drawings by Aboriginals have also been reported across Australia (Green, 2009). Important points of departure may exist between the systems used between these communities, yet such differences have not yet been discussed extensively. I will thus refer to this "visual language family" as Central Australian Visual Language (CAVL).

Given that this chapter serves as an overview of this work, I will discuss the properties of these systems broadly under the umbrella of CAVL with the knowledge that systems may vary for individual communities, such as comparisons between Warlpiri and Arrernte sand drawings (for a start to such comparisons, see Green, 2009).

# Cultural Role

At the outset of this discussion, we must first situate the context of these representational systems in Central Australian communities. Sand drawings' role as a communicative system intrinsically ties to the cultural role of the ground itself in these cultures. Many daily and social interactions might occur while people are seated or reclining on the ground. The ground thus provides a readily accessible and "readable" surface for aesthetic and embedded meaning, either produced (sand drawings) or naturalistic (tracks). Many scholars have commented that, for these people, the ground serves as a huge and natural "drawing board" that can be "read" (Green, 2009; McRae, 1991; Munn, 1986; Strehlow, 1951; Wilkins, 1997).

Sand drawings as a performative genre are predominantly used in narratives made by women, although similar conventions are used like gestures as a part of daily communicative acts for women, men, and children. Indeed, drawing in the sand is thought of as an integral part of the notion of "talking" (Munn, 1986; Wilkins, 1997). The pervasive use of drawings as an accompaniment to casual conversation while seated on the ground extends so far that women clear the ground (for a drawing surface) almost automatically when sitting down (Green, 2009).

In their most full-blown context, sand stories integrate drawings with speech, an alternate sign language, gesture (separate from sign language, both conventional gestures and novel gesticulations), and possibly a sung language. Narratives rarely exist solely in drawn form, and at its core the practice of sand narratives is a multimodal activity. In fact, the combination of just signing and drawing can entirely supplant the use of speech (Wilkins, 1997).

In many places, the modalities may intertwine with each other in inseparable ways. This is a point worth stressing, since, although we will primarily focus on the components of the visual language, any full account of these communicative systems must consider all of these components. Multimodality is the norm, both here and in the broader context of human communication (be it speech with gesture, text with images, etc.). Thus, just as "comics" *are written in* a visual language in combination with a verbal language, sand stories *are told using* CAVL, speech, and manual signs. As in the rest of this book, I emphasize here the visual language to provide focus to the identity and structure of this modality with the expectation that such knowledge can further an investigation of the whole of human expression. For an approach to sand stories that is particularly sensitive to the interaction of all modalities, see Green (2009, In Press).

Sand narratives are used to tell several types of stories, which include themes about social behavior and deviation from moral codes, along with fairly universal themes of romance, revenge, retribution, or supernatural monsters. Many sand narratives may be regarded as "Dreaming stories"—related to the fundamental genesis myth of Australian Aboriginal cultures—but also narrate daily events (Green, 2009). Ultimately, however, since the practice of sand drawings passes down through the generations, it is believed to be derived from the Dreaming along with all other social practices. The ground serves as a conduit between the visible world and the spiritual realm of ancestors. Thus, to some people, these stories are not necessarily conceived of as "drawn" on the ground and then erased at their finale, but rather that the stories reside in the ground with the spirits, and storytelling merely uncovers them for a period of time.

## Graphic structure

Unlike the structure of AVL or JVL where narrative units unfurl spatially across a sequence of images, the signs in CAVL unfurl temporally into (mostly) a single narrative space. Because they are ultimately multimodal, sand stories involve two loci for expressing representations (Green, 2009). A "ground space" in front of a speaker is used to draw on the sand and/or set up props such as leaves (Figure 9.1). This surface is defined at the outset by wiping the space clean and clearing it of twigs or rocks. A second "air space" above this ground is used to articulate manual signs. Because actual drawing on the ground involves bodily actions, the articulation of various

**FIGURE 9.1** *Ground and air space in sand narratives (adapted from Green 2009).*

drawings may involve starting in the air space and moving to the ground, or drawing on the ground and moving into the air. This dynamic nature of articulating signs, beyond the static aftermath of their creation, should be remembered because of the real-time interactive nature of sand drawing.

The actual graphic structure of CAVL is very simple—lines are drawn in sand with the fingers, a stick, or a wire. These may be supplemented (or fully replaced) with non-graphic elements, such as leaves, twigs, and other elements that can play roles as objects in narratives like a miniature theatre. Similar to how speech sounds involve different articulators in the mouth, sand drawings are created using several articulatory hand shapes (Green, 2009). A loose open-handed shape with palm touching the ground is used to drag across the surface for broad lines or to wipe it clean. The back of the hand may be used for this as well. Fingers may be spread to create a series of parallel lines. Fingertips of a bunched or spread hand may be used for individuated marks or dots. Precise lines are drawn using the middle finger, or pairs of the middle-index fingers or middle-ring fingers. Noticeably, drawing with the index finger is often avoided, and it is often kept crooked or raised to stay out of the way while drawing. Slapping the ground with the back of the hand may indicate violent events in the narrative, and both hands can be used if needed to convey plurality. Slapping the ground with the palm rarely occurs outside of signaling a story's ending. Also, the drawing hand may simultaneously articulate a sign from the sign language, adding a further layer of meaning to the drawing.

The shapes created by these articulations are often fairly simple, including straight or curved lines, enclosures (boxes, circles, ovals), and dots created by stabbing the sand. As will be discussed, these lines and shapes can be used in many versatile ways and the interpretation of the physical graphic structure may vary based on an articulation's context in a narrative (Green, 2009; Munn, 1986). Also, some marks require the dynamism of the bodily motion that creates them, not just the static end result, in order to be meaningful. Finally, the system of representations used in sand narratives also appears in other contexts, which include the preparation of ceremonial grounds, women's body painting, men's sacred objects, and the acrylic "dot" paintings that appear in the contemporary art market (Green, 2009; Munn, 1986; Wilkins, 1997). This is similar to the cultural use of other visual languages, such as how the graphic structure of JVL appears in cultural contexts beyond just printed manga.

## *Spatial orientation*

A broader system of spatial orientation situates the basic graphic structure of CAVL. Wilkins (1997) recounts an interesting story where he presented various Arrernte children with a drawing of a horse like that in Figure 9.2, and asked them to describe what they saw. While all of the respondents

FIGURE 9.2 *Drawing of a horse, redrawn from Wilkins (1997).*

replied that it was indeed a horse, several did not describe it in the same way that we might (i.e. as a "running horse" with puffs of dust/smoke around its legs to show motion). Rather, some replied that the horse was lying down, or even dead!

Why might some Australian Aboriginals describe this image as a horse lying down or dead? One reason is the orientation of space in sand narratives. Rather than take a lateral, sideways viewpoint on drawings similar to canonical drawings in AVL or JVL (Cohn, 2011), sand drawings use a fixed *aerial viewpoint*. Thus, Wilkins' horse was described as lying down, because that's how the image would look from a bird's eye view. Individuals who replied that the drawing showed a dead horse interpreted the puffs of smoke, with their curved lines, as either wind blowing across the horse or as marks representing crows eating at the horse (Wilkins, 1997). In discussing these results with older adults, Wilkins found confirmation of the children's interpretations for this horse lying down or being dead.[1]

This pervasive aerial viewpoint is actually consistent with spatial cognition found across communicative systems used by Aboriginal Australians, including spoken languages, sign languages, and gestures. All of these systems, as well as sand drawings, predominantly use a system of *absolute space* (Figure 9.3b), which describes spatial locations in terms of cardinal directions (north, east, south, west). This is contrasted with systems that use *relative space* (Figure 9.3a) in reference to a human body (left, right, etc.) (Levinson, 1996). Thus, in speech, words for cardinal directions are preferred when describing locations in space over terms for relative space as found in languages like English or Japanese.

Sand drawings employ this absolute frame of space by setting a default assumption to orienting objects and events with how they would be in the real world (Wilkins, 1997). For example, if a girl walks north in a story, her movements drawn in the sand will coincide with *actual* north in reality. This means that spatial relationships within a story are highly sensitive to the actual cardinal directions in which a narrator is oriented. Thus, if a real place is discussed in the story, representations of it will be mapped to the ground in ways that preserve its accurate orientation in real life.

This effect is strong enough in the interpretation of sand narratives that, in a study by Green (2009), Aboriginals who viewed sand stories on computer screens interpreted motion based on the real-life cardinal direction more than the original directions in the videos. Gestures accompanying sand drawings as well as those in daily conversation have also been found to be locked to the accurate compass directions (Wilkins, 2003), which appears to be common with the gestures of various aboriginal peoples who use absolute space (Haviland, 1993; Levinson, 1996). Thus, sand drawings maintain the same cognitive orientation to absolute space that permeates all expressive modalities amongst members of these communities.

It is also worth considering the relationship between maintaining absolute space and the aerial viewpoint. First, the fixed absolute space locks sand drawings into the context in which they are represented (i.e. drawn on sand in real time). If these narratives were drawn on a wall or drawn on paper and moved, cardinal directions would need to be accurately noted to orient the narrator and audience. Without such notation, rotating the paper could completely change the spatial orientation—and the meaning—of the

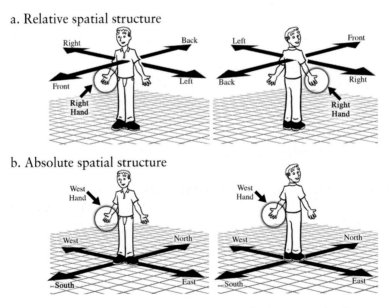

**FIGURE 9.3** *Different types of spatial frames of reference used in language and other communicative systems. In relative systems, the spatial reference rotates with the speaker's body (and thus "right hand" changes with that hand), but in absolute reference it maintains the same no matter how the speaker is situated (and thus "West hand" changes based on which hand is Westward).*

narrative. In contrast, AVL and JVL use lateral viewpoints that require no such contextual spatial cues. They can easily be portable and retain the same intrinsic relative space.

Second, the fixed aerial viewpoint facilitates the use of absolute space. If sand drawings used a lateral viewpoint, cardinal directions would be much harder to maintain throughout a narrative and would require a sense of depth that is not afforded by the morphology of sand narratives (as discussed in the next section). Thus, the drawing system is structured in a way that coincides with other aspects of cognition and expression.

Despite the permeating orientation to absolute space across domains, drawings by pen or in sand by younger Aboriginals sometimes deviate from the pervasive aerial viewpoint. In these drawings, large locative objects, such as automobiles, swing sets, or the whole scene, may be drawn with a lateral side-view perspective into which the conventionalized CAVL figures are situated (Cox, 1998; Green, 2009; Wilkins, 1997). The introduction of this lateral viewpoint no doubt reflects the influence of Western style representations into Australian culture and schooling. In linguistic terms, these mixed representations represent a type of *language contact* where the properties of one visual language become introduced into another (similar to how conventions from JVL have begun permeating dialects of AVL, as discussed in the last chapter).

These examples are also useful for illustrating that these drawings do not necessarily represent how the children (or adults) perceive the world. They do not "see" what they draw with aerial or mixed viewpoints, nor do these viewpoints reflect the habitual perspectives taken on the world. Rather, these spatial orientations are part of the graphic structure and conceptual structure of the visual language and other expressive modalities (Munn, 1973; Wilkins, 1997).

## Lexicon and morphology

In previous chapters, I argued that American and Japanese VLs can be thought of as similar to "synthetic" languages, where units are built of several novel schematic parts. In contrast, CAVL is more like "analytic" languages, where each expression encompasses its own gestural-temporal moment in the narrative stream. These expressive units are fairly simple in representation: most full figures of people, animals, places, etc. constitute only a few lines and shapes, reflecting the economy of representation demanded by a real-time communicative interaction. While many signs are conventionalized and systematic, the same graphic structure—lines and shapes—may appear with different meanings, making the physical marks highly polysemous (Munn, 1986) and often open to different interpretation if presented without the contextual influence of other modalities (Green,

2009). This disambiguation does not necessarily have to come through labeling signs explicitly, but rather the way in which signs interact with others (drawn, spoken, or signed) can provide enough context to clarify their meanings (Green, 2009; Wilkins, 1997).

Related to the aerial viewpoint, markings made in the sand represent "tracks" on the ground similar to the imprints of actual objects (Dubinskas and Traweek, 1984; Green, 2009, In Press; Strehlow, 1951, 1964; Wilkins, 1997). Things that do not make tracks are "invisible" to the ground and are not depicted in the sand (Wilkins, 1997). These elements are either inferred from the visible marks, or are represented through a different modality, either vocalized in speech or signed manually. For example, birds flying in the air would not be drawn—only signed—until they landed on the ground where their tracks would become visible. Signs that do not represent tracks may include waterholes, hills, creek beds, and other natural landforms, or the floor plans of houses and other urban spaces. In these cases, the signs act more as iconic outlines from an aerial viewpoint (Wilkins, 1997), similar to what one might find on a stylized map.

Because sand drawings are created using dynamic articulations of the hands in real time, some signs may be *static* and while others are *dynamic* (Green, 2009). Static signs derive their meaning from the end result of the articulation of the hands (i.e. the production script is a means to the end of creating the sign). In dynamic signs, the motion and articulation of the hands may actually play a meaningful role in the interpretation of the sign (i.e. the production script itself carries meaning).

## Static signs

Many of the "track"-type signs are iconic of an object's actual tracks or imprints. For example, people are conventionally drawn with a "U" shape, where the open part represents the front of a person and the curvature the backside. This shape is iconic of the prototypical imprint that people make when sitting in a cross-legged position on the ground. It may also be used for standing figures, although sometimes drawn smaller in size (Green, 2009). Figures lying down are commonly drawn using an elongated straight line, again iconic of the imprint a body makes on the ground. This line does not necessarily have a head that is explicitly drawn (although heads do appear in drawings by younger people). Sleeping individuals culturally place their head to the east and thus the direction of the head can be inferred through the pre-established absolute space of the depiction (Green, 2009).

Several other basic static signs are conventionalized as well. For example, shorter straight lines often represent a digging stick or a spear, while oval shapes can be a type of dish, stone, pillow, or shield. Fire is depicted by two or more lines converging on a central point, which creates a small mound at their center (alternatively, a circle), resembling the prototypical way of

Person (sitting)  Person (lying down)  Digging stick, spear  Boomerangs  Water dish, stone, pillow, shield

Seed or fruit, small item standing up (stick, spear)  Fire  Windbreak  Humpy/cave

Bush, tree, plant, "thing"  Water hole, billycan, cooking hole  Creek, blanket, women dancing  Meandering line: water, space in a room

Two people  Group of elongated objects (e.g. goannas or pencil yams)  Plural small objects (e.g. seeds, feathers), water, plural standing objects (e.g. spears)

**FIGURE 9.4** *Selection of vocabulary items from the CAVL lexicon, including pluralized forms. Redrawn from Green (2009).*

stoking a fire or piling wood (Green, 2009). Windbreaks are drawn with a long curved line, sometimes with a central circle representing a supporting post, running north-to-south alongside an encampment to protect against easterly winds. Circles of varying sizes can represent waterholes, water in a billycan, or cooking holes. A small sample of these conventionalized static lexical items appears in Figure 9.4 (for further detailed listings of these signs, see Green, 2009, In Press; Munn, 1962, 1986).

Static shapes may be drawn multiple times to express plurality. Two U-shapes might be two people. Large numbers of items may be less numerically specific and aimed at showing a mass or group, as in several dots to show seeds or bushes for plants. Within the narrative world, the precise number of signs is not important, but rather their repetition implies multiplicity. Depending on the hand articulation, this multiplicity may be drawn all at once, as with using multiple fingers to create dots for seeds, or dragging multiple spread fingers to make parallel lines showing several yams.

## Static compounds

While CAVL signs are predominately analytic, they allow for conventionalized combinations of basic signs to form more complex signs. Munn (1962, 1986) classified one group of these combinations as "actor-item" signs, since they involve a person or actor with another inanimate object, such as a stick or dish. These combinations provide additional context to further disambiguate the meanings of both signs, or create a recognized conventional combination (for further detailed listings of these signs, see Green, 2009, In Press; Munn, 1962, 1986). We may think of highly conventionalized combinations as analogous to compound words, where (often) the meaning of two or more words creates an additional meaning beyond just the component parts (e.g. a *house boat* is a boat that is also a house, but looks like neither a prototypical house nor boat). Similarly, the combination of multiple CAVL signs may elicit additional inferences about a broader meaning for the whole construction.

One type of compound shows one shape surrounding another, to represent that the surrounded object is on or in the other (Green, 2009). This might include food in a dish, objects on a stone, or person in or behind a windbreak (Figure 9.5). Notably, no explicit graphic convention marks something as inside versus on top of another. For example, an oval surrounding dots can represent both food *in* a dish and seeds *on* a grinding stone. In this case, context may aid in clarifying the meaning, although the same graphic structure shows two different spatial relationships.

Composite signs involving multiple figures may provide valuable information about the relationships between characters and their actions (Green, 2009). For example, a large U-shape with a smaller U-shape may imply a parent and child. This is especially true if one U-shape is

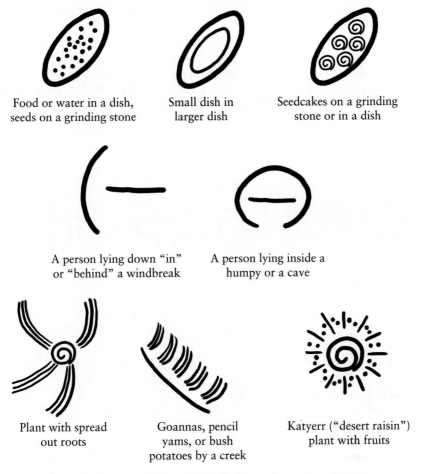

Food or water in a dish,
seeds on a grinding stone

Small dish in
larger dish

Seedcakes on a grinding
stone or in a dish

A person lying down "in"
or "behind" a windbreak

A person lying inside a
humpy or a cave

Plant with spread
out roots

Goannas, pencil
yams, or bush
potatoes by a creek

Katyerr ("desert raisin")
plant with fruits

**FIGURE 9.5** *Static compounds in CAVL. Redrawn from Green (2009).*

enclosed within the concave portion of another U-shape, which represents a child sitting on a mother's lap. Several people drawn facing each other in close configuration might be interpreted as a group sitting in mourning (Green, 2009; Munn, 1986), and figures facing away from each other may represent sulky or uncooperative behavior (Green, 2009). Actions may also be implied, such as two women sitting with a honey ant hole which implies that they are *digging* for honey ants (Munn, 1986). Other examples are shown in Figure 9.6.

People are also often depicted alongside items in certain orientations, including objects—like domestic items and plants—and locations—like windbreaks and creeks. The meaning of these constructions often draws upon inferences about the causal or cultural relationships between such items. For example, a person sitting away from a plant may represent

Mother with child (on lap)

Facing each other (e.g. spousal couple, two women, etc.)

Facing away (e.g. sulky, non-cooperative behavior

Facing each other (plural), as in mourning or cooperative behavior

Person with spears and boomerangs in front of another item

Person/people with an object (e.g. fire, food, waterhole)

People surrounding another person lying down or an object (e.g. spear or fighting stick)

Person sitting in shade

Person collecting food from a plant

Two people eating

Person (woman) with digging stick and dish

Person lying on a headrest (for women, a dish, for men, a shield)

Three people sleeping behind a windbreak

A prone person and a seated person behind a windbreak

**FIGURE 9.6** *Static compounds involving humans. Redrawn from Green (2009).*

that they are using it for shade (despite no shadow being drawn in sand), but facing towards the plant may mean they are gathering food (Wilkins, 1997). Person-item pairs can also inform about gender. A person alongside a spear is usually male, while a person alongside dishes or food is usually female (Munn, 1962, 1986). Again, Figure 9.6 depicts further examples.

## Dynamic signs

Just as sand naturally can depict the static imprint of objects on the ground, it can also show the tracks of moving objects. Beyond the aerial viewpoint, the interpretation of Wilkins' horse described above (Figure 9.2) as lying down or dead may have also related to the lack of tracks to indicate movement. If an object moves, it should leave tracks, and without such marks, the horse in that position must be lying down, not moving.

Tracks often involve dynamic motions to create paths similar to motion lines. These simple lines extend from a starting Source to an endpoint Goal. Sometimes, locations along a path may be represented using circles (Munn, 1962). Because sand drawings unfurl in real time, the actual gestural act of depicting the path represents the narrative creation of that path (not simply the aftermath of creating the line representing the "to and from" of the path). For example, the speed and rhythm of the articulation may affect meaning, as in the sporadic or staccato movements related to certain types of dancing or a ritualized skipping motion indicative of women preparing to fight (Green, 2009). Also, a "flick" of the fingers into the air at the end of path line implies that the motion continues beyond the visibly drawn line (Green, 2009).

Several modifying shapes of a path line can elaborate on its manner (see Figure 9.7). A basic straight line represents a straight path, such as a person's trajectory while running or walking, or the path of an action like a spear thrown from a person (Munn, 1986). Footprints can accompany path lines, either added to already drawn lines or created along with the path, suggested by leaving portions of the path broken (Green, 2009) or by piercing the ground with fingertips (but not wires) to create indentions (Munn, 1986; Strehlow, 1964).

Wilkins (1997) described a similar path created by pressing two adjacent fingers into the ground repeatedly—one finger for each foot. Shapes also can vary: wavy lines can represent a meandering path, for the path of snakes, rain, or lightning (Munn, 1962); bumpy lines may represent a figure dancing (Munn, 1986); circular lines may show the path of a person going around an object (usually a plant); while shapes spiraling from the center outward are used in Arandic "monster" stories (Green, 2009). Also, plurality can be applied to nearly every path by simply drawing more lines, often simultaneously with various fingers, or by redrawing existing lines to imply other people walking the same path (Green, 2009).

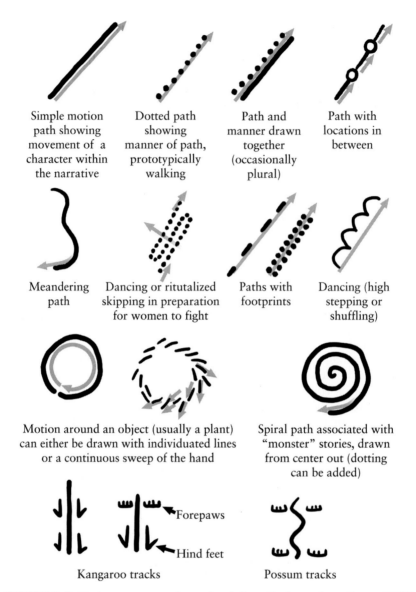

**FIGURE 9.7** *Various representations of path lines. Redrawn from Green (2009) and Munn (1962, 1986).*

Another type of track represents the footprints of animals, particularly kangaroos, possums, and marsupial mice. These prints consist of a central path line, representing the imprint of the animal's tail dragging on the sand, while footprints alongside this line differentiate the type of animal (Munn, 1962). These lines are more common amongst Warlpiri men's storytelling and designs than the prevailing women's sand stories.

## Dynamic compounds

Just as static compounds can be created from certain combinations of signs, dynamic compounds can also imply certain actions or events. In these cases, dynamic signs often combine with static ones. A simple example is the drawing of a motion line followed by a U-shape, which depicts a person moving to a location and then stopping (Green, 2009). The reverse depiction, where a path line emerges from a U-shape, implies that the figure threw a spear. In this case, the single path line represents both the spear and its trajectory (Munn, 1986). Both are shown in Figure 9.8. This example highlights how the dynamic action of creating the signs influences the meaning: the resulting static signs look identical, but the order and direction of drawing (i.e. the production script) differentiates their meanings.

Person moves to a               Person throwing a spear
location and stops

**FIGURE 9.8** *Combinations of path lines with people. Redrawn from Green (2009).*

# Narrative grammar

As mentioned, a sand narrative unfolds in time within a single drawing space. Typically, drawn items remain present unless they move within the scene or the whole scene is erased to clear space for the next scene. This means that the elements that are not erased persist throughout the scene as the episode builds progressively, especially aspects of the setting (windbreaks, trees, creeks, etc.) or actual tracks on the ground (Wilkins, 1997).

In general, the order in which objects and events are expressed coincides with their progression through the narrative (Green, 2009; Munn, 1986;

Wilkins, 1997). Because of the complex multimodal interactions involved in sand stories, the contribution of the drawn form alone may be difficult to extract. Nevertheless, all three modalities appear to run in parallel with each other, with speech and sign providing information unavailable in the drawings, while the drawings provide spatial relationships unavailable to speech (Green, 2009). Below, I focus on the properties of sand drawings relevant to their representations as narrative sequences.

## *Erasure*

A sand story starts by clearing the sand for drawing, creating an empty canvas of sand. Similarly, this drawing space is erased at the narrative's end, often using slower, more deliberate movements, and a concluding slap of the drawing space with the hand. In general, erasure plays an important role throughout the course of a narrative. By wiping away all or parts of a scene, erasure allows the narrative to temporally unfurl in a single ground space without the need for spatial juxtaposition (such as with adjacent panels). Because of this role, higher rates of erasure appear when narratives are told with just drawings and sign language than when accompanied by speech, because these modalities bear a larger load of communicating the meaning (Wilkins, 1997). Erasure is rarely used to make corrections, even though narrators may recognize that mistakes occur (Green, 2009, In Press).

Partial erasures may serve several functions within a story and these types of changes can sometimes be achieved through redrawing over an existing mark (Green, 2009; Munn, 1986; Strehlow, 1964). A portion of the ground space may be wiped away as a prelude to full erasure, while individual signs may be erased to signal changes in location or posture of a figure or object. For example, a person erased from one location may then move to another location where they are redrawn. Alternatively, erasure can signal changes in body posture. For example, wiping away a straight line to be redrawn as a U-shape may mean that the person gets up after lying down while sleeping. Erasure can also aid in changing a U-shape from facing one direction to another. Objects may also be erased to indicate a change in local space, such as how erasure of an object next to a U-shape implies that the person picks it up off the ground (Wilkins, 1997). Generally, only objects that can possibly move or change are subject to erasure, while fixed spatial information like windbreaks or creeks are not wiped away until a scene finishes (Green, 2009, In Press; Wilkins, 1997).

Erasure can also occur on a larger level within the story, such as wiping the entire ground space. These major erasures of a scene usually signal a shift in location, in time, or to the actions of a different character (Green, 2009, In Press; Munn, 1986; Wilkins, 1997), and are often preceded by articulations that start on the ground and move to the air (Green, 2009).

Erasures of this type signal shifts between different narrative episodes. This is consistent with the theory of narrative grammar presented in Chapter 4, where shifts in characters, space, and location often mark the boundaries between narrative constituents. In this case, erasure provides an articulated cue for the boundaries between narrative constituents (whether at the level of phases or full Arcs).

## *Narrative structures*

Some basic combinatorial rules constrain the sequence of sand drawings, and several constraints guide the unfurling of a drawn scene. For example, locations precede the depictions of people, and people precede the depictions of objects. In general, this is consistent with the structure of the narrative grammar, in that Orienters (introduction of places) precede Establishers (introduction of characters), which precede the rest of the narrative sequence. We will explore these aspects of visual narrative grammar in CAVL in more depth.

After clearing a space, locative information is first drawn to situate the narrative. These are most often a "domestic" space indicated by windbreaks or fireplaces and the placement of tools and artifacts. Young people often situate stories in contemporary settings like houses, shopping complexes, or football grounds, sometimes drawing complete floor plans of the internal structures of buildings. Structurally, these settings all serve as Orienters—the superordinate place in which the rest of a narrative might take place. The windbreak of a traditional shelter is an especially important locative, represented as a curved line. This establishes that the story may be of a domestic nature, but it also locates the representation in absolute space (Wilkins, 1997). Because the backs of windbreaks usually face to the east to protect from the easterly winds, they provide a visual cue for reinforcing the absolute directions of a drawing.

Besides domestic spaces, scenes may also take place outside the camp, involving searching for food or hunting, localized by drawings of a grove of trees or a water hole (Munn, 1986). Another type of scene can provide a "juncture" between other scenes, such as a person traveling from one location to another (Munn, 1986). These scenes often follow erasure of a previous scene, and show the movement of a person without reference to a setting. Since they purely show the trajectory of a character along a path that connects narrative constituents, these scenes function similarly to Prolongations in the visual narrative grammar, which provide a medial state between Initials and Peaks, often showing a trajectory of a path.

The endings of sand narratives are often less defined than their opening locatives. They often lack formal endings altogether. However, a conventional finale (Release) involves the characters returning to the earth. This is represented with a circular hole, a dead body, a dead body in a hole,

| People converging on a hole | People converging on a hole (possibly a hole surrounded by trees) | People converging on burial place for dead person | People converging on burial place for dead person in a hole |

**FIGURE 9.9** *Various representations used to depict the finale of a sand story. Redrawn from Munn (1986).*

etc. toward which the paths of various people converge (Green, In Press; Munn, 1986), as depicted in Figure 9.9. This type of ending is consistent with the idea that the sand stories actually reside in the earth and are simply "uncovered" by storytelling. Thus, the characters (and the narrative as a whole) return to their natural place at the end of a story, signaled further by the ultimate erasure of the story space and the slap of the ground.

Just as other visual languages use modifiers like Refiners or Conjunction, an additional feature of the narrative grammar described by Wilkins (1997) modifies the time an object spends in a particular location. He noted that a narrator may continually draw over already depicted lines in order to make them deeper, thereby signaling that the object remains in that place for a longer period of time. Deeper imprints signify longer time. In a related fashion, redrawing an element in the narrative can function to focus attention onto that particular character or object, and it often co-occurs with demonstratives in speech (Green, 2009; Wilkins, 1997). This type of focus is consistent with the "zooming" effect of Refiners.

## Sequential constraints

Finally, as has been stressed, CAVL unfurls narratives temporally in a single space as a *temporally-sequential* system, as opposed to a *spatially-sequential* system like in AVL or JVL where panels become juxtaposed in a spatial sequence. This difference in navigational structure has several ramifications on the actual structure of the expressions (discussed below), but it is worth considering how this difference impacts actual comprehension. When he presented Arrernte children with the sequential images from comics, Wilkins (1991, 1997) found that some children expected each panel to constitute its own enclosed narrative, and they did not make the connections between and across panels. Instead, they perceived each panel as belonging to its own scene, since CAVL temporally unfolds a scene in a single space (temporally-sequential), as opposed to juxtaposing temporal snapshots across an extended physical space (spatially-sequential). This suggests that not only is fluency required to understand visual languages generally, but that fluency in the structures of a specific visual language can create different assumptions about the comprehension of other visual languages—just like spoken or signed languages.

## Culture meets structure

The study of CAVL plays an important role within the scope of visual language theory because it offers an important contrast with the other predominant visual languages of the world. Without this contrast, we may be falsely led into believing that the structures found in the systems used in comics are universal traits of all visual languages. The cultural context and ecology of CAVL has resulted in a vastly different structure, thereby offering another perspective on underlying typological variation that may exist across visual languages. In this broad endeavor, we might ask: 1) How are visual languages across the world similar? 2) How do they differ? 3) Can we generalize these differences as part of a broader universality underlying visual languages?

As discussed, CAVL overlaps in many ways with visual languages like AVL or JVL. For example, they all use highly conventionalized iconic schemas, they all combine discrete signs to form larger morphological meanings, they all use motion lines to depict paths, and they all divide narratives into constituent parts that share at least some structural features. However, even more interesting are the differences between these systems, particularly how the spatial versus temporal nature of the sequence may change broader aspects of the system as a whole (see Table 9.1).

I will argue that many properties of CAVL structure arise because of the cultural context of sand stories as real-time interactive communication, along with the ready availability of sand as a drawing surface throughout many areas of Central Australia (Munn, 1986). Consider, for example, the demands placed on a graphic system that is used dynamically in interactions with other people. A sign must be economical enough in production to accommodate the fast pace of communicative interaction, resulting in simple, analytic graphic morphology. This graphical simplicity, demanded by temporal economy, further enhances a high degree of polysemy in the signs (since disambiguating details would require even more time to draw that can more easily be expressed through other domains like speech or signing). The "canvas" furthers this simplicity, since a high degree of detail is not easy to imbue in sand when articulated with fingers, sticks, or wires.

Time also directly effects structure. Since these drawings unfurl over time, the actual temporal actions and production scripts involved with signs may be meaningful. This temporal sequence also means that figures need not be repeatedly drawn for them to stay meaningful across a discourse—they statically remain present throughout the narrative and only need to be redrawn if they change. Also, the aftermath of the drawing process is not as important as the process itself. The final representation does not reflect a single utterance, but the accumulation of numerous utterances in constant flux throughout the discourse. Finally, their real-time depiction in sand means that stories are meant to be experienced in the context they are created. Unless they are filmed (whereby they lose their embedded absolute space), these stories are much less portable. All of these traits directly tie to the context of sand drawings in society, and are facilitated by the sand that pervades these societies as a simple, accessible surface allowing such interactions to happen without additional tools or technology (like pencils, pens, paper, or portable computer tablets).

**TABLE 9.1.** *Differences in structure as a result of a sequence arising through spatial versus temporal juxtaposition*

| Spatially-Sequential | Temporally-Sequential |
| --- | --- |
| Drawer and audience separated in time | Drawer and audience interacting in time |
| Sequential units laid out spatially without sensitivity to time | Sequential units unfurl temporally across space |
| Production script plays no meaningful role (and is independent of the audience's experience) | Production script can play meaningful morphological and narrative role, accessible to audience |
| Units are built of many component schemas (Synthetic) | Units largely stand alone as schemas (Analytic) |
| Signs allow potential for large amount of disambiguating complexity | Signs remain simple with large affordance for polysemy |
| Representation can be understood out of the context of the time of its creation (portable) | Representations meant to be comprehended in the context of their creation (somewhat non-portable) |
| Production script is lost, and aftermath of drawing is all that is salient to an audience | Aftermath of representation is not as important as the real-time expressions comprising it |
| Elements in a narrative that persist must be redrawn across frames, regardless of changes | Elements in a narrative that persist need only be drawn once, and redrawn if they change |

By comparison, spatially-sequential visual languages like AVL or JVL are also artifacts of their cultural context. These visual languages are created outside the constraints of a real-time communicative interaction, and thus result in a different type of structure. Because the drawer and audience are separated in time and space, no temporal demands force a drawer to remain economical in their representations—they are free to have as much complexity in the representation as they want. This complexity means signs can have far more specific, disambiguating properties built out of *numerous* graphic morphemes synthetically combined together.

Also, being drawn with pencils or pens on paper allows for fine-grained details to be depicted onto the surface, facilitating further complexity (and allowing for mass-produced portability, but requiring additional tools). This separation in time between production and comprehension also means that the audience cannot see the production script, making the temporal act of drawing play no meaningful role in discourse. The audience only sees the completed aftermath of a representation, with no view on the process used to create it. Since sequence cannot arise from the temporality of representation, it must be artificially created by spatial juxtaposition: a temporal sequence in a single space would be lost if viewed after it is created. This requires panels to carry the "temporal" sequence spatially, thereby demanding that anything that persists throughout a narrative span must often be redrawn in subsequent frames, whether they change or not. Such redundancy is a direct result of the contextual separation between drawer and audience.

These comparisons illustrate the influence of culture—entwined with physical environment—on the structure of graphic systems. Such influence must be considered in any endeavor to characterize the universals of visual language or its comprehension. Nevertheless, the same biological brains that yield spatially-sequential systems also yield temporally-sequential systems. The task then lies in learning what is culturally constrained, what is universal, and where those properties meet.

# Note

1  Wilkins also mentioned that the position of the horse's legs may have contributed to this interpretation of a static figure rather than a moving figure. Additionally, the lack of "tracks" to show movement contributed to this interpretation as well (a point to which we will return).

# CHAPTER TEN

# The Principle of Equivalence

In the previous chapters, I have argued that the human ability to create graphic images constitutes a visual-graphic modality of language that is unconnected from associations with verbal language (as in writing). This visual language is a natural, instinctive capacity for expressing concepts in the visual-graphic domain that can be put into discrete sequences governed by a rule system (a grammar). As a result, humans can develop three types of languages: a spoken, verbal language; a bodily, signed language; and a graphic, visual language.

When concepts are not ordered sequentially with a grammar, the visual-graphic modality produces single images, just as the manual modality may create gestures that are not embedded within a broader sign language. In both of these cases, the modality persists resiliently in its ability to convey concepts, despite lacking full fluency achieved without a grammar. Together, these modalities—whether they use a grammar or not—can create multimodal expressions that combine speech with gesture or drawings, or text with visual language.

Overall, this perspective assumes that structure, development, and processing across domains obey what I call the "Principle of Equivalence":

*We should expect that the mind/brain treats all expressive capacities in similar ways, given modality-specific constraints.*

This principle falls into two parts. Let's start with the first clause: "*We should expect that the mind/brain treats all expressive capacities in similar ways.*" This notion expresses the idea that various human behaviors should be structured, processed, and developed in comparable ways, because they all emerge from the same brain, with the same cognitive building blocks. Throughout, I have argued that particular general properties of cognition emerge in the visual-graphic modality just as they do in verbal and signed languages. These properties may include (but are not limited to):

1   The large-scale storage of schematic patterns of varying sizes into long-term memory (i.e. a lexicon).

2   Classes of productive (open-class) and fixed (closed-class) schematic patterns.

3   The ability for basic schematic patterns to act as units unto themselves (analytic), or to combine in order to form novel units (synthetic).

4   Stored knowledge of sensorial forms that make correspondences with meaning in various types of reference (e.g. iconic, indexical, symbolic).

5   Combinatorial strategies to create larger schematic meanings out of basic meanings (e.g. morphological strategies like affixation, suppletion, reduplication, and compounding).

6   Larger groupings of units can form constituents that can be embedded hierarchically and recursively (i.e. a grammar).

The implication is that the mind uses these (and other) general strategies across numerous expressive domains. Many of these same cognitive capacities also factor into other types of human behaviors, such as music, which makes great use of patterns in memory as well as hierarchic embedding (i.e. properties 1 and 6), yet does not link those musical notes to any type of conceptual meaning (i.e. property 4). Thus, while various facets of cognition overlap across domains, not all structures overlap in all domains. Different human behaviors then arise from which properties are (or are not) engaged in their respective modalities.

The second clause further constrains this idea: "...*given modality-specific constraints.*" This clause aims to wards off an overextension of the similarities between domains. We should absolutely expect that different human behaviors have some cognitive differences. However, the nature of those differences should be a *direct result* of the channel and properties of the behavior itself. In other words, the precise manifestation of the above-listed properties differs between domains because, for example, the verbal-auditory and visual-graphic modalities put different demands on their expressive systems. For example, using the medium of sound, the verbal-auditory channel forces a linear sequence, while the visual-graphic channel using light does not. Producing and hearing verbalized sounds occurs throughout a temporal span, making the linearity of language an artifact of its medium. It needs no additional "navigational structure" except the time in which it is uttered.

In contrast, while visual language does unfurl temporally, this linearity may disappear once the production script has ended, leaving a spatially preserved whole image. In many cases, the perceiver of a drawing never sees the temporal unfolding of the image, leaving the production and comprehension of that expression separated both in nature (socially interactive versus non-interactive communication) and processing (seeing an unfolding representation versus a whole representation). Beyond comprehension, this impacts development: if given only a finished representation, a learner cannot acquire a production script, making learning to draw it that much harder. Thus, several levels of differences between modalities all result from basic departures between the modalities themselves.

As is hopefully clear by breaking down the Principle of Equivalence into two parts, the challenge posed to research is in identifying which under-lying traits of domains overlap and which do not. However, this Principle affirms the general processes of the mind: why should the brain create several unique and diverse ways to handle different behaviors when it can efficiently make use of various general underlying structures (like those listed above) in a variety of capacities?[1]

Given the context of this Principle of Equivalence and the research presented throughout, contrary theories should bear the onus of answering the key question: Why should the mind/brain *not* treat drawing and visual language (...and other human behaviors) like other expressive capacities? The cultural notions about the nature of drawing and sequential images—what I referred to previously as the "Art Frame"—at present do not regard them like language at all. Here, they hold that drawings reflect a person's unique and individualistic creative nature, and each individual draws differently because it depicts their own perception on the world.

This is very different from the notion of visual language outlined in this book, and goes against the Principle of Equivalence. So, why should the cognition of drawing be completely *unlike* any other human behavior? (Similarly, why should *language* be unlike other domains?) Why would it be advantageous to cognition or behavior for drawing (or language) to be unlike other domains?

# Other investigations

Of course, beyond the structures we have discussed, visual language involves several other factors. The previous chapters lay a foundation for a more detailed study of visual language in linguistics, cognitive psychology, and cognitive neuroscience. Truly, any way in which language is studied should apply to the visual form. These might include (but are not limited to):

- *Conceptual structure/semantics*—We have only addressed certain aspects of meaning, but many other more complicated aspects of semantics have not been covered. What sort of deeper conceptual mappings (i.e. metaphor, blending, etc.) can occur in visual morphology and across panels? How are inferences created across and between panels? How might the aspects of the visual lexicon tie to embodied aspects of cognition? (e.g. Cohn, 2010a; Forceville, 2005; Forceville and Urios-Aparisi, 2009).

- *Multimodality*—How do multiple channels of expression (verbal, manual, visual) connect to each other to create a larger whole of meaning? How do they interface together? Do modalities share a common conceptual structure? Are there constraints on how much each modality contributes to the whole of meaning? What does a whole "language system" that can distribute semantics into various modalities at the same time look like?

- *Language acquisition*—How is visual language acquired? What is the process of learning to draw? Does this development resemble the development of other language modalities, such as in the verbal or manual form? (e.g. Cohn, 2012b).

- *Linguistic typology*—What is the range of variation in the visual languages of the world and are there consistencies that lead to underlying universals?

- *Historical linguistics*—How might the structure of a visual language change over time? What are the properties of visual languages no longer in use? (e.g. Nielsen and Wichmann, 2000).

- *Comparative linguistics/Language contact*—How does the structure of a visual language change with exposure to another? Might existing visual languages share historical roots?

- *Anthropological linguistics*—What are the characteristics of the cultures that arise around visual languages of the world? How might aspects of the broader culture influence the structure of the visual language, and vice versa?

- *Sociolinguistics*—How is visual language used in sociocultural settings, and how does it frame a person's identity? What biases does one's own visual language create towards the perceptions of other visual languages?

- *Computational linguistics*—How might statistical modeling be used to study the properties of visual language? (e.g. Laraudogoitia, 2008, 2009).

- *Cognitive neuroscience*—What neural circuitry is activated in the processing of visual language? What can cognitive impairments (aphasia, genetic disorders, etc.) teach us about the biological and neural structuring of visual language? (e.g. Bihrle, Brownell, Powelson, and Gardner, 1986; Huber and Gleber, 1982).

The questions that motivate all of these fields apply equally to verbal, sign, and visual languages. Insofar as visual language is a real and actual language on par with other domains in terms of its structure and cognition, research in nearly any domain related to language should both be conceivable as well as possible. Truly, the theory of visual language not only applies to linguistics and the language sciences, but it can serve to unify disparate research topics, such as that of comics with that of sand narratives, and in fields as diverse as art history, literature, linguistics, psychology, cognitive science, and art education. This broad accessibility is a testament to the linguistic status of visual language and its potential to be researched across the study of language.

## Closing remarks

By now, it should be very apparent that this book is less about "comics" than it is about language and the mind/brain. As we close this discussion, it is worth returning to the interface of these ideas with artistry. In particular, it is important to address the pernicious, yet untrue, claim that studying an "art form" somehow robs it of its "artistry." Knowing that drawing and visual language are based on schematic patterns stored in memory that combine to make novel forms does not lessen anyone's creative capacity to use these forms. Nor does the mechanism of learning these patterns—exposure and imitation—weaken anyone's creativity. If anything, knowledge of such structures can enhance one's appreciation, not lessen it. Artistry can no more be robbed of its impact by the science of visual language than sunsets are robbed of their beauty by knowing that the earth spins on an axis in reference to the sun.

One of the primary emphases of linguistics research since the 1950s is how "infinite uses can be made of finite means." With a vocabulary of roughly 20,000 words in English—shared by members of a community—we are able to create an infinite amount of novel sentences, utterances, conversations, and narratives. This tension between the systematic/conventional and the unique/creative is intrinsic to the understanding of language and its structure. We all rely on the same words, but how we use them is what we judge as artistic or not.

In the spirit of this Principle of Equivalence, there is no reason that the same standards and practices should not hold true of visual language: artistry comes from what is done with a (visual) language, not from its properties. And great things have been done with it, if the history of the visual language used in comics over the past century is any indication. Just imagine how much more could be done if this visual language was used and treated like other languages.

# Note

1  Lest I extend too much, such permeating aspects of cognition offer a way to address the "Creative Explosion" of technological and expressive capacities in the evolutionary record of human history. The idea would be that many behaviors could emerge because of the development of their underlying cognitive properties.

# GRAPHIC REFERENCES

Aragonés, Sergio (2002) *Actions Speak*. Milwaukie, OR: Dark Horse Comics.

Cannon, Zander (1997) *Replacement God*. San Jose, CA: Slave Labor Graphics.

Cham, Jorge (2004) *PhD Comics*. April 7, 2004. www.phdcomics.com

Godek, Tym (2006) *One Night*. Originally posted on March 20, 2006. http://www.yellowlight.scratchspace.net/comics/onenight/onenight.html

Kibuishi, Kazu (2003) *Copper*: "Somersaults." www.boltcity.com

Koike, Kazuo, and Goseki Kojima (1995) *Lone Wolf and Cub: A Taste of Poison*. Vol. 20. Milwaukie, OR: Dark Horse Comics.

Larsen, Erik (1996) *Savage Dragon: A Force to be Reckoned With*. Anaheim, CA: Image Comics.

—(2010) *Savage Dragon: Back in Blue*. Berkeley, CA: Image Comics.

Mahfood, J. (2002) Grrl Scouts in "Just Another Day". In *Dark Horse Maverick: Happy Endings*. Edited by D. Schutz. Milwaukie, OR: Dark Horse Comics.

McFarlane, Todd and Greg Capullo (2000) *Spawn*, #100. Orange, CA: Image Comics.

Mignola, Mike, Ryan Sook et al (2003) *Mike Mignola's B.P.R.D.: Hollow Earth and Other Stories*. Milwaukie, OR: Dark Horse Comics.

—(2004) *Butternutsquash*: "Ladies Man." May 28, (2003) www.butternutsquash. net

Perez, Ramon and Rob Coughler (2004) *Butternutsquash:* "Sweet Horror!" August 18, (2004) www.butternutsquash.net

O'Malley, Bryan Lee (2005) *Scott Pilgrim vs. The World*. Portland, OR: Oni Press.

Ottaviani, Jim and Big Time Attic (Kevin Cannon and Zander Cannon) (2005) *Bone Sharps, Cowboys, and Thunder Lizards*. Ann Arbor, MI: G.T. Labs.

Sakai, Stan (1987) *Usagi Yojimbo: Book One*. Seattle, WA: Fantagraphics Books

Shanower, Eric (2001) *Age of Bronze: A Thousand Ships*. Berkeley, CA. Image Comics

Weing, Drew (2002) *Journal Comic*. December 12, 2002. www.drewweing.com

Wood, Wally. "Wally Wood's 22 Panels that Always Work."

# REFERENCES

Abbott, M., and Forceville, C. (2011) Visual representation of emotion in manga: Loss of control is Loss of hands in *Azumanga Daioh* Volume 4. *Language and Literature, 20*(2), 91-112.

Abel, J. and Madden, M. (2008) *Drawing Words and Writing Pictures*. New York: First Second Books.

Arijon, D. (1976) *Grammar of the Film Language*. London: Focal Press.

Arnheim, R. (1978) Expressions. *Art Education, 31*(3), 37–8.

Barber, J. (2002) *The Phenomenon of Multiple Dialectics in Comics Layout*. Masters Thesis, London College of Printing, London.

Bihrle, A. M., Brownell, H. H., Powelson, J. A. and Gardner, H. (1986) Comprehension of humorous and nonhumorous materials by left and right brain-damaged patients. *Brain and Cognition, 5*, 399–411.

Bloomfield, L. (1933) *Language*. New York: Holt, Rinehart and Winston.

Bordwell, D. (1985) *Narration in the Fiction Film*. Madison, WI: University of Wisconsin Press.

—(2007) *Poetics of Cinema*. New York: Routledge.

Bordwell, D. and Thompson, K. (1997) *Film Art: An Introduction* (5th Edition edn) New York: McGraw-Hill.

Bouissou, J.-M., Pellitteri, M., Dolle-Weinkauff, B. and Beldi, A. (2010) Manga in Europe: A short study of market and fandom. In T. Johnson-Woods (Ed.), *Manga: An Anthology of Global and Cultural Perspectives* (pp. 297–314) New York: Continuum Books.

Brenner, R. E. (2007) *Understanding Manga and Anime*. Westport, CT: Libraries Unlimited.

Bresman, J. (2004) *Test of Sequential "Sense" of Comics*. Class Essay: MSTU 5510.008: Social and Communicative Aspects of the Internet and Other ICTs, Teacher's College, Columbia University, New York.

Brewer, W. F. (1985) The story schema: Universal and culture-specific properties. In D. R. Olson, N. Torrance and A. Hildyard (eds), *Literacy, Language, and Learning* (pp. 167–94). Cambridge: Cambridge University Press.

Brewer, W. F. and Lichtenstein, E. H. (1981) Event schemas, story schemas, and story grammars. In J. Long and A. D. Baddeley (eds), *Attention and Performance IX* (pp. 363–79). Hillsdale, NJ: Erlbaum.

—(1982) Stories are to entertain: A structural-affect theory of stories. *Journal of Pragmatics, 6*(5–6), 473–86.

Bridgeman, T. (2004) Keeping an eye on things: attention, tracking, and coherence-building. *Belphégor, 4*(1), 1–18.

—(2005) Figuration and configuration: mapping imaginary worlds in BD. In C.

Forsdick, L. Grove and L. McQuillan (eds), *The Francophone Bande Dessinée* (pp. 115–36). Amsterdam, Netherlands: Rodopi.

Brooks, P. H. (1977) The role of action lines in children's memory for pictures. *Journal of Experimental Child Psychology, 23*, 93–107.

Burr, D. C. and Ross, J. (2002) Direct evidence that "speedlines" influence motion mechanisms. *The Journal of Neuroscience, 22*(19), 8661–4.

Butcher, S. H. (1902) The Poetics of Aristotle (3rd edn). London: Macmillian and Co. Ltd.

Caldwell, J. (2012) Comic panel layout: A Peircean analysis. *Studies in Comics, 2*(2), 317–38.

Callaghan, T. C. (1999) Early Understanding and Production of Graphic Symbols. *Child Development, 70*(6), 1314–24.

Carello, C., Rosenblum, L. D. and Grosofsky, A. (1986) Static depiction of movement. *Perception, 15*(1), 41–58.

Carroll, J. M. (1980) *Toward a Structural Psychology of Cinema.* The Hague, Netherlands: Mouton.

Carroll, J. M. and Bever, T. G. (1976) Segmentation in cinema perception. *Science, 191*(4231), 1053–5.

Ceglia, S. and Caldesi Valeri, V. (2002) Maison Ikkoku. *Image [and] Narrative, 1*(1).

Chan, T. T. and Bergen, B. (2005) Writing direction influences spatial cognition. *Proceedings of the Twenty-Seventh Annual Conference of Cognitive Science Society* (pp. 412–17).

Chatman, S. (1978) *Story and discourse.* Ithaca, NY: Cornell University Press.

Chomsky, N. (1957) *Syntactic structures.* The Hague, Netherlands: Mouton.

—(1965) *Aspects of the theory of syntax.* Cambridge, MA: MIT Press.

Čižek, F. (1927) *Children's coloured paper work.* Vienna, AT: Scholl.

Clark, H. H. (1996) *Using language.* Cambridge: Cambridge University Press.

Cohn, N. (2003) *Early writings on visual language.* Carlsbad, CA: Emaki Productions.

—(2007) A visual lexicon. *Public Journal of Semiotics, 1*(1), 53–84.

—(2009) *Action starring narrative and events.* Paper presented at the Comic Arts Conference, San Diego, CA.

—(2010a) Extra! Extra! Semantics in comics!: The conceptual structure of *Chicago Tribune* advertisements. *Journal of Pragmatics, 42*(11), 3138–46.

—(2010b) Japanese Visual Language: The structure of manga. In T. Johnson-Woods (Ed.), *Manga: An Anthology of Global and Cultural Perspectives* (pp. 187–203). New York: Continuum Books.

—(2010c) The limits of time and transitions: Challenges to theories of sequential image comprehension. *Studies in Comics, 1*(1), 127–47.

—(2011) A different kind of cultural frame: An analysis of panels in American comics and Japanese manga. *Image [and] Narrative, 12*(1), 120–34.

—(2012a) Comics, linguistics, and visual language: The past and future of a field. In F. Bramlett (Ed.), *Linguistics and the study of comics* (pp. 92–118). New York: Palgrave MacMillan.

—(2012b) Explaining "I can't draw": Parallels between the structure and development of language and drawing. *Human Development, 55*(4), 167–92.

—(2012c) *Structure, meaning, and constituency in visual narrative comprehension.* Doctoral Dissertation, Tufts University, Medford, MA.

—(2013a) Visual narrative structure. *Cognitive Science*, 37(3), 413–52.

—(2013b) Navigating comics: An empirical and theoretical approach to strategies of reading comic page layouts. *Frontiers in Cognitive Science*, 4, 1–15.

—(In Press-a) Beyond speech balloons and thought bubbles: The integration of text and image. *Semiotica*.

—(In Press-b) You're a good structure, Charlie Brown: The distribution of narrative categories in comic strips. *Cognitive Science*.

Cohn, N., Paczynski, M., Jackendoff, R., Holcomb, P. J. and Kuperberg, G. R. (2012) (Pea)nuts and bolts of visual narrative: Structure and meaning in sequential image comprehension. *Cognitive Psychology, 65*(1), 1–38.

Cohn, N., Taylor-Weiner, A. and Grossman, S. (2012) Framing attention in Japanese and American comics: Cross-cultural differences in attentional structure. *Frontiers in Cultural Psychology, 3*, 1–12.

Costall, A. (1997) Innocence and corruption: Conflicting images of child art. *Human Development, 40*, 140–4.

Cox, M. V. (1998) Drawings of people by Australian Aboriginal children: the intermixing of cultural styles. *Journal of Art and Design Education (JADE), 17*(1), 71–80.

Cox, M. V., Koyasu, M., Hiranuma, H. and Perara, J. (2001) Children's human figure drawings in the UK and Japan: The effects of age, sex, and culture. *British Journal of Developmental Psychology, 19*, 275–92.

de Saussure, F. (1972) *Course in general linguistics*. Trans R. Harris. Chicago, IL: Open Court Classics.

Dean, M. (2000) *The ninth art: Traversing the cultural space of the American comic book*. Doctoral Dissertation, University of Wisconsin-Milwaukee, Milwaukee, WI.

Drucker, J. (2008) Graphic devices: Narration and navigation. *Narrative, 16*(2), 121–39.

Dubinskas, F. A. and Traweek, S. (1984) Closer to the ground: A reinterpretation of the Walbiri iconography. *Man, New Series, Vol. 19*(1), 19–30.

Duncan, H. F., Gourlay, N. and Hudson, W. (1973) *A study of pictorial perception among Bantu and White school children*. Johannesburg, South Africa: Witwatersrand University Press.

Duncan, R. and Smith, M. J. (2009) *The power of comics*. New York: Continuum Books.

Eerden, B. (2009) Anger in Asterix: The metaphorical representation of anger in comics and animated films. In C. Forceville and E. Urios-Aparisi (eds), *Multimodal Metaphor* (pp. 243–64). New York: Mouton De Gruyter.

Eisenstein, S. (1942) *Film sense*. Trans. J. Leyda. New York: Harcourt, Brace World.

Eisner, W. (1985) *Comics and sequential art*. Florida: Poorhouse Press.

Favorito, E. and Baty, K. (1995) The silphium connection. *The Celator, 9*(2), 6–8.

Fein, O. and Kasher, A. (1996) How to do things with words and gestures in comics. *Journal of Pragmatics, 26*(6), 793–808.

Fodor, J. and Bever, T. G. (1965) The psychological reality of linguistic segments. *Journal of Verbal Learning and Verbal Behavior, 4*(5), 414–20.

Forceville, C. (2005) Visual representations of the idealized cognitive model of anger in the Asterix album *La Zizanie*. *Journal of Pragmatics, 37*(1), 69–88.

—(2011) Pictorial runes in *Tintin and the Picaros. Journal of Pragmatics, 43,* 875–90.

Forceville, C. and Urios-Aparisi, E. (2009) *Multimodal metaphor*. New York: Mouton De Gruyter.

Forceville, C., Veale, T. and Feyaerts, K. (2010) Balloonics: The visuals of balloons in comics. In J. Goggin and D. Hassler-Forest (eds), *The rise and reason of comics and graphic literature: Critical essays on the form*. Jefferson: McFarland and Company, Inc.

Freytag, G. (1894) *Technique of the drama*. Chicago, IL: S.C. Griggs and Company.

Friederici, A. D. (2002) Towards a neural basis of auditory sentence processing. *Trends in Cognitive Sciences, 6*(2), 78–84.

Friedman, S. L. and Stevenson, M. B. (1975) Developmental changes in the understanding of implied motion in two-dimensional pictures. *Child Development, 46,* 773–8.

Gardner, H. (1980) *Artful scribbles*. New York: Basic Books.

Garrett, M. F. and Bever, T. G. (1974) The perceptual segmentation of sentences. In T. G. Bever and W. Weksel (eds), *The structure and psychology of language*. The Hague, Netherlands: Mouton and Co.

Gauthier, G. (1976) Les Peanuts: une graphisme ideiomatique. *Communications, 24,* 108–39.

Genette, G. (1980) *Narrative discourse*. Trans. J. E. Lewin. Ithaca, NY: Cornell University Press.

Gernsbacher, M. A. (1985) Surface information loss in comprehension. *Cognitive Psychology, 17,* 324–63.

Goffman, E. (1974) *Frame analysis: An essay on the organization of experience*. Cambridge, MA: Harvard University Press.

Goldberg, A. (1995) *Constructions: A construction grammar approach to argument structure*. Chicago, IL: University of Chicago Press.

Goldin-Meadow, S. (2006) Talking and thinking with our hands. *Current Directions in Psychological Science, 15*(1), 34–9.

Gravett, P. (2004) *Manga: Sixty years of Japanese comics*. New York: HarperCollins.

Green, J. (2009) *Between the earth and the air: Multimodality in Arandic sand stories*. Doctoral Dissertation, University of Melbourne, Melbourne, Australia.

—(In Press) Multimodal complexity in Arandic sand story narratives. In L. Stirling, T. Strahan and S. Douglas (eds), *Narrative in intimate societies*. Amsterdam, Netherlands: John Benjamins.

Groensteen, T. (2007) *The system of comics*. Trans B. Beaty and N. Nguyen. Jackson, MI: University of Mississippi Press.

Gross, D., Soken, N., Rosengren, K. S., Pick, A. D., Pillow, B. H. and Melendez, P. (1991) Children's understanding of action lines and the static representation of speed of locomotion. *Child Development, 62,* 1124–41.

Gubern, R. (1972) *El lenguaje de los comics*. Barcelona, Spain: Peninsula.

Hagoort, P., Brown, C. M. and Groothusen, J. (1993) The syntactic positive shift (SPS) as an ERP measure of syntactic processing. In S. M. Garnsey (Ed.), *Language and cognitive processes. Special issue: Event-related brain potentials in the study of language* (Vol. 8, pp. 439–83). Hove, UK: Lawrence Erlbaum Associates.

Halliday, M. A. K. and Hasan, R. (1976) *Cohesion in English*. London: Longman.

Harvey, R. C. (1994) *The art of the funnies: An aesthetic history*. Jackson, MI: University of Mississippi Press.

Hatfield, C. (2012) *Hand of fire: The comics art of Jack Kirby*. Jackson, MI: University Press Of Mississippi.

Haviland, J. (1993) Anchoring, iconicity, and orientation in Guugu Yimithirr pointing gestures. *Journal of Linguistic Anthropology, 3*(1), 3–45.

Haviland, S. E. and Clark, H. H. (1974) What's new? Acquiring new information as a process in comprehension. *Journal of Verbal Learning and Verbal Behavior, 13*, 512–21.

Hayashi, H., Matsuda, G., Tamamiya, Y. and Hiraki, K. (2012) *Visual cognition of "speed lines" in comics: Experimental study on speed perception*. Poster presented at the 34th Annual Conference of the Cognitive Science Society. Sapporo, Japan.

Herman, D. (2003) *Narrative theory and the cognitive sciences*. Stanford, CA: CSLI.

—(2009) *Basic elements of narrative*. West Sussex, UK: Wiley-Blackwell.

Hick, D. H. (2012) The language of comics. In A. Meskin and R. T. Cook (eds), *The art of comics: A philosophical approach* (pp. 125–44). West Sussex, UK: Wiley-Blackwell.

Hobbs, J. R. (1985) *On the coherence and structure of discourse*. Stanford, CA: CSLI Technical Report 85–37.

Hockett, C. F. (1977) Logical considerations in the study of animal communication. In C. F. Hockett (Ed.), *The view from language: Selected essays, 1948–1974* (pp. 124–64). Athens, GA: University of Georgia Press.

Hoey, M. (1991) *Patterns of lexis in text*. Oxford: Oxford University Press.

Horn, C. G. (1996) American manga. *Wizard Magazine, 56*, 53–7.

Horrocks, D. (2001) Inventing comics: Scott McCloud defines the form in *Understanding comics*. *The Comics Journal, 234*, 29–39.

Huber, W. and Gleber, J. (1982) Linguistic and nonlinguistic processing of narratives in aphasia. *Brain and Language, 16*, 1–18.

Huffman, D. A. (1971) Impossible objects as nonsense sentences. In B. Meltzer and D. Mitchie (eds), *Machine intelligence* (Vol. 6). Edinburgh, Scotland: Edinburgh University.

Hünig, W. K. (1974) *Strukturen des comic strip*. Hildensheim, Germany: Olms.

Huntsinger, C. S., Jose, P. E., Krieg, D. B. and Luo, Z. (2011) Cultural differences in Chinese American and European American children's drawing skills over time. *Early Childhood Research Quarterly, 26*(1), 134–45.

Ishibashi, K. and Okado, T. (2004) How copying artwork affects students' artistic creativity *Proceedings of the 26th Annual Conference of the Cognitive Science Society* (pp. 218–623).

Ito, H., Seno, T. and Yamanaka, M. (2010) Motion impressions enhanced by converging motion lines. *Perception, 39*(11), 1555–61.

Jackendoff, R. (1983) *Semantics and cognition*. Cambridge, MA: MIT Press.

—(1990) *Semantic structures*. Cambridge, MA: MIT Press.

—(2002) *Foundations of language: Brain, meaning, grammar, evolution*. Oxford: Oxford University Press.

—(2010) *Meaning and the lexicon: The parallel architecture 1975–2010*. Oxford: Oxford University Press.

—(2011) What is the human language faculty?: Two views. *Language, 87*(3), 586–624.

Jahn, M. (2005) Cognitive narratology. In D. Herman, M. Jahn, and M.-L. Ryan (eds), *Routledge encyclopedia of narrative theory* (pp. 67–71). London: Routledge.

Kaufman, A. S. and Lichtenberger, E. O. (2006) *Assessing adolescent and adult intelligence* (3rd edn). Hoboken, NJ: Wiley.

Kawabe, T. and Miura, K. (2006) Representation of dynamic events triggered by motion lines and static human postures. *Experimental Brain Research, 175*(2), 372–5.

Kawabe, T., Yamada, Y. and Miura, K. (2007) Memory displacement of an object with motion lines. *Visual Cognition, 15*(3), 305–21.

Kehler, A. (2002) *Coherence, reference, and the theory of grammar.* Stanford, CA: CSLI Publications.

Kennedy, J. M. (1982) Metaphor in pictures. *Perception, 11*(5), 589–605.

Kennedy, J. M., Gabias, P. and Piertantoni, R. (1990) Meaning, presence and absence in pictures. In K. Landwehr (Ed.), *Ecological perception research, visual communication and esthetics* (pp. 43–56). New York: Springer-Verlag.

Kennedy, J. M., Green, C. D. and Vervaeke, J. (1993) Metaphoric thought and devices in pictures. *Metaphor and Symbolic Activity, 8*(3), 243–55.

Kennedy, J. M. and Ross, A. (1975) Outline picture perception by the Songe of Paua. *Perception, 4*, 391–406.

Kerr, S. and Durkin, K. (2004) Understanding of thought bubbles as mental representations in children with autism: Implications for theory of mind. *Journal of Autism and Developmental Disorders, 34*(6), 637–48.

Kim, H. and Francis, G. (1998) A computational and perceptual account of motion lines. *Perception, 27*(7), 785–97.

Kirby, J. (February 1999) Interview with Ben Schwartz. *The Jack Kirby Collector, 23*, 19–23.

Kistler, M. (1988) *Mark Kistler's draw squad.* New York: Simon and Schuster Inc.

Kloepfer, R. (1977) Komplentarität von sprache und bild – am beispiel von comic, karikatur und reklame. In R. Zeichenprosesse Posner and H.-P. Reinecke (eds), *Zeichenprozesse. Semiotische foxschung in den einzelwissenschaften* (pp. 129–45). Wiesbaden, Germany: Athenaion.

Koch, W. A. (1971) *Varia semiotica.* Hildensheim, Germany: Olms.

Koelsch, S. and Siebel, W. A. (2005) Towards a neural basis of music perception. *Trends in Cognitive Sciences, 9*(12), 578–84.

Korzenik, D. (1979) Socialization and drawing. *Art Education, 32*(1), 26–9.

Kraft, R. N., Cantor, P. and Gottdiener, C. (1991) The coherence of visual narratives. *Communication Research, 18*(5), 601–16.

Kuleshov, L. (1974) *Kuleshov on film: Writings of Lev Kuleshov.* Trans R. Levaco. Berkeley, CA: University of California Press.

Kunzle, D. (1973) *The history of the comic strip* (Vol. 1). Berkeley, CA: University of California Press.

Kuperberg, G. (2007) Neural mechanisms of language comprehension: Challenges to syntax. *Brain Research, 1146*, 23–49.

Kutas, M. and Federmeier, K. D. (2011) Thirty years and counting: Finding meaning in the N400 component of the Event-Related Brain Potential (ERP). *Annual Review of Psychology, 62*(1), 621–47.

Kutas, M. and Hillyard, S. A. (1980) Reading senseless sentences: Brain potential reflect semantic incongruity. *Science, 207*, 203–5.

Lakoff, G. and Johnson, M. (1979) *Metaphors we live by*. Chicago, IL: University of Chicago Press.

Lamme, L. L. and Thompson, S. (1994) "Copy?...Real artists don't copy!" but maybe children should. *Art Education, 47*(6), 46–51.

Langacker, R. W. (2001) Discourse in cognitive grammar. *Cognitive Linguistics, 12*(2), 143–88.

Laraudogoitia, J. P. (2008) The comic as a binary language: An hypothesis on comic structure. *Journal of Quantitative Linguistics, 15*(2), 111–35.

—(2009) The composition and structure of the comic. *Journal of Quantitative Linguistics, 16*(4), 327–53.

Lau, E. F., Phillips, C. and Poeppel, D. (2008) A cortical network for semantics: (De)constructing the N400. *Nature Reviews Neuroscience, 9*, 920–33.

Lefèvre, P. (2000) Narration in comics. *Image [and] Narrative, 1*(1).

Lent, J. A. (2010) Manga in East Asia. In T. Johnson-Woods (Ed.), *Manga: An anthology of global and cultural perspectives* (pp. 297–314). New York: Continuum Books.

Lerdahl, F. and Jackendoff, R. (1982) *A generative theory of tonal music*. Cambridge, MA: MIT Press.

Levi, A. (1996) *Samurai from outer space: Understanding Japanese animation*. Chicago, IL: Open Court.

Levin, D. T. and Simons, D. J. (2000) Perceiving stability in a changing world: Combining shots and intergrating views in motion pictures and the real world. *Media Psychology, 2*(4), 357–80.

Levinson, S. (1996) Language and space. *Annual Review of Anthropology, 25*, 353–82.

Liddell, S. K. (2003) *Grammar, gesture, and meaning in American Sign Language*. Cambridge: Cambridge University Press.

Lowenfeld, V. (1947) *Creative and mental growth* (3rd edn). New York: The Macmillan Company.

Mandler, J. M. (1978) A code in the node: The use of story schema in retrieval. *Discourse Processes, 1*, 14–35.

—(1984) *Stories, scripts, and scenes: Aspects of schema theory*. Hillsdale, NJ: Lawrence Earlbaum Associates.

Mandler, J. M. and DeForest, M. (1979) Is there more than one way to recall a story? *Child Development, 50*, 886–9.

Mandler, J. M. and Johnson, N. S. (1977) Remembrance of things parsed: Story structure and recall. *Cognitive Psychology, 9*, 111–51.

Masuda, T., Gonzalez, R., Kwan, L. and Nisbett, R. E. (2008) Culture and aesthetic preference: Comparing the attention to context of East Asians and Americans. *Personality and Social Psychology Bulletin, 34*(9), 1260–75.

McCloud, S. (1993) *Understanding comics: The invisible art*. New York: Harper Collins.

—(1996) Understanding manga. *Wizard Magazine, 56*, 44–8.

—(2000a) Follow that trail. *I can't stop thinking! 3*, Retrieved from http://www.scottmccloud.com/comics/icst/icst-4/icst-4.html

—(2000b) *Reinventing comics*. New York: Paradox Press.

—(2006) *Making comics*. New York: HarperCollins.

McNeill, D. (1992) *Hand and mind: What gestures reveal about thought.* Chicago, IL: University of Chicago Press.

McRae, J. F. K. (1991) *Story as sovereignty: A study of the relationship between the sand stories of the Warlpiri Aborigines and their country.* School of Teacher Education, University of Technology Sydney (Kuring-gai Campus).

Mori, K. (1995) The influence of action lines on pictorial movement perception in pre-school children. *Japanese Psychological Research, 27*(3), 183–7.

Munn, N. D. (1962) Walbiri graphic signs: An analysis. *American Anthropologist, 64*(5), 972–84.

—(1966) Visual categories: An approach to the study of representational systems. *American Anthropologist, 68*(4), 936–50.

—(1973) The spatial presentation of cosmic order in Walbiri iconography. In A. Forge (Ed.), *Primitive art and society* (pp. 193–220). London: Oxford University Press.

—(1986) *Walbiri iconography: Graphic representation and cultural symbolism in a Central Australian society.* Chicago, IL: University of Chicago Press

Nakazawa, J. (1997) *Development of manga reading comprehension: Developmental and experimental differences in adults.* Paper presented at the Proceedings of the 8th Annual Conference of Japan Society of Developmental Psychology.

—(1998) Development of manga notation understanding *Proceedings of the 9th Annual Conference of Japan Society of Developmental Psychology* (p. 182).

—(2002) Analysis of manga (comic) reading processes: Manga literacy and eye movement during Manga reading. *Manga Studies, 5*, 39–49.

—(2004) Manga (comic) literacy skills as determinant factors of manga story comprehension. *Manga Studies, 5*, 7–25.

—(2005) Development of manga (comic book) literacy in children. In D. W. Shwalb, J. Nakazawa and B. J. Shwalb (eds), *Applied developmental psychology: Theory, practice, and research from Japan* (pp. 23–42). Greenwich, CT: Information Age Publishing.

Nakazawa, J. and Nakazawa, S. (1993a) Development of *manga* reading comprehension: How do children understand *manga*? In Y. Akashi (Ed.), *Manga and child: How do children understand manga?* (pp. 85–189): Research report of Gendai Jidobunka Kenkyukai.

—(1993b) How do children understand comics?: Analysis of comic reading comprehension. *Annual of Research in Early Childhood, 15*, 35–9.

Nakazawa, J. and Shwalb, D. W. (2012) *The comparison of manga literacy between Japanese and U.S. university students.* Paper presented at the Meeting on the Psychology of Manga, Chiba University, Japan.

Natsume, F. (1998) The future of manga (Japanese comics). Retrieved from http://www.fpcj.jp/e/gyouji/br/1998/980917.html

Neff, W. A. (1977) *The pictorial and linguistic features of comic book formulas.* Doctoral Dissertation, University of Denver, Denver, CO.

Neville, H. J., Nicol, J. L., Barss, A., Forster, K. I. and Garrett, M. F. (1991) Syntactically based sentence processing classes: Evidence from event-related brain potentials. *Journal of Cognitive Neuroscience, 3*(2), 151–65.

Newtson, D. and Engquist, G. (1976) The perceptual organization of ongoing behavior. *Journal of Experimental Social Psychology, 12*, 436–50.

Nielsen, J. and Wichmann, S. (2000) America's first comics? Techniques, contents, and functions of sequential text-image pairings in the classic Maya period *Comics and Culture: Analytical and Theoretical Approaches to Comics* (pp. 59–77). Copenhagen, Denmark: Museum of Tusculanum Press.

Nisbett, R. (2003) *The geography of thought: How Asians and Westerners think differently... and why*. New York: Nicholas Brealy Publishing Ltd.

Nisbett, R. and Masuda, T. (2003) Culture and point of view. *Proceedings of the National Academy of Sciences, 100*(19), 11163–70.

Nisbett, R. and Miyamoto, Y. (2005) The influence of culture: Holistic versus analytic perception. *Trends in Cognitive Sciences, 9*(10), 467–73.

Nöth, W. (1990) *Comics handbook of semiotics* (pp. 472–5). Indianappolis, IN: University of Indiana Press.

Ohtsuka, K. and Brewer, W. F. (1992) Discourse organization in the comprehension of temporal order in narrative texts. *Discourse Processes, 15*, 317–36.

Omori, T., Ishii, T. and Kurata, K. (2004) *Eye catchers in comics: Controlling eye movements in reading pictorial and textual media*. Paper presented at the 28th International Congress of Psychology, Beijing, China.

Oomen, U. (1975) Wort-Bild-Nachricht: Semiotische aspekte des comic strip "Peanuts". *Linguistik und Didaktik, 24*, 247–59.

Osterhout, L. and Holcomb, P. (1992) Event-related potentials elicited by syntactic anomaly. *Journal of Memory and Language, 31*, 758–806.

Osterhout, L. and Nicol, J. L. (1999) On the distinctiveness, independence, and time course of the brain responses to syntactic and semantic anomalies. *Language and Cognitive Processes, 14*(3), 283–317.

Paget, G. W. (1932) Some drawings of men and women made by children of certain non-European races. *The Journal of the Royal Anthropological Institute of Great Britain and Ireland, 62*, 127–44.

Paine, S. (1992) Conflicting paradigms of vision in drawing development research. In D. Thistlewood (Ed.), *Drawing research and development* (pp. 1–13). Harlow: Longmans.

Pallenik, M. J. (1986) A gunman in town! Children interpret a comic book. *Studies in the Anthropology of Visual Communication, 3*(1), 38–51.

Palmer, S. and Rock, I. (1994) Rethinking perceptual organization: The role of uniform connectedness. *Psychonomic Bulletin and Review, 1*, 29–55.

Parsons, S. and Mitchell, P. (1999) What children with autism understand about thoughts and thought bubbles. *Autism, 3*(1), 17–38.

Patel, A. D. (2003) Language, music, syntax and the brain. *Nature Neuroscience, 6*(7), 674–81.

Patel, A. D., Gibson, E., Ratner, J., Besson, M. and Holcomb, P. J. (1998) Processing syntactic relations in language and music: An event-related potential study. *Journal of Cognitive Neuroscience, 10*(6), 717–33.

Peeters, B. (1998 [1991]) *Case, planche, et récit: Lire la bande dessinée*. Paris, France: Casterman.

Peirce, C. S. (1931) Division of signs. In C. Hartshorne and P. Weiss (eds), *Collected papers of Charles Sanders Peirce: Vol. 2: Elements of logic*. (pp. 134–73). Cambridge, MA: Harvard University Press.

Pemberton, E. F. and Nelson, K. E. (1987) Using interactive graphic challenges to foster young children's drawing ability. *Visual Arts Research, 13*(2(26)), 29–41.

Piaget, J. (1951) *Play dreams and imitation in childhood*. New York: W. W. Norton.

Premack, D. and Woodruff, G. (1978) Does the chimpanzee have a "theory of mind"? *Behavioral and Brain Science, 4*, 515–26.

Reid, V. M., Hoehl, S., Grigutsch, M., Groendahl, A., Parise, E. and Striano, T. (2009) The neural correlates of infant and adult goal prediction: Evidence for semantic processing systems. *Developmental Psychology, 45*(3), 620–9.

Richardson, M. (1937) *Lecture to the Royal Society of Arts (Item No. 3047)*. Marion Richardson Archives, University of Birmingham.

Rommens, A. (2000) Manga story-telling/showing. *Image [and] Narrative, 1*(1).

Rumelhart, D. E. (1975) Notes on a schema for stories. In D. Bobrow and A. Collins (eds), *Representation and understanding* (pp. 211–36). New York: Academic Press.

Sakurai, S., Narumi, T., Tanikawa, T. and Hirose, M. (2011) *Augmented emotion by superimposing depiction in comics*. Paper presented at the Proceedings of the 8th International Conference on Advances in Computer Entertainment Technology, Lisbon, Portugal.

Saraceni, M. (2000) *Language beyond language: Comics as verbo-visual texts*. Doctoral Dissertation, University of Nottingham, Nottingham.

—(2003) *The language of comics*. New York: Routeledge.

Sasse, H.-J. (1987) The thetic/categorical distinction revisited. *Linguistics, 25*, 511–80.

Schank, R. C. and Abelson, R. (1977) *Scripts, plans, goals and understanding*. Hillsdale, NJ: Lawrence Earlbaum Associates.

Schodt, F. L. (1983) *Manga! Manga! The world of Japanese comics*. New York: Kodansha America Inc.

—(1996) *Dreamland Japan: Writings on modern manga*. Berkeley, CA: Stonebridge Press.

Shamoon, D. (2011) Films on paper: Cinematic narrative in Gekiga. In T. Perper and M. Cornog (eds), *Mangatopia: Essays on manga and anime in the modern world* (pp. 21–36). Westport, CT: Libraries Unlimited.

Shinohara, K. and Matsunaka, Y. (2009) Pictorial metaphors of emotion in Japanese comics. In C. Forceville and E. Urios-Aparisi (eds), *Multimodal metaphor* (pp. 265–93). New York: Mouton De Gruyter.

Shipman, H. (2006) *Hergé's Tintin and Milton Caniff's Terry and the Pirates: Western vocabularies of visual language*. Paper presented at the Comic Arts Conference, San Diego, CA.

Silverstein, M. (1976) Shifters, linguistic categories, and cultural description. In K. Basso and H. A. Selby (eds), *Meaning and anthropology* (pp. 11–56). New York: Harper.

Sinclair, R. (2011) Christ, it works for everything. Retrieved from http://www.robertsinclair.net/comic/asshole.html

Sitnikova, T., Holcomb, P. J. and Kuperberg, G. (2008) Two neurocognitive mechanisms of semantic integration during the comprehension of visual real-world events. *Journal of Cognitive Neuroscience, 20*(11), 1–21.

Slepian, M. L., Weisbuch, M., Rutchick, A. M., Newman, L. S. and Ambady, N. (2010) Shedding light on insight: Priming bright ideas. *Journal of Experimental Social Psychology, 46*, 696–700.

Smith, N. R. (1985) Copying and artistic behaviors: Children and comic strips. *Studies in Art Education, 26*(3), 147–56.

Sonesson, G. (2005) From the linguistic model to semiotic ecology: Structure and indexicality in pictures and in the perceptual world. *Semiotics Institute Online, Lecture 4*. Retrieved from http://semioticon.com/sio/courses/pictorial-semiotics/

Stainbrook, E. J. (2003) *Reading comics: A theoretical analysis of textuality and discourse in the comics medium*. Doctoral Dissertation, Indiana University of Pennsylvania, Indiana, PA.

Stein, N. L. (1988) The development of children's storytelling skill. In M. B. Franklin and S. Barten (eds), *Child language: A reader*. New York: Oxford University Press.

Stein, N. L. and Glenn, C. G. (1979) An analysis of story comprehension in elementary school children. In R. Freedle (Ed.), *New directions in discourse processing* (pp. 53–119). Norwood, NJ: Ablex.

Stein, N. L. and Nezworski, T. (1978) The effects of organization and instructional set on story memory. *Discourse Processes, 1*(2), 177–93.

Sternberg, M. (2001) How narrativity makes a difference. *Narrative, 9*(2), 115–22.

Strehlow, T. G. H. (1951) Forward. In R. Batterbee (Ed.), *Modern Australian Aboriginal art*. Sydney, Australia: Angus and Robertson.

—(1964) The art of circle, line, and square. In R. M. Berndt (Ed.), *Australian Aboriginal art* (pp. 1-7). Sydney, Australia: Ure Smith.

Sully, J. (1896) *Studies of childhood*. London: Longmans, Green.

Takashima, M. (2002) The development of young children's understanding of representation using thought-bubbles. *The Japanese Journal of Developmental Psychology, 13*(2), 136–46.

Talmy, L. (2000) *Toward a cognitive semantics* (Vol. 1). Cambridge, MA: MIT Press.

Tanaka, T., Shoji, K., Toyama, F. and Miyamichi, J. (2007) *Layout analysis of tree-structured scene frames in comic images*. Paper presented at the International Joint Conference on Artificial Intelligence.

Thorndyke, P. (1977) Cognitive structures in comprehension and memory of narrative discourse. *Cognitive Psychology, 9*, 77–110.

Todorov, T. (1968) La grammaire du récit. *Langages, 12*, 94–102.

Toku, M. (2001) Cross-cultural analysis of artistic development: Drawing by Japanese and U.S. children. *Visual Arts Research, 27*, 46–59.

—(2002) *Children's artistic and aesthetic development: The influence of pop-culture in children's drawings*. Paper presented at the 31st INSEA Convention, New York.

Töpffer, R. ([1845] 1965) *Enter: The comics: Rodolphe Töpffer's essay on physiognomy and the true story of Monsieur Crépin*. Trans E. Wiese. Lincoln, NE: University of Nebraska Press.

Trabasso, T. and Nickels, M. (1992) The development of goal plans of action in the narration of a picture story. *Discourse Processes, 15*, 249–75.

Trabasso, T., Secco, T. and van den Broek, P. (1984) Causal cohesion and story coherence. In H. Mandl, N. L. Stein and T. Trabasso (eds), *Learning and comprehension of text* (pp. 83–111) Hillsdale, NJ: Erlbaum.

Trabasso, T. and Stein, N. L. (1994) Using goal-plan knowledge to merge the past with the present and the future in narrating events on line. In M. M. Haith,

J. B. Benson, R. J. Roberts Jr. and B. F. Pennington (eds), *The development of future-oriented processes* (pp. 323–49). Chicago, IL: University of Chicago Press.

Trabasso, T. and van den Broek, P. (1985) Causal thinking and the representation of narrative events. *Journal of Memory and Language, 24*, 612–30.

van Dijk, T. (1977) *Text and context*. London: Longman.

Viola, W. (1936) *Child art and Franz Cizek*. Vienna, Austria: Austrian Junior Red Cross.

von Flue, N. (2004) Set-up, (beat), punchline. Retrieved from http://ape-law.com/hypercomics/beat

Walker, M. (1980) *The lexicon of comicana*. Port Chester, NY: Comicana, Inc.

Wellman, H. M., Baron-Cohen, S., Caswell, R., Gomez, J. C., Swettenham, J., Toye, E. and Lagattuta, K. (2002) Thought-bubbles help children with autism acquire an alternative to a theory of mind. *Autism, 6*(4), 343–63.

Wellman, H. M., Hollander, M. and Schult, C. A. (1996) Young children's understanding of thought bubbles and thoughts. *Child Development, 67*, 768–88.

Wertheimer, M. (1923) Untersuchungen zur lehre von der gestalt (Laws of organization in perceptual forms). *Psychol. Forsch., 4*, 301–50.

West, W. C. and Holcomb, P. (2002) Event-related potentials during discourse-level semantic integration of complex pictures. *Cognitive Brain Research, 13*, 363–75.

Wilkins, D. P. (1991) The semantics, pragmatics, and diachronistic development of "associated motion" in Mparntwe Arrernte. *Buffalo papers in linguistics*, 207–57.

—(1997) Alternative representations of space: Arrernte narratives in sand. In M. Biemans and J. van de Weijer (eds), *Proceedings of the CLS opening academic year '97 '98* (pp. 133–64). Nijmegen, Netherlands: Nijmegen/Tilburg Center for Language Studies.

—(2003) Why pointing with the index finger is not a universal (in sociocultural and semiotic terms). In S. Kita (Ed.), *Pointing: Where language, culture, and cognition meet* (pp. 171–215). Mahwah, NJ: Erlbaum.

Willats, J. (1997) *Art and representation: New principles in the analysis of pictures*. Princeton, NJ: Princeton University Press.

—(2005) *Making sense of children's drawings*. Mahwah, NJ: Lawrence Erlbaum.

Wilson, B. (1988) The artistic tower of babel: Inextricable links between culture and graphic development. In G. W. Hardiman and T. Zernich (eds), *Discerning art: Concepts and issues*. Champaign, IL: Stipes Publishing Company.

—(1992) Primitivism, the avant-garde and the art of little children. In D. Thistlewood (Ed.), *Drawing research and development* (pp. 14–25). Harlow: Longmans.

—(1997) Child art, multiple interpretations, and conflicts of interest. In A. M. Kindler (Ed.), *Child development in art* (pp. 81–94). Reston, VA: National Art Education Association.

—(1999) Becoming Japanese: Manga, children's drawings, and the construction of national character. *Visual Arts Research, 25*(2), 48–60.

Wilson, B. and Wilson, M. (1977) An iconoclastic view of the imagery sources in the drawings of young people. *Art Education, 30*(1), 4–12.

—(1982) *Teaching children to draw*. Englewood Cliffs, NJ: Prentice-Hall.

—(1984) Children's drawings in Egypt: Cultural style acquisition as graphic development. *Visual Arts Research, 10*(1), 13–26.

—(1987) Pictorial composition and narrative structure: Themes and creation of meaning in the drawings of Egyptian and Japanese children. *Visual Arts Research, 13*(2), 10–21.

Winter, W. (1963) The perception of safety posters by Bantu industrial workers. *Psychological Africana, 10*(2), 127–35.

Witek, J. (2012) Comics modes: Caricature and illustration in the Crumb family's *Dirty laundry*. In M. J. Smith and R. Duncan (eds), *Critical approaches to comics: Theories and methods* (pp. 27–42). New York: Routledge.

Wolk, D. (2007) *Reading comics: And what they mean*. Cambridge, MA: Da Capo Press.

Yamazaki, M. (1984) *On the art of the no drama: The major treatises of Zeami*. Trans J. T. Rimer. Princeton, NJ: Princeton University Press.

Yannicopoulou, A. (2004) Visual aspects of written texts: Preschoolers view comics. *L1- Educational Studies in Language and Literature, 4*, 169–81.

Zacks, J. M., Braver, T. S., Sheridan, M. A., Donaldson, D. I., Snyder, A. Z., Ollinger, J. M., Buckner, R. L. and Raichle, M. E. (2001a) Human brain activity time-locked to perceptual event boundaries. *Nature Neuroscience, 4*(6), 651–5.

Zacks, J. M. and Magliano, J. P. (2011) Film, narrative, and cognitive neuroscience. In D. P. Melcher and F. Bacci (eds), *Art and the senses* (pp. 435–54). New York: Oxford University Press.

Zacks, J. M., Speer, N. K., Swallow, K. M. and Maley, C. J. (2010) The brain's cutting-room floor: Segmentation of narrative cinema. *Frontiers in Human Neuroscience, 4*, 1–15.

Zacks, J. M. and Tversky, B. (2001b) Event structure in perception and conception. *Psychological Bulletin, 127*(1), 3–21.

Zacks, J. M., Tversky, B. and Iyer, G. (2001c) Perceiving, remembering, and communicating structure in events. *Journal of Experimental Psychology, 130*(1), 29–58.

—(2004) The immersed experiencer: Toward an embodied theory of language comprehension. In B. H. Ross (Ed.), *The psychology of learning and motivation* (Vol. 44, pp. 35–62). New York: Academic Press.

Zwaan, R. A. and Radvansky, G. A. (1998) Situation models in language comprehension and memory. *Psychological Bulletin, 123*(2), 162–85.

# INDEX